Hey, Hun

EMILY LYNN PAULSON

Hey, Hun

Sales, Sisterhood, Supremacy, and the
Other Lies Behind Multilevel Marketing

Row House Publishing recognizes that the power of justice-centered storytelling isn't a phenomenon; it is essential for progress. We believe in equity and activism, and that books—and the culture around them—have the potential to transform the universal conversation around what it means to be human.

Part of honoring that conversation is protecting the intellectual property of authors. Reproducing any portion of this book (except for the use of short quotations for review purposes) without the expressed written permission of the copyright owner(s) is strictly prohibited. Submit all requests for usage to rights@rowhousepublishing.com.

Thank you for being an important part of the conversation and holding sacred the critical work of our authors.

Library of Congress Cataloging-in-Publication Data Available Upon Request

ISBN 978-1-955905-89-3 (TP)
ISBN 978-1-955905-91-6 (eBook)

Printed in the United States
Distributed by Simon & Schuster

Design by Neuwirth & Associates, Inc.
Interior illustrations by Jillian Thalman

First paperback edition 2024
10 9 8 7 6 5 4 3 2 1

To all the women who are brave enough to speak

out about destructive systems that benefit them,

and to those harmed by them day in and day out.

Contents

Contents

Introduction

"Okay, ladies, before our morning session, let's get together! Pose, hang on . . . Kelsey, I can't see your face, get over to the left . . . Amy, I can't see you! Okay, here we go . . . *Smile!*"

I stand up straight in the back row, like I'm posing for a cheerleading photo, except I'm thirty-five, I'm slightly drunk, and technically, I'm at work. Becky takes the picture with her iPhone and looks at it. I can tell she's not pleased with every woman in it, but clearly, it's good enough for the ones who count. I'll let you in early: I'm one of those who count. I have been a consultant for Rejuvinat, a multilevel-marketing company (MLM), for two years—and already, I am one of their top earners. If all goes well, I'll be getting the white Mercedes by the end of the year.

Fair warning: This is the pretty much true, absolutely ridiculous, definitely catty story of my life in an MLM, but it's more than that. It's also about how MLMs operate, their role in the lives of suburban women across the United States, and the belief systems, systemic racism, and white supremacy that course through their trainings, marketing, and one-on-one interactions. (Think white supremacy is a stretch? To that, I give you the Merriam-Webster dictionary definition of supremacy: "The state or condition of being superior to all others in authority, power, or status.")

Because what I learned during my time at one of the biggest MLMs in the world is that it wasn't just a way for stay-at-home moms (SAHMs) to earn money, it was actually a way for women to exploit other women, demanding that they be remade in their (well-filtered) image. We required that initiates subscribe not only to the products we peddled but to a worldview that championed old, imperial ideas of success, class, race, and beauty.

And to think, all I wanted was a stupid white car.

MLM is a marketing strategy for the sale of products or services where the MLM's revenue comes from contractors who are non-salaried, selling the company's products or services to friends and family, while the participants' earnings are derived from a multilevel commission system. This strategy is also called direct selling, network marketing, pyramid selling, and social commerce, among many other monikers. The compensation plan pays people based on product sales and recruitment of more people to sell the products. It requires people like me to sell to and attempt to recruit others into the same organization. You probably know many people in MLMs. You might purchase products from them without even knowing it.

At first glance, it seems so benign—women selling leggings and makeup and cookware in their spare time, with the hope of building more income and more friendships. "Cute" social media posts suggest that lonely suburban gals can build meaningful community with other success-oriented women and become the best version of themselves. What's wrong with a little girl power? As it turns out, a lot. What makes the whole enterprise so sticky (and icky) is the fact that distributors make more money from recruitment and the sales of those they recruit than from the products they sell directly. To succeed in the industry, sales reps must consistently recruit new distributors. This is sold as a flexible option for busy moms, but it can be very hard to succeed if you don't have a large network (and firm resources) to draw from.

It's easy to overlook these factors because MLMs are everywhere, so they can't be that bad, right? I didn't think so. In fact, to my last days, I still defended and wanted to believe in what I had done, even though I felt immeasurable guilt and shame. It took me a long time to gather the guts to write this book, for fear of offending people I loved and still do. A part of me wanted to say it wasn't that bad, but if you keep reading, you'll probably disagree. After I left the world of MLM, I began to see it for what it was. I began to see that Rejuvinat, and the many MLMs just like it, employed specific methods to maintain control over people, just like cults. Steven Hassan, former cult member and defector, describes this phenomenon in his dissertation as the BITE (behavior, information, thought, and emotional control) Model, which I will reference in greater detail in this book.

Using these methods, MLMs not only promote a specific vision of feminism, patriotism, and capitalism, they also create a system of exploitation that leaves many women financially, emotionally, and morally bankrupt. During my time at Rejuvinat, I saw deep-rooted racism, classism, religious discrimination, antisemitism, bias, and cult behavior, which isn't surprising, because MLMs work like most colonial structures: They recruit their members through social engagement, economic control, exploitation, and entrapment, creating a breeding ground for white violence in the absence of any economic, racial, or ethnic diversity. And if you decide to leave, exiting MLMs can feel akin to taking on the class bully in middle school, except the mean girls are all in their thirties and forties, wielding luxury SUVs and Louis Vuitton Neverfulls. And once you do escape, the healing process can be overwhelming.

Important note: Yes, I am a white chick talking about white supremacy. When I began writing this book, I didn't think it would contain much about white supremacy and racism, because as a white woman, I was naive to how those forces were at play in the work and culture of MLM life. I thought the book would just be a juicy story about my involvement, the realizations I had during my experience, and why I couldn't be involved anymore, and it is, but there is so much more. As I researched and interviewed former MLM members, I began to see just how insidious the culture was, and with the rise of QAnon and other conspiracy theories, I saw the links between the pseudoscience, white supremacy, and, yes, racism that permeated MLM life.

But I'm not an antiracist educator, and I have no interest in making money from teaching white chicks how to be better white chicks. I've benefited from the privilege of being white, pretty, financially sound, and thin most of my life. I still do, and I likely always will. I'm not here to wag fingers or win the Woke White Olympics. I'm a white chick who profited off a system that I believe exploits people (including other white women). Period. And I think it's our duty as humans to speak out about things that are unfair and unjust, even if they benefit us. *Especially* if they benefit us. Because if the benefit is only for a few, the detriment is for many.

Throughout the 2010s, MLMs took off through Instagram and influencers and the cult of suburban moms who were catapulted into guru status (such as, ahem, rhymes with Hachel Rollis), all because they knew how to use a filter and parrot personal development clichés. And I understand the allure because I was one of those moms. In some ways, I still am, as I find myself counting the social media likes and nitpicking my appearance in selfies just like anyone else. But during my time at Rejuvinat, I saw what those filters did to the women behind them, and I discovered the hard way what they did to me.

Because somewhere between day 1, when I signed the consultant enrollment form, and day 2,568, when I faxed in my termination notice, I became a person I didn't like, and I was one of the few who "made it."

It is reported by most sources that between 96 and 99.7 percent of people who buy into MLM schemes lose money. The odds of turning a profit in any MLM are lower than the odds of winning roulette. But

I did win. As I said before, I was a success story in the MLM world. I made well over a million dollars during my residency as a #bossbabe. I walked stages adorned with sparkly gowns and waved a pageant wave toward a crowd of adoring fans praying to be where I was. I earned every bonus, gift, luxury purse, and diamond-encrusted piece of jewelry the company had to offer (and I also paid hefty taxes on them). I went on so many shopping sprees and international trips that it made my head spin (and the nonstop drinking didn't help). I led convention trainings, got to be a keynote speaker at numerous company events, and was a corporate darling for nearly my entire run in my MLM.

But I did a lot more than that. During my years at Rejuvinat, I also pushed away friends and family. I burned bridges. I wasted precious time being distracted with "my business" instead of spending time with my children, who were still very much children at that time. I spent hours parroting company scripts to my downline (the people I recruited to be on my "team") and tens of thousands of dollars on retreats, trainings, personal development, products, and gifts. I recruited *hundreds* of women into a dream that wasn't achievable or sustainable for the majority of them, and taught others to do the same. I got wrapped up in all things #girlboss with designer shoes and white cars and the full MLM bling lifestyle. I sent cut-and-paste texts and emails that make me cringe, and I regularly added and cold-messaged random strangers on social media with the salutation "Hey, hun" (hence the name of this book), because I was following a "system of operation." I can see now how influenced (brainwashed) I was. As horrible as it feels to compare to a mass suicide, I believe the figure of speech fits here: I drank the Kool-Aid. And I made it a double.

Speaking of doubles, I also sank into severe substance-use disorder and deep depression. The night I got the car (oh yes, I did!), I found myself in handcuffs only hours later. If you really want to know what fuels many of those MLM sales parties, you don't need to look much further than the bar. I certainly didn't. My drinking took off during my time with Rejuvinat. I drank as much as I sold, and I was very successful at both. So successful that I got a DUI the night of my "car party." And after I hit rock bottom and got sober, I was trotted out at every Rejuvinat event as their "inspirational tale." Though it wasn't long before they started to complain that my star was shining a little too bright. Because despite being camouflaged as empowering, MLMs are deeply anti-feminist. They aren't about women succeeding; they are about using the appearance of female success to help the company succeed.

As I escalated in the ranks, the things I saw over the course of the next few years changed my viewpoint. Despite parroting every toxic-positive mantra in the MLM world, including "You only fail if you quit!," ad nauseum during my indoctrination, I did just that: I quit.

Among MLM circles, there's a common belief that those who fail do so because of their limited beliefs, fixed mindset, shitty priorities, and unwillingness to do what it takes to succeed. But I did what it took. I earned all the things. Yet I still felt the entire time that I was failing, and by the end of my seven years of captivity, I couldn't wait to get the hell out.

When I left, I began to wonder, *Why aren't more people talking about this?* And I found out that they were.

As I began diving into podcasts, reading books, watching YouTube channels, surfing Reddit pages, looking at the sources of information (formerly banned by my company), as well as personally interviewing hundreds of current and former MLM members who describe their experience as "cultlike," I realized we were a silenced majority. Though there are many people who gleefully attack and condemn MLMs, few of them have actually been in one. Most women I spoke with are embarrassed and afraid to tell their story.

This book is my amends, my celebration, my cautionary tale, and a glimpse into the stories of many. The women who have lost money, friends, self-esteem, and more, all because they wanted to join a "life-changing opportunity." This is me not staying silent.

Though I may (will) be labeled a hater by those still in the MLM community (it's a common practice to shun anyone who dissents from MLMs), I don't hate MLMs, and I don't hate the people who run them or join them. I have friends who are still in them, many of whom I recruited into the system. Many of the people I met who are involved in MLMs helped me a great deal in my personal life and my sobriety journey. Some are my best friends. If anything, I feel extremely connected to women (especially moms) who are still immersed in the culty MLM world, on a level that people who haven't been involved in them don't understand. I love MLM people. One of my favorite quotes from Roberta Blevins, host of the *Life After MLM* podcast and star of the documentary series *LuLaRich*, is "Everyone in an MLM is a victim and a perpetrator." And I believe that. I now view people in MLMs as victims and predators, simultaneously, whether they want to see it that way or not.

Just like almost everyone who joins an MLM, I joined believing I was helping people, helping myself, and creating a legacy for my family. I joined for a community and a purpose. I sold that dream to others, and at the core, I do believe most people who join MLMs are good people who believe the exact same thing. They want to make a difference in their own and others' lives. They want to have fun, friendships, and community, all the things that MLMs promise. Like I once did, they truly believe the things they are saying: that they intend to sell a dream. But intention and impact don't always match.

Speaking of intention and impact: I use a fictitious company name and list arbitrary products. There is no Rejuvinat. I do this not to protect the particular company, but because I believe they're all similar. Though there are minute differences in structure and finances, MLMs all function the same way and exploit the same characteristics and vulnerabilities in people. Regardless of their rank, time in their MLM, or background, the women I talked to who left MLMs had so much in common with me: a desire for self-improvement, to help their family, or to be part of something bigger than themselves. There were more commonalities than differences, which is a nod to the homogeneous nature of the people targeted to be in MLMs, and also the blueprint for how vulnerable people get sucked in.

I'm certainly not winning any popularity contests, but I'm not here to ruin the party for anyone else. I'm no stranger to dissenting from something that mass amounts of women love and consider a personality trait. Along with speaking out about the harm of MLMs, I am a vocal recovery advocate who shares about substance-use disorder and prevention regularly. I shout my sobriety from the mountaintops and sing the praises of living alcohol-free. I've written a book about it, run a large community app for moms in recovery, and have talked about it openly for almost seven years. Yet I have tons of friends and loved ones who drink, and I could give a shit if alcohol is sold or consumed around me. I'm pro-sobriety, not anti-drinker. I'm also not anti–people in MLMs. This is simply my story woven in with what I've learned throughout.

Additionally, the women I write about in this book don't actually exist. There is no Becky, Kimberly, Hannah, or Madison; rather, they are composites of the hundreds of different women I interacted with over my tenure in MLM. While similar qualities and behaviors were combined into these protagonists and antagonists, the truth is, there might be a little Becky, Kimberly, Hannah, and Madison in all of us. Timelines have been lengthened or shortened for storytelling, and some circumstances such as location have been changed for context or to protect identities. However, all the conversations, scenarios, and interactions took place, and they are shared here with as much accuracy as my memory can provide. Though I have a hard time looking back and believing some of the things that were said to me and the circumstances I placed myself in over the past decade, it's all true. A dozen years ago, I would have thrown this book in a fire. And now, I'm writing it instead, because I think this is how we change things.

So, whether you've been in an MLM, hate MLMs, or just want to read about white women behaving badly (and why), hey, hun, I hope you enjoy this book.

Hey, Hun

BECKY

ME

VANESSA

The Best Fake Friends You'll Ever Have

＊ ＋
＋

I was recruited into an MLM by someone who convinced me that we were friends because she "saw herself in me." She played on my emotions, knowing I wanted to leave the military, and told me to put the kit cost on my credit card because she could train me to earn it back. Fast-forward a few months and despite doing everything she "coached me to do," I was exhausted and losing money. It got so bad financially that I quit, with loads of credit-card debt. And that "friend"? She told me that I gave up, blocked me, and never spoke to me again.

—JANICE, former MLM rep

I n early 2014, by all accounts, my life was pretty great. I had a supportive spouse, beautiful kids, and a comfortable life. And yet, something felt like it was missing. I couldn't quite put my finger on it. After our last child was born, I remembered thinking, *What's next?* Despite being busy with five kids, I felt like I had to be doing more. Was being a SAHM enough? I looked around at other moms who worked from home or worked full-time and thought, *How do they do it?* and they probably looked at me and asked the same thing. Did anyone actually have it figured out? Why did we all feel like we should be doing more? I felt like a martyr most days, and I knew I wasn't alone.

In many ways, women have internalized the idea that we must do it all, while also taking on the brunt of housework, childcare, and the emotional and mental labor of managing a household full of different people with varying needs, all at our own expense. I'd tried many coping mechanisms to fill the void—wine, other people, overscheduling myself—but I always ended up feeling less than, alone, and isolated. That was, until I found what could be the solution to all my problems: a business in a box.

"Babe! I left Rowan's blanket downstairs. Can you grab it when you come up?"

I'm snuggling with my two-year-old, crammed into a toddler bed where I end up falling asleep many nights, much to the chagrin of my aching back. But not tonight. Tonight, I'll be meeting a friend I haven't seen in almost twenty years. Okay, "friend" is a bit of a stretch. Becky is from my hometown, and we went to the same high school but were never close. In fact, I'm pretty sure we've never spoken. She was a few years younger than me in school and quiet, but always very sweet. She friended me on Facebook a while back and I happily accepted. (Back then, Facebook was still pretty new and a fun place for sharing pics of kids with people you hadn't seen in ten years—instead of the minefield of ads, sales, politics, misinformation, and anxiety driven by bizarre algorithms that it is today—so getting friend requests from past acquaintances wasn't out of the ordinary. The good old days.) A few weeks prior, Becky had reached out via Messenger and told me she'd be in Seattle for a work trip; she asked if I'd like to get wine during her visit. An IRL visit? From a human woman? A night out away from my kids? Truly, she had me at "wine." I said yes without much thought, and here we are, on the precipice of our first official live conversation.

I grab my coat, load the map on my phone, and head off. It's been a while since I've been out alone without my husband, or any of the kids. Truth be told, the past year has been pretty rocky between my husband

and me. Adding a fifth kid to the mix has been a challenge, as has his travel schedule. On top of that, finances have been tough, and juggling all the things has been overwhelming. Preschool, piano lessons, soccer practice, driving *everywhere*, and packing all the lunches between naps and diaper changes. Maybe that's why I jumped at the chance to meet with someone I hardly know, and her "colleagues." It's funny how constantly being surrounded by six other people can still leave you feeling so damn lonely sometimes.

In many ways, feeling isolated and alone is what drives many women and moms to find "coping mechanisms," little escapes from reality. Though they are innocent from the outset—who doesn't love a "mom's night out with wine!" or to "shop at home with Kelsi"?—they never address the actual problem: that women don't have a village. We are alone. Even if we are married or partnered, even if we have friends, the day-to-day tasks fall completely on our shoulders.

Since the birth of my first son, I have been wondering where that idyllic village people keep talking about is, or if it even exists. Is there a phone number to call or something? Plenty of people offer to "help" in their own way, but the odds are stacked against moms. We take time off from our jobs while our partners go back to work, maybe have a little maternity leave, or assume more of the household duties in lieu of working outside of the home. Yet days are stretched out, the calendar is empty, and we're busier than ever trying to keep a human alive. The smallest tasks we took for granted before, even buying groceries, seem daunting with a new squealing ball of flesh in tow. Despite this being the norm for every woman who has a baby, most of us do it by ourselves. Studies show that 90 percent of new moms consider themselves lonely, and 54 percent consider themselves friendless.

This loneliness, plus overwhelm from caring for children, on top of the new routine of being alone most of the time, can lead to isolation, which is ironic, because you're *never* actually alone. You can't even pee alone. But the lack of adult interaction and the loss of your previous life feels lonely. And though the stigma around postpartum depression is lessening, many moms still don't reach out for help because they don't want to be seen as weak or unable to cope. Friendship circles change because it can be hard to relate to women without children or with children of a different age, and there is an endless struggle and cycle of guilt over the choices you need to make as a mom—and no matter what, according to someone, you're making the wrong choice. No wonder a night out getting drunk with friends or an annoying sales pitch from Kelsi down the street seems so much more inviting than anything that actually fixes the problem. Rachel Allender, a licensed therapist who works with couples and parents, says, "You can change your job or career. But you can't divorce your kids. And there is a negative impact on you when you can never power down."

But who has time when we are busy doing it all?

So, this is how it started: a promise of wine and an opportunity to overcome the loneliness, just for one night. Wine and shopping are already regular escapes for me, and now, I am being led into an evening that offers more. Becky works for one of "those" companies. Lately, they've been popping up more and more on social media—you know, *opportunity of a lifetime, join my team, blah blah blah.* Don't get me wrong, I've been intrigued. How could I not? I've seen some of the fun trips Becky has been on. Apparently, she's making great money, and best of all, she has a host of new friends according to her social media posts. It would seem that this "opportunity" has truly changed her life, even if it does make my Facebook feed annoying. I am skeptical, and guarded, though I can't put my finger on what doesn't sit well with me. But if she brings it up, what's the harm in learning more? Plus, the idea of jetting off to wine country to spend a week hanging out with other women and not my kids sounds like a freaking lottery ticket. I check the rearview mirror and shake off my anxiety. Why am I spending my drive overthinking this? It's a night out! I turn the tunes up for the rest of the ride (Britney Spears? Yes!) and after another fifteen minutes of bliss, alone in my car, I pull into a parking lot to a wine bar. I check my lipstick, take a deep breath, and head inside.

"Emily! So good to see you!" Becky throws her arms around me. It's funny after so many years that people look exactly the same as your memory. She hasn't changed a bit! Or maybe we've both changed a lot and our old brains have adjusted to our new reality. She introduces me to a few other ladies at the table and gestures to the waitress to come over as we sit down.

The first thing I notice is the product lineup on the table. There are some supplements, shakes, beauty products, and pamphlets with pictures of business kits on them. I quickly realize that the other ladies here each have "guests" with them who apparently were invited to learn about the business. Initially, I'm a little crestfallen. I'd thought that Becky wanted to catch up with me, when in reality, she wants to give me the MomBoss version of a timeshare presentation. I pull myself down to earth with some reassuring self-talk: *Come on, this is someone you know from Facebook who told you in advance she was here for work— lighten up, Emily!*

As the waitress brings my large pour of prosecco, I forget what I was so worried about, and I settle in for the spiel.

"I lost all the baby weight in the first few months when I became a consultant," sings one rep. "My skin has never been more glowy," echoes another.

I down my first drink as I listen to praises of the products from all of these women who use them. They sound very genuine. And these women look like completely normal moms my age, not sleazy vacuum salesmen. In fact, they all sort of look like me—upper middle class, wearing cool mom clothes, and sporting trendy handbags. They continue, "And the products were so good, I couldn't pass up the business opportunity. Why wouldn't I want my own products at a discount? I'm going to use them anyway!"

"Same!" continues another. "People were asking me what I was using on my hair, so why wouldn't I want to get in on that? Wash my hair and talk about it? It's so easy!"

Hmmm, they have a point. I can feel my earlier hesitation subside. As the endorsements ring out, one after another, every single one targets an example of most women's insecurities, mine included. I can't help but perk up at the not-so-subtle subtext: *Get rid of that mom bod! Heal your postpartum acne and hair loss. Not enough money or friends? This opportunity's for you!* It's nothing new in marketing and not singular to MLM, but MLMs have found a particularly effective, approachable way to target women's insecurities—by offering us a neat little bundle of lifestyle solutions, with a community of perky and positive "friends" to boot.

I find myself picking which area of myself I want to start improving: my skin, my hair, my waistline, or my loneliness? Hell, why not all of it? Now I understand *exactly* why people go for the giant product kit— might as well have it all!

In this moment, it feels reassuring to know I can become the perfect mom, wife, woman—and it might have a hefty price tag attached to it, but that's nothing new. Take a gander at the makeup or diet section of any store, which is abundant with ways to make you look better or feel younger—at a price. By the same token, sisterhood at a price has been around since time immemorial. Sororities are the gold standard of paid sisterhood. While the stats on sororities show that women who are members of Greek organizations are more likely to report feeling emotionally supported in college, that support is costly. Add to that the cost of higher education in the United States, which through a process of elimination ices out the ones who can't afford access to this exclusive sisterhood.

I remember going through sorority rush the first time and feeling so much love, and then participating in it the following year, only to realize how much judgment went into it. The attractive, thin, well-to-do co-eds were the benchmark. If you were "wanted" by your favorite house, it felt like an achievement. Yet, when you pulled back the curtain, you realized you were just another pretty face to fill their lineup. But now, years later, standing in this wine bar and admiring the products and the new gaggle of girlfriends, I once again feel *seen*, the same way I did when I initially rushed my sorority. And even though I know how that went down (not well), the high is enough to make me fantasize about the possibilities.

Becky continues to tout the benefits of her products, her company, and of course, the highly vaunted friendships that come with the territory.

Because of this combination of aggressive sales tactics, empty promises, and sisterhood at a price, MLMs have often been described as cultlike.

First, I recognize *cult* is a strong word, generally drawing allusions to the Jonestown massacre or the Children of God, but the same mind-control tactics are used by high-pressure organizations (ranging from educational institutions to corporations) in similar ways, sometimes destructively and sometimes very innocently. Cultism is a spectrum. As Amanda Montell describes in her book *Cultish*, "Though the stakes and consequences of respective affiliations differ considerably, the methods used to assert power—to create community and solidarity, to establish an 'us' and a 'them,' to align collective values, to justify questionable behavior, to instill ideology and inspire fear—are uncannily, cultishly similar."

Essentially, we are all exposed to and influenced by *cults*. For example, there are plenty of culty behaviors in workout programs; Orangetheory (which I personally love) and CrossFit talk about splat points or

WODS, which is loaded insider language you'd only understand if you were part of the group. We are *all* involved in cultish communities, whether it's our bunco group, our church, our sorority, or even our workplace. And that's all fine and good; just because something is culty doesn't mean it's harmful! I'm not hurting anyone by posting my splat points on social media, even if nobody knows what the hell I'm talking about. Although communities are important (even if they contain weird jargon and rituals people outside of them seldom understand), creating financially exploitative, competitive divides is harmful. Instead of being obvious and sensational, MLMs and other commercial cults are small and sinister, like death from a thousand paper cuts. Because they are readily disguised as positive and business-building, they are easy to miss.

The best way I've found to calculate the harm of a cultish system, as I referenced previously, is through the BITE Model by Steven Hassan. Hassan is a mental-health counselor and a leading expert on cults and mind control. He has personal experience, having escaped the Unification Church (also known as the Moonies) in 1976; he has since dedicated his time to educating people about the ways many organizations use the same cult tactics we associate with Jonestown, the Waco compound, and other stories of community gone bad.

According to Hassan, cults are organizations that exercise undue influence over their members to make them dependent and obedient. They take advantage of their position of power over another in ways that are constructive/healthy, destructive/unhealthy, and everything in between. This undue influence is often called brainwashing. *Brainwashing* is a term most people have heard, but they may not realize how easy it is to be influenced in a destructive and unhealthy way. In MLMs, this is first done by showering an individual with praise and promising them something: money, a group of friends, a better lifestyle. Then, once a member is hooked, the organization systematically disrupts that person's ability to think for themselves. Sound sensational?

And are we still talking about those innocent jewelry and leggings salespeople? Yes. Yes, we are. That process of gaining undue influence is what Hassan calls the BITE Model:

- **Behavior control:** Cults can dictate what a person does and who they are, by restricting what they eat and wear, how much they sleep, whom they associate with, and how they use their money. Rewards and punishments are used to modify behavior, and individualism and critical thinking are discouraged. Permission is required for major decisions, and thoughts, feelings, and activities are reported to superiors. Behavior control is used to instill dependency and obedience.

- **Information control:** Cults may distort, withhold, or lie about information by controlling access to non-cult information, encouraging spying, or producing propaganda like YouTube videos, movies, or newsletters. Members are kept busy so they don't have time to think or investigate on their own, and information is compartmentalized into insider/outsider doctrines or different levels of leadership.

- **Thought control:** Cults will attempt to control thought through toxic positivity, clichés, loaded language, and buzzwords. Constructive criticism, questions, and opposition are not allowed. Black-and-white thinking is instilled, and denial, rationalization, and wishful thinking are encouraged.

- **Emotional control:** Cults will use love bombing (excessive praise and attention), emotional highs and lows, and fear of losing friendship or community if you leave or question authority. Anything good is the product of the cult; anything bad is your fault. Feelings of guilt or unworthiness are promoted if the system is not followed, and there is a required ritualistic and sometimes public confession of sins or vulnerabilities.

The comparison between cults and MLMs is nothing new. *Amway: The Cult of Free Enterprise* was written in 1999 by former Amway distributor Stephen Butterfield and describes the cultlike tactics used in one of the longest-standing MLMs in the world. When it was published, it exposed the mysterious terminology, mass meetings, focus on recruitment, toxic positivity, and complete and unquestioning dedication to the company—qualities that are very similar to those associated with cults. Many former members have made this comparison, and virtually every MLM functions this way.

I certainly hadn't driven all the way out to that wine bar to join a cult, nor did I believe that was what was being sold to me at the time, but hindsight is twenty-twenty.

As I continue to admire the deluxe consultant package on the table, a bundle of products that is expensive but discounted enough to make even the most unassuming bargain shopper salivate, I remind myself that I'm not interested in bugging my friends. The prospect of asking friends and family to buy crap makes me very uncomfortable. And adding up the cost of products in my head, I decide to ask more questions. It's the math that makes me bite.

"If I *did* buy the big product kit—I mean, because I'd love to use all that stuff—how much would I be obligated to sell? Can I just buy it for myself and not sell anything?" This will be the deal-breaker, for certain. The last thing I want is to have a garage full of skincare I can't unload.

"Oh, that's the beauty," Becky says. "You can do as little or as much as you want! No minimums."

Huh. Really? That seems too good to be true (it is, and we will get to that later). But, if I can get the products (which I now *need* to have, even though I didn't know about them until tonight!) at a discount (is it *really* a discount?), *maybe* with an interested friend or two, that wouldn't be a terrible waste of time, right? At least it will be a nice distraction from my life right now, which I could use. If I can make some money, that's a bonus! I raise my glass to the waitress to order another prosecco as I'm convincing myself by the minute. After all, going back to my previous job (I used to be a chemist before kids) would require full-time childcare, which would eat up a huge chunk of my paycheck. Plus, getting recertified and sprucing up my resume isn't exactly appealing. Isn't buying a business kit an easier solution? What options do moms have once they've been out of the workforce for so long? This sounds like the perfect fix.

"All right, why the heck not? I'll use all this stuff, anyway," I tell Becky. "Where do I sign?" Kale's not going to be thrilled with me dropping $500 on a bunch of serums, shakes, and supplements, but what he doesn't know is that I can earn the money back! Oh yes, I will!

The other women squeal with excitement, "If you need *anything*, you just let me know."

Another woman adds, "Same—I'm in the area. Happy to help in any way."

Wow, I'm actually blown away by the immediate support! Here it is—my village! An instant sisterhood! I'm feeling the love already. The other women start sharing stories about how the community has saved them, and I'm all ears.

"When my husband and I got divorced, most of my friends chose him. This company gave me an instant tribe," one woman says, starting to tear up. "I know," another goes on. "I don't know what I'd do without my Rejuvinat family!" A woman named Lilly adds, "When I joined this company, my friends thought I was crazy. They all unfriended me on Facebook and stopped talking to me. But whatever—I had a whole slew of new friends."

So, how did I go from ready and willing to deflect Becky's bossbabe advances to seriously considering signing on the dotted line within an hour? Because I was the perfect target for an MLM, which preys on the cultural epidemic of isolation. They don't exist because millions of

SAHMs are just dying to sell beauty products. They exist because those women feel lonely, trapped, and bereft of other solutions. Consultants in the organization share their vulnerability, which makes you feel drawn to their openness and kindness; you find commonality and connection, and assume the company and products are the solution to your mutual pain. Any person who is vulnerable, or struggling to have a meaningful friendship or connection, is going to be drawn to that experience, just as I was drawn to this meeting of "friends" over wine to get away from my family for the evening.

This was the *B* in the BITE Model: behavioral control. Ignoring my intuition and buying some products doesn't sound like that big of a deal, but it is. Because when you join for a community and stay for a community, you will ignore red flags. Eventually, even if the results don't match up, if the MLM ruins your finances, damages other relationships, or preys upon your insecurities, you are still drawn to it because you want this seemingly safe, welcoming environment. Feeling financial pressure? Loneliness? Shame in being a working parent? The need to lose some baby weight? All of a sudden, the MLM is the way to eradicate those pain points. And even if you do push friends away (like Lilly, who was blacklisted from her friend group and picked up by her MLM friends), you are sucked into the MLM even further, since it seemingly provides support. Remedying loneliness is the real draw. It is conditional friendship, at a price. Sociology generally defines community as a social unit that shares something in common, such as customs, characteristics, values, beliefs, or norms; no financial strings are attached. Because there is a financial hierarchy in an MLM, with women making money off one another's sales, this recruiting tool can never create true community. Still, I joyfully skipped right into it with a glass of bubbly in my hand.

As I sit across from a glowing Becky and reach that glass back out for the waitress to fill, I am thrilled with my decision.

Becky squeezes my hand and says, "You're going to love this. You have such a huge network—you will be amazed at how far you can take this."

Huh. Okay. Shit. She reminds me that I need to actually *do* something. Hmm. I don't know, I guess I know a lot of people. But, like I told her before, I'm not interested in having parties and shilling products. The power structure that seems to be inherent in female relationships is already at play.

"So, what would I start with? Say, if I do want to recommend this stuff to friends," I inquire timidly. "What do I say? What do I show them?" I wave my hands around the table of products. So far, all I've done is share my Social Security number and credit card info, but I've had no formal training of any kind and have never really been in sales. But I do like to buy stuff!

"Oh, it's no problem," Becky assures me. "The best thing to do first is to make lists. Make one dirt list—that's the people who would buy dirt from you, people who would support you no matter what. Then, make a dream-team list of people you'd want on your team."

"Hold up. What if I don't want to have a 'team'?" I say with actual air quotes. "What if I just want to sell products?" Frankly, I'm not even sure I want to do *that*; I just want the huge kit filled with everything, and the discount, but I'm throwing her a bone here.

Becky looks deflated. "Yeah, I mean . . . totally, you can do that. Let's just start with who would like these products. Let's start there!"

She hands me a pen and a notebook emblazoned with *#goaldigger* right across the table. Oh, hey, we're doing this *now*, right here? Got it. I tap the pen on the paper and stare blankly at her.

"When you recommend your favorite mascara or jeans to friends, who do you recommend them to? Write those people down. That's your dirt list! People who would buy dirt from you because they respect your opinion *so much*. I mean, they're already buying this stuff somewhere—why wouldn't they buy it from you?"

The language, as well as her insistence on me doing this right now, is cringey. I mean, dirt list? But she has a good point. I recommend my favorite stuff all the time. The other day, I shared on Facebook about a vacuum that didn't suck (I mean, it *did* suck—it's a vacuum) and no joke: four people bought it! Same with a printer I purchased, and a pair of boots. People ask what I use on my skin all the time, too. This is starting to make more sense to me. Sure. I nod and agree. "Okay, I can work on a dirt list."

She smiles back, satisfied with my compliance. The indoctrination is working, even if I can't see it yet. I don't realize that I will be repeating this recruitment script with my friends only hours later. It's so effective, because for that evening, I have hope. Hope that I can make money, hope that somehow my life will be better, and I'll be happier, more fulfilled, less alone. And now, I have all these new friends here to cheer me on! I just have to convince other people they can have this, too. Even though I have no proof that this will work for me yet, the power of positive thinking is beating out logic.

Now I'm thinking about how I'm going to get all this shit in my house. Hopefully, it gets delivered during the week when Kale's at work. It's nice that they come right to my door! I try not to worry about it. When the goods arrive, I'll dig in and figure out how I'm going to get rid of it all.

"So, I get my products in a week or so, and then how long do I need to use the products first before I can endorse them?" I ask Becky. She quickly fires back, "Oh, why wait? Talk now! That's the beauty of social media. Fake it till you make it! You can post, you can message people, you can see people in person, you can call them, you can reach people so many different ways! And I have language for you I can share!" She pushes a stack of paper with training documents across the table. I flip through and see memory joggers to think of friends, scripts to cut and paste when I message people, ideas for Facebook photos and posts. Well, they certainly do make it easy!

"Seriously, people eat this shit up!" She smiles. "The more people you share this with, the more people who can purchase from you or join you! It's really just a numbers game!" I nod and try to soak it all in.

"A numbers game," I repeat back. Becky is right. Who needs the products when all I'm really selling is the image of the lifestyle this "opportunity" affords? The instant gratification of thinking that you can click a "buy now" button and actually solve something about your life, your appearance, your pocketbook, your social life. We do it all the time.

And because people already know, like, and trust you, they are going to already be vulnerable to whatever you are selling. Or better yet, just like you, they can also "Be your own 'She-EO'! Build your own business! Get your leggings and change your life!"

Back in our moms' generation, the plasticware and makeup parties were transparent, and you knew what you were getting into. But when I met up with Becky, MLMs were just starting to infiltrate social media. That Facebook message: Surprise, it's a friend from high school you hated but who just so happens to be selling nail wraps! That coffee with a friend: Ta-da, a chick from church who usually gives you death stares but now wants you to sign up for her training program and collagen pudding! The bait and switch was everywhere in the 2010s. That's how I was roped in, through a Facebook message!

Even as I sit across Becky staring down at the sales material she has just slid across the table, my intuition is telling me it's icky. But I don't listen to that nagging voice that seems to know it's all too good to be true. After all, the women sitting before me appear to be smart, reasonable people, and they all seem so happy . . . and successful!

I shake off my buyer's remorse, say goodbye, and hop back in the car for the long drive home. It's still kind of early. Kale will be up, and I *really* don't want to explain this to him tonight. He's always supportive of projects I get involved in, but we are trying to communicate better these days and I should not be spending this kind of money right now without talking to him. I ring up my friend Vanessa and ask her to meet up with me for a drink on the way home.

"V! Wine! Mission Cantina, ten minutes?"

"You got it. See you there. You'd better not look cute," Vanessa warns me. "I'm coming from the gym."

I actually *am* cute for the first time in a long time. I figure I'll use it to my benefit. She can be my first tester client.

"Two Grey Goose sodas!" I yell to the bartender as Vanessa looks through the pamphlets I've brought.

"So, what is this? Like a home party makeup thing?" she giggles.

"I don't even know. God, what have I done?" We laugh as I admit, "I seriously got sucked in." I pull out another pamphlet. "But you know I've been wanting to try different vitamins, and I've been all over the place with my skincare lately. I figure this checks all the boxes. I mean, look at this!" I show her the impressive before-and-after pictures.

"Dang!" Her eyes get big. "Will it make me skinny?"

"I don't know—worth a shot!" I say, shrugging. My persuasion skills need improvement.

"So, you can make money with this, yeah?" she asks, more interested as we talk. "I need to figure out a way to make some cash soon or I'm never going to be able to live on my own."

She shakes her head and digs into the chips and salsa. Ahh. Her crappy marriage is near its end. I perk up. She's right—this could really help her! The ladies at the wine bar all sang the praises of this business, which they asserted had helped them get their groove back. Becky had said something about offering this "gift" to other people. She told me about a woman in the MLM who only had $40 in her bank account and used it to buy product, and now she's one of the top earners in the company. She said that people who were "hungry" to change their circumstances could do really well. What if that could happen for Vanessa, and I could be the catalyst? How awesome would that be?

In many ways, the economics of isolation are most pronounced in women like Vanessa and me. According to a study from Yale University, women like us (traditional marriage roles, upper middle class, privileged) experience a higher degree of isolation, as we have smaller meaningful social groups than women in lower socioeconomic levels. This has to do with the fact that more-advantaged women are less likely to know other women from their same socioeconomic group than less-advantaged women are. And as I had experienced, though I had a large network, a lot of it was superficial. I only had a handful of friends I'd consider close. Since social connections are fundamental to well-being, if you're a person-of-privilege who doesn't have a community but needs one because you're also still a living, breathing human being with feelings, why not just buy your community?

With stars in her eyes, Vanessa asks, "Is this what you bought?" as she points to a product lineup. I nod.

She begins to beam as she drinks her second Grey Goose. "Okay, I'm in! How fun would it be to work together?"

It *would* be fun! *Wow, this is easier than I thought it would be*, I think to myself. I already have my first business partner and I haven't even received my products yet! Now I'm racking my brain for more people who'll be perfect for this opportunity. Wait . . . is this the dream team Becky was talking about?

"All right, you want to start working on your dirt list?" I ask her.

"What the fuck is a dirt list?"

It certainly would be awesome if Vanessa made it to the top, but sadly, what I don't know at this point is that it's unlikely. Highly unlikely. Yet stories like these, of people who are "hungry" enough to fulfill their wildest dreams, lead the most unsuspecting and desperate people to believe that just maybe they could be at the top, too. The archetypal rags-to-riches stories of being poor and now being adorned head-to-toe in Chanel lift their hopes and open their wallets. They manipulate emotions to drown out both our deeper intuition and our logic—and if someone preys on emotion (look how strong you are! I want to be a strong, independent woman, too!), both intuition and logic lose.

This myth of meritocracy denies the many other factors that go into "success" as we tend to frame it. The idealization of hard work and the "anyone can do this" mentality don't translate when the playing field isn't level. Vanessa and I have money, and our friends are similarly well-heeled. We have plenty of acquaintances with enough disposable income to buy their friends' products. Despite Vanessa's rocky marriage and my stretched bank account, we will always have stability—and an extensive network, no matter how superficial. A product purchase didn't break the bank for me, and it won't for Vanessa, either. Not everyone is primed with such privileges. MLMs are designed so people without long dirt lists will fail. You cannot sell products to people who can't afford products, offering less return for those with fewer resources while expecting the same investment.

I WAKE UP the next morning with a hangover—and that buyer's remorse I vaguely felt when I left the wine bar after reconnecting with Becky is back. Yikes. I need to think of a series of excuses before I talk to Kale. Usually, we "ask" each other before we spend more than $200 on something outside of our normal expenses. Rather than ask for permission, I'll be asking for forgiveness, but he's already off to work. I get breakfast started, open my phone, and check Facebook. I see that "my business" has been announced (yikes), and I've been added to about ten "team pages." Holy shit. Didn't know that was going to happen. You see, I'm in the downline of the person I purchased from, Becky, but also in the downline of anyone else who makes money off me. It's a reverse family tree of sorts, I guess. Or a pyramid. I've also been added to other huge team pages of people who apparently don't make money off me, but I'm part of their "family," too—or something. It's a little confusing at this point, and I'm slightly weirded out. I didn't know I was going to be "outed" on social media, especially since I haven't even talked to my husband yet! My mom even sends me a text: "Did you really sign up for one of those Mary Kay thingies?" I didn't exactly give my consent to be announced, but I guess I didn't know I needed to. At the same time, look at all these people!

I'm already being besieged by tons of friend requests: people who also probably feel awkward AF about this! They offer welcome messages and kind comments; it's a bit overwhelming but in a good way. Being accepted into a new community is so much more than just friendship and acceptance. Even if it's just proximity and not actual friendship, it's a lifeline to humanity. What's being offered by Rejuvinat is necessary; we cannot survive without connection, and it feels *so* real. What I don't consider is that maybe it shouldn't cost anything or require being exploited to make some ladybosses (or white dude CEOs) rich. I ignore it at the time, but I should have noticed that there were only a few people at the top; that the success stories shared by many were only the success stories of the people looking down at us from the apex of the pyramid. My involvement only legitimized the MLM for them, to their own networks; their jubilant declarations of acceptance were for them, not me.

I dig a little deeper on the team pages to see other women being "shouted out" on leader lists, top tens, incentives, etc. It's a little dizzying going down the rabbit hole of all this stuff, and there's so much vocabulary I don't understand (why so many acronyms and what the hell are *PV* and *QV* and *SED* and *MP*?), but I get the gist. It seems like everyone here is happy, fulfilled, and making money. They all have beautiful photos of their perfect families, with blown-out hair and fun manicures. They seem to go on lavish trips and shopping sprees and have beautiful homes. Who wouldn't want to look like this? I need to sit down and figure all this stuff out, finish my lists, and apparently also plan a business launch party. Tonight! Wait, no, I have marriage counseling tonight. I check the calendar. Yeah, I may have to stay up after the babysitter leaves. Well, I guess that'll be a good time to drop the bomb that I spent $500 on this shit! Unless Kale sees it on Facebook first.

For now, I'll focus on breakfast and children and all the things that feel like the biggest gifts I could ever receive . . . yet somehow, leave me feeling like I need more.

"Pancake!" my four-year-old yells as she throws said pancake in the air and it drops onto the floor. We both giggle as the toddler runs after it. "No no no! Dirty!" I warn him.

"Five-second rule, Mama?" she asks.

I shrug and check my phone again for more notifications. I could get used to these accolades and attention. I don't even notice as the toddler eats the pancake off the floor.

I have a real job now.

KIMBERLY

JAMIE

BECKY

ME

JUNE

VANESSA

I'm Positive That You Suck

✦

Over the years of being in my MLM, I was taught to stop questioning the system and to get my mindset right. I was making money, so I fell into the trap pretty easily. What changed things for me was watching my downline work harder than me and still lose money. My upline assured me that they must not be doing the work, but I saw with my own eyes that they were. I realized that I looked successful because so many people were buying kits and failing. I couldn't unsee how ugly it was. No amount of money was worth making people feel that everything was their fault.

—MELISSA, former MLM rep

Mama! The dewivery man is here!" my four-year-old yells from the living room as UPS brings a package to the door. My toddler is on my hip as I peer around the corner. Wow! It's big, it's pink, and it's adorned with the Rejuvinat logo! It's not the first one I've received of late. Or second. Or twentieth. Between Rejuvinat and my Amazon habit, I've had to increase the capacity of our recycling service. But it's a small price to pay for the joy of boxes on my porch—like every day is Christmas!

My husband wasn't initially thrilled that I signed up to do something "like this," and sadly, he *did* find out via Facebook, but as I started bringing home a little bit of money, he was happy to see me finding some joy in my contribution to the family. I'm not going to be the one to burst his bubble and let him know I technically haven't made any money yet because I've been buying more products and promotional items, paying a babysitter for nights out with "clients," and indulging that darn Amazon habit—but he's generally fine with my new side hobby.

It's just a few months into my #bossbabe journey, and I've already amassed quite a large dream team, which is comical considering I had no desire to build a team. Apparently, recruiting is the name of the game, and I keep getting more bonuses and gifts as I sign up new recruits. Vanessa was just the start! Several other friends decide to jump on board with me, too, trusting my endorsement of this gig, and with each signup, I receive an additional bonus. So much better than trying to sell a $20 collagen powder! The lingo is different depending on the person you ask, but *inviting, signing up, building a team, networking, linking arms,* and *partnering* mean the same thing: recruit humans. As my recruitments increase, not only is the company showering me with praise, gifts, and bonuses—my uplines are spoiling me, too! In fact, one of the gifts arriving today—in a big pink box, of course—is from one of my uplines, someone I haven't even met yet.

"More cream?" my daughter asks as she points to the package, since the last box included multiple hand creams that you can now find in every goddamn bathroom of our house. Isn't it funny how even though I'm not expected to carry inventory, I somehow have this shit everywhere?

"Not sure, let's see—want to help?" I open the top of the box, read the card, and realize who it's from. Gasp, it's Kimberly! Kimberly is *the* biggest consultant in the company. I think she may have been one of the very first reps! Almost everyone in the entire company falls somewhere under her. I'm definitely on one of her many Facebook teams, and (lucky her) I happen to be on the same pay level as her. Let me explain: The commission structure of every MLM is a little different, but the "multilevel" is what's important here. I make money on products I sell to customers. Becky (my upline, who recruited me) also makes money on those sales. So does Allison (her upline who recruited her), and her upline, and her upline, and so on. Depending on the company, the number of levels you get paid on differs, but the structure is basically the same.

DATA : SECURITIES
AND EXCHANGE
COMMISSION

6
36
216
1,296
7,776
46,656
279,936
1,679,616
10,007,696
60,466,176
362,796,056
2,176,782,336
13,060,694,016

The website Relatively Interesting, which promotes science, reason, and critical thinking, gives a great simple example of a "product-based pyramid scheme" mathematical proof using data from the US Securities and Exchange Commission.

- Cassidy recruits 6 reps who each pay $100 for a starter kit.
- Cassidy gets 10 percent of each starter kit that's sold.
- Cassidy also gets 10 percent of each product that any of her reps sold, including additional starter kits.
- Cassidy tells her reps that the fastest way to make money isn't by selling product, but by recruiting more people.
- The people at the top of the pyramid get commissions from everyone in the downline (the people below them in the pyramid).

Using simple math and these figures, by the time you're at the twelfth level of the pyramid, you'd need to recruit two billion people so that everyone could make back their money. At the ninth level, you'd need thirteen billion people—you know, twice the population of the planet. Most MLMs stop payment at a certain level; for example, in Rejuvinat, we can only earn commissions six levels down, but as you can see, 46,000 reps would still be needed for everyone to earn back their money. Can't exactly get those numbers from your book club or your bunco group, Jan.

Also, those alleged 46,000 reps are not going to be on the same level playing field.

This is why the product cost is so inflated—because so many levels of pay are built in. Kimberly is far enough upline that I haven't met her, but she still gets paid for everything I sell. Hence, this gracious thank-you gift.

I grab the scissors as my daughter tugs on my leg and digs through the Styrofoam peanuts. "What is it, Mama?"

I shrug. "Let's see." I open the plastic packaging, and it's a black leather, structured Kate Spade bag, with that new purse smell and all.

Ahh. What on earth did I do to deserve this? Best gig ever! My toddler remarks, "Pretty purse, Mama!"

"It is, isn't it? Oh, I have to thank her! Let's send a thank-you note, okay?" I put my toddler in the highchair with a handful of Cheerios and open up Facebook. There is no return address on the box (this came from *her*, not the company, so it's a true honor); I'll have to send a Facebook message to thank her. I log in, and before I can even type her name, I see a few posts on my wall from other people in my upline:

"You're killing it! Congrats on two new business partners!"

"It's a pleasure working with you, keep up the great work!"

"You're on FIRE hotshot!"

Along with that, *so* many new followers, mostly women from the company. Look how my community is growing! I sit back and try to think of the last time I was complimented for something other than my cooking, which isn't often, by the way. This business is making me feel the love.

But the love I'm feeling is actually thanks to a very effective manipulation technique called love bombing. It's used by many cultlike groups to push the idea of a sense of friendship and community. It's the *E* in the BITE Model: emotional control. I was already a vulnerable target as an isolated SAHM, so the idea of having a community of close friends was appealing, but being spoiled and shouted out by them was next level. It's why you hear so much about MLM reps' excitement when they join, and why they post *every* gift, *every* social media shoutout, and *every* leaderboard (a social media tier list ranking you against your other MLM cohorts). It's the dopamine hit that keeps on giving. And it makes it easy to ignore the warning signs and that gut feeling that everything about this is problematic. Eventually, this turns into other things—shopping at the same stores and buying the same studded heels and the same fedora hats because you need to match the other bossbabes—and before you know it, your entire social media feed turns into curated photos of sisterhood and togetherness at the expense of all others.

But lest I get ahead of myself.

I grab my camera and take a photo with my new purse. I take a few ... *hmm, that one is no good* ... *crap, let me grab some lipstick* ... *ahh, the lighting* ... *okay, that one will do.* I post on my wall, "I love this gig! I love getting spoiled for doing what I love doing anyway!" Whatever the hell that means. It's a script I found on the printout Becky gave me the day she recruited me at the wine bar. I post and tag Kimberly as a public "thank you" for the kind gift. Perfect! I go to her Facebook wall and notice that she's been tagged about twenty-five times by other reps in her downline—they all got the same purse, and they've all posted the same curated photo. I can't help but notice the rest of them are filtered much better than mine. I feel a temporary sting, then remember I'll be that big one day. Someday I'll be buying Kate Spade bags for all the kickass chicks in my downline!

My daughter tugs on me again. "Mama, come on!"

Ugh, crap, look at the time. I have to finish the laundry, get on a call with Vanessa and her new potential recruit, and pick up the other kids from school. Shit. As great as I feel, time is still a limited resource, eaten up by all the minutes and hours I find myself on the phone, glued to my Facebook feed.

As I'm packing up to leave, a notification pops up from a comment on the photo I just posted: "For fuck's sake, enough with the MLM bullshit!" The message is from a pretty close friend of mine from college. Ouch. What's up her ass? But I remember what I've been taught, and I quickly block her. She wouldn't say that if she were a real friend! No time for haters, or so I've been told. I don't realize at the time that I am isolating myself further from people in real life to dive deeper into the insular fantasy world of this commercial cult. I just feel like I'm siding with the people who "love and support me," but as I'll figure out much later, my allegiance to the MLM and the products at the cost of real friendships is actually a bonus for the company. By blocking the haters, the MLM is only gaining more control of me.

MLMs encourage reps to see any concerned family member or friend as a negative person. You are told that they are simply "jealous," but the truth is, in their dissuasion, they are shining light on the truth of what is really going on, and that truth is a threat to your uplines and the company.

Thus, any critic (even if they are a close friend or family member) must be discredited and ignored. This is the *T* in the BITE Model: thought control. And thought control forbids critical questions about the leader, doctrine, or policy. This is common practice in cults. Scientology, for example, says that anyone who questions the religion is a "suppressive" person. Ouch. In MLM, we use our own parlance: "Think my face cream sucks? You're dead to me!"

Even if the so-called "hater" happens to be a member of your family (your sister, or mother, or even your spouse) who genuinely expresses concern, you are supposed to attempt to dispel their worries, and if you can't, you need to distance yourself from them, block them on social media, and toe the company line. While the MLM will tell everyone that true friends and family "support" you, buying crap from you isn't authentic support. And those who *don't* want to buy your crap can be made to feel pressured and uncomfortable, which can ultimately cause genuine friends who would legitimately support you with love and kindness to turn away and distance themselves.

A common post floating around social media from MLM reps is: "Support your friends and families just the way you support the big-box stores and celebrities you don't know." It's a guilt trip. The MLM indoctrinates you to expect your friends to support you instead of allowing them to spend their money, time, and life the way they see fit. Your friends' financial and leisure activities become a target for recruiting: "Hey, Michelle, you could spend that $5.95 a day on skincare, not a latte! Karen, you could spend an hour working a side gig instead of sitting on Netflix!" It's social harassment. So, you gain a community of bossbabes, but you risk pushing away those who love you, no matter how many people you recruit. You also risk shutting off the voice of reasonable skepticism and emotional honesty in the back of your head.

Gatekeeping doesn't just limit who you are allowed to call "friends," but also what you can say and where you can say it. On the team pages, I see such warnings as:

> Your social media is NOT the appropriate place for you to vent, share opinions, bash, etc. Anything you post now affects whether or not you get business! If you post about how much you hate your job, people will assume it's the business. If you are sick all the time, people will assume our products suck. If you post hot topics that have strong opinions, you're going to offend half of your audience. If you post about how you're broke or about your husband's job, people will assume this business doesn't work. EVERYTHING you post will now be in association with your business. No negativity!

This comes not just from the field of consultants and uplines, but also those at the corporate level. If there were any negative articles, blogs, lawsuits, YouTube videos, or other critical media or press, we were sent strict instructions from the company *not* to talk about it, and not to click on the link because it would increase the site's Search Engine Optimization (SEO). Instead, we were given a CliffsNotes version of what the article or video (allegedly) stated, in addition to a curated script of what to say if anyone asked about it. The company would tell us not to read anything negative, not to form our own opinion and come up with our own rebuttals. We were to parrot the company statement and not our formulated view, in order to "get back to income-producing activity." This is the *I* in the BITE Model: information control. Minimize access to non-cult sources, critical information, and former members. Don't click; here's what you say, instead. Then, get back to work. Whatever you do, don't look behind the curtain.

After posting my thank-you to Kimberly, I hang up my fancy new purse, recycle the boxes, and throw the laundry in the dryer. It's cool that I can fit this business into my life, but unfortunately, I still find myself scrambling to keep up with all my other responsibilities. I'm cash-rich (or at least, getting there) and time-poor. I put the littles in the car and hop in to pick up the others. I'm leaving a little early because I need to call Vanessa on the way. We have a conference call scheduled with another potential new recruit. It's been fun growing my team and also helping my downline grow theirs, though the bigger it gets, the more of these car calls I'm doing, which is becoming trickier to fit between juggling five kids. Becky assures me that if I put in the time now, it will pay off later. I am being as coachable as possible and doing whatever she tells me.

"Hey, you, sorry I'm a little late. You have Brianna on?" I fumble with the Bluetooth button on my phone and pull out of the driveway.

"Hey, Em. Yes, one sec!" Vanessa adds Brianna to the call.

On my drives to and from school pickup, I'm multitasking three-way calls. Oh, the three-way—yes that's really what it's called, and no, the innuendo never gets old. Here's the way it works: A consultant brings a prospective recruit to a phone call with their upline—in this case, Vanessa (my recruit) is calling me with Brianna (her potential recruit), so I can answer Brianna's questions. This is meant to accomplish a few things:

- **Emotional control:** makes the new recruit feel like they are special by talking to the "guru/expert" (me).
- **Behavior control:** trains the consultant on what to say about the company.
- **Thought control:** dispels any valid questions/concerns that the new potential recruit may have.
- **Information control:** indoctrinates them into the system of doing this all over again with new people themselves.

Yes, it's as gross as it sounds. And it feels very similar to rushing a sorority; the planned conversation with the more important sorority sisters, always pretty, usually white, who've already gone through a list of photos and have their favorites pegged and the answers to their questions preloaded. "Oh, no way! You were a cheerleader, too?! So was I! You'll fit in so well in our house!" Meanwhile, we, of course, knew she was a cheerleader because we spent days studying the rushee's photos and applications, and we already knew which ones we'd be attacking. And here I am, in my mid-thirties, re-creating the same behavior to sell a similar promise of a different sisterhood. I already know everything about this chick because Vanessa has filled me in on all of Brianna's pain points: She wants more money for activities with her kids but doesn't want to go back to full-time work after maternity leave.

"Hi, Brianna, I'm Emily, Vanessa's friend and business partner. I'm here to help answer any questions you may have about this business opportunity!"

This script never feels good, because ultimately, you aren't listening to people's concerns—you're just squashing them. But I'm getting so used to not feeling good, I can already practically ignore it . . . almost.

"Yeah," Brianna stammers. "I just really don't want to sell to friends and family. Honestly, I was just interested in some products, and Vanessa mentioned getting a bigger discount. But it feels weird to sell to other people."

Oh, honey, don't I know it! "Well, Brianna, do you feel as though Vanessa has been bugging you?" There is an awkward silence before she replies, "No, not at all. I actually have been asking her about it."

I feel like a snake about to strike, gaslighting her with my response. "Well then, you should have no reason to feel that anyone would think you're bugging them. You've been in good hands with Vanessa!"

The language is effective, but it's all smoke and mirrors. God, I could use a drink. I shush my youngest in the back seat, who is starting to get antsy as I pull into a parking spot at school. After about ten minutes of back and forth, we say goodbye to Brianna, who ultimately says, "Hell to the no," and I chat with Vanessa for a bit.

"Ugh, Em, I just don't think this is for me. I *hate* trying to convince people! I suck at it!" she complains.

I understand the sentiment; it's soul-crushing to have to try to talk people into this. The reality is, some people come to these calls interested, but most are coerced, like poor Brianna, who was just asking about some damn product discounts. We are taught to make it no big deal. As soon as someone asks *any* questions about "the business," you segue to "Hey, that's a great question. I'd love to have you chat with my friend and business partner about this. She's great because [insert fake reason here: she's been at this longer . . . lives in your town . . . also has twins . . . whatever]. She's free at two or four. What works for you?" More behavior, information, thought, and emotional control. People feel pressured, so they show up already defensive, and it's beyond awkward. But we do it this way because it's easier to dispel the concerns of a stranger; you don't feel as bad about blowing sunshine up the ass of someone you hardly know. Plus, the more you lather, rinse, and repeat, the more natural it becomes, and the more you start to truly believe what you're saying. You conclude that you have a secret, that they need to know the secret, and that they will be better off if they join you so they can be in on it.

How's that logic for you?

Although I have complete empathy and understanding for Vanessa—because I hate these conversations, too—I still have to sell the dream. If she doesn't keep doing these calls, her team won't either, and so on and so on. Duplication is something that is taught in the MLM: Be coachable, do things the way your leader does them, and your team will do them the way you do them, and so on. Copy and paste is the way this works, or so Becky tells me.

Ugh. Time to charm.

"Vanessa," I tell my best friend. "You are doing *so* awesome!" And she is. That part is genuine. She has had so many new customers and got a new business partner just last week, and this was her third three-way this week! "Listen, I've heard no so many times. Sometimes it takes people a little longer to see the vision, you know? Just remember it's only a no right now. Remember Tessa? We had two calls with her, and she finally came around."

"True," Vanessa agrees. "Same with Lori . . . and Kelsi. You're right. I just need to keep plugging away!"

Phew. Disaster averted.

Let's pause here. Maybe you're a bit triggered by the "never take no for an answer" speak? Yes, I really did say, "It's only a no right now." Quite a mindfuck, as a woman, to constantly be reminding yourself, your children, the world, that no means no—unless you're talking MLM. Because wearing people down is something you're taught from the beginning, and it comes in many flavors:

"Keep reaching out, and eventually people will say yes."

"People take twelve nos before they get to a yes."

"You're sharing something great—help them see how they fit into this."

I believed this; I really did. But it's coercion disguised as "just sharing something fun!" Of course, it feels skeevy to push products on friends and family, or to cut and paste messages on Facebook, or to cold-call people and bring in your upline on a three-way call. It's skeevy to call it a three-way! But when you're indoctrinated into an MLM, you're taught to ignore your own intuition from the outset, for the sake of the numbers game. My upline taught me to never take no for an answer. Ever. Her upline taught her. Every corporate training taught all of us. And I was now teaching it to my new recruits. It's amazing how much you can ignore your intuition when everyone around you is doing the same thing.

None of these things intuitively feel good because they *aren't* good. Yet the goal of MLM training is to get you to ignore those nagging feelings. Eventually, it becomes second nature: That gross generic message feels okay when you've copied and pasted it for the twentieth time. Before long, that script feels natural when you've memorized and recited it over and over. It's amazing what you can be conditioned to do. And that doesn't mean you've lost your fear or leveled up. It just means you've become used to it, like staying with an abusive boyfriend or becoming addicted to cocaine.

Make no mistake: MLMs will promise you all kinds of things— community, connection, and opportunity—but they're lying. This isn't personal growth. This is getting gradually accustomed to ignoring your intuition, dismissing warnings from people who love and care about you, and negating the red flags that ask you to go against the values you hold dear. It's natural to take it personally when someone blocks you on social media because of something *you* did. It's natural to feel scummy about sending a message that isn't aligned with who you are. And it's absolutely natural to feel bad when you don't take no for an answer. All of these feelings are there for a reason—and being asked to shrug them off and do the same thing over and over will erode your sense of self over time.

But here I am, ignoring my intuition and helping Vanessa to ignore hers, like a good little MLM soldier. Because even if something feels bad, it's better than getting kicked out of the sisterhood—and for a bunch of lonely women who are desperate for connection, that community is everything.

"Thanks, Em, that helps. See you tonight!"

Tonight? Wait, what's tonight? Ah, yes! The biz op! Shit, it's Thursday! How could I forget? Another local consultant who is pretty high up has rented out an event space to do a business presentation. A biz op is a leveled-up version of the "wine and opportunity" meeting Becky invited me to just a few short months before. It's row seating, someone from the corporate office, a PowerPoint presentation, speakers, and a call to action to sign up at the end. Consultants bring guests or just themselves to become further indoctrinated—er, trained—in the system of operation.

These retention events, as described by Jason Jones, an attorney and advocate for victims of manipulation fraud, are designed to keep people in the commercial cult as long as possible. He describes three levels on the path of retention: recruits (the people at the bottom of the pyramid), grinders (those who do the greatest amount of work and put on these events), and profiteers (the people at the very top, who do very little work and make most of the money). The objective of these events—whether they are biz ops, conventions, or Zoom calls—is to move people from the recruits into the grinders category, keeping them there as long as possible, at least three to four years. The goal is not to get them to the profiteers level, because, mathematically, virtually nobody makes it there.

Grinders usually have no sales experience yet still become deeply involved in the MLM, thanks to these constant retention events. They likely will not be making a lot of money but may be doing enough to keep going and possibly cover their own costs. The events are at the local, regional, and national levels, and consultants are encouraged to attend, even if they have to travel; these are often labeled as success trainings. By attending, you are immersed further into the retention process. You see stories like yours, a never-ending series of testimonials, and you can visualize yourself having the same success. With the electric crowds and events, your hope becomes belief, and if your belief fades because of the obvious lack of results you're getting, these events continue to rekindle the possibility that next year, it might be you . . . so you keep grinding.

It's the kind of emotional manipulation that happens in all MLMs, consistently, all around the country.

This is actually going to be my first one, and as an added bonus, I have been asked to speak! Apparently, I'm a "good example" of what this business can do, since I'm so new and have already grown a good-sized team. But whatever, I'm just excited to get a night out again. Honestly, this business has been the best excuse to escape from my day-to-day. If nobody signs up, at least I'll have some wine and friends to hang out with.

"Yes!" I happily chirp back. "I'll be there! Actually, I'll pick you up?"

"Perfect, I even have a couple guests meeting us there."

"See, you're already turning this around! Remember, the only way you fail is if you give up."

I feel good that I've turned a negative into a positive, even if it feels like I'm reciting lines from an inspirational quote cat poster, but it seems to work, so I add, "Also, I'm going to bring you this book Becky gave me about positive mindset. See you later!"

Books, mantras, courses, cat poster wisdom—these are the name of the game because the cure for negativity in MLM is positivity. T-o-x-i-c positivity!

Every MLM is dishing out the same narrative. Follow the system and you will see immediate and incredible benefits! Be positive, and if you work hard enough, you'll make it! Just keep your head down and keep working! This is the falsehood of white supremacy: that you should always be striving for the next level, the next promotion, more money, more recognition, to be the best at all costs. And if you reach your potential, it's because of what the MLM taught you, but if you don't, it's because you didn't try hard enough.

Over my time with Rejuvinat, I began to notice on team pages, and even the company's public social media accounts, that any negative comments (about crummy products, poor customer service, claims about a predatory business model) would always get deleted. Product not working for you? You must not be using it correctly. Someone didn't like the return policy? They should have read it thoroughly beforehand. Not getting enough customers? You must not be imbibing enough personal development material. It didn't matter how benign the complaint was, or what it was about. Only positive comments and questions were allowed. Instead of questioning it, I emulated this with my own team.

You're taught not to complain, because if you complain, it will attract negativity. And you don't want your negativity to spread and become contagious. That's exactly the same recipe for success used by cults: behavior control. The personal intentions of individual reps attempting to stay positive might be good (I just want her to feel better!), but toxic positivity minimizes, denies, and invalidates very real human emotions. It makes you feel you are doing wrong by having negative emotions or questioning things.

Instead of recognizing that you are feeling guilty for *doing* bad, the MLM inspires shame, making you feel that you *are* bad. Not that you are a human with normal emotions and critical-thinking skills, because those are reactions the MLMs require you to quell.

Every time I was struggling, someone suggested a new book or a mantra, and I found it quite helpful. I can't say whether any of it actually fixed my mindset—I never came away with tools or skills per se—but it did work to distract me and convince me to keep going. Why not pay it forward?

MLMs are built on the belief that if it works for me, it will work for you, despite any differences in resources, backgrounds, skill sets, or networks. MLMs believe everyone is truly equal, in the most abusive way possible. At the same time, this so-called equality only holds true to a certain point. Some people will never succeed as much as others, and MLMs already know this. This is exactly why the business model is tiered—it's by design.

So, what about people who don't make it? The more than 90 percent who never make a dime? Easy: They should have done more. Failure to succeed is on you, even if it's the norm, not the exception. When someone "fails," it must be due to a negative mindset, lack of faith, or not working hard enough. At least that's what you're told, and what you're expected to repeat. "It works if you work!" Ignore the fact that very few MLM members ever *break even*. A very small percentage make a little bit (less than $5,000 a year, which is before taxes, by the way). The ones who make $100,000 per year (again, before taxes)? Less than *half* a percent. The ones with photos of opulent lifestyles dripping with designer bags and friendships galore that you see on social media? Those are the people who make up 0.05 percent (yes, five *hundredths* of a percent) of MLM reps. All the others are faking it until they make it. Unfortunately, they never make it.

Now, positivity in and of itself isn't a bad thing; it's, well, positive! Looking for the inherently good things around you—the sunny day, a roof over your head—and having a general gratitude for positive things is great. However, conditioning people to believe the only reason they could fail is their own fault rather than the fault of systemic issues fundamental to the business model is victim blaming and gaslighting. And it may sound familiar, since our capitalist society frequently rewards a few at the expense of the many (hard-working Amazon employees busting ass for a living wage watching Jeff Bezos being launched into space on a dick rocket, or Kim Kardashian telling women everywhere to "get off their fucking asses and work"). Yet MLMs don't rely solely on capitalism. They want you to worship at the altar of meritocracy, which is far more sinister; this is the belief that the harder you work, the more likely it is that you'll succeed. But the problem is not people's work ethic. It may sound plausible in theory, but the MLM model is not designed to help everyone succeed.

The "pull yourself up by the bootstraps" ideology relies on consumerism and a focus on self-improvement and mindset culture. It conveniently ignores socioeconomic status. It ignores race, ethnicity, religion, culture, gender, sexuality, and marginalized identities. It ignores those who live below the poverty line, who don't have access to cash or technology, and those with disabilities or exceptions. It relies on privilege in the statement "If I can do it, so can you."

It's a lie—an intentional one. If people blame themselves, they turn away from the real flaws in the system.

After I get the kids home and set them up with homework/snacks/ TV shows/babysitter (again), I sneak upstairs and dig through my closet to find something to wear for my biz op tonight. Ugh, nothing screams businesswoman to me. Jeans and a T-shirt? This is not gonna cut it; I'll be standing in front of the crowd and telling my story! I need to dress the part. When the field development leader asked me for a headshot for the promotional materials for this event, I had to send her an old Easter picture and she had to crop out my family. That doesn't scream #bossbabe at all. Last week on a Zoom call with one of the top leaders, we were told that in our social media photos, we "should dress for the title you want."

I can appreciate that, but all the top leaders are typically dressed head-to-toe in Chanel or Gucci or other brands I've never owned, let alone had any interest in buying. Maybe I can run to Nordies later and find something presentable, so I can pass? But Kale is not going to be happy if I put more purchases on the credit card this month. I've already bought so much product! Maybe in a few months I can redirect my attention and invest in attire. Again, I remind myself I have to spend money to make money. Or something like that.

I throw an old blazer over a T-shirt and jeans and put on some heels I haven't worn in years. I fiddle with my hair and throw on some more mascara. This will do. It will be a good trial run for the next time. Because there *will* be a next time, I'm sure of it. If I'm already being asked to speak at these events now, I can only imagine what the future holds. I'm excited to tell my story, and I'm optimistic that some guests might join our team, but I'm mostly looking forward to finally meeting some of the people from corporate in person, as they've been gushing over me the last couple of months.

"Thank you, Jessica!" I wave goodbye to the sitter, kiss the kids, and head out.

I pull up to Vanessa's house and she hops into my car, visibly annoyed. "What's up?" I ask as she slams the door.

"Ugh. Jake. He's such a dick," she fumes, fixing her hair in the mirror.

Ah, Jake, the hubby—well, soon-to-be ex-hubby. Thanks to Rejuvinat and her generous parents, Vanessa was able to afford her own apartment and get away from him, but Jake doesn't love that she's more independent. "He called five minutes before he was supposed to pick the kids up and told me that he couldn't come. Luckily, my mom came over. It was my fault for telling him it was a work thing—"

I interrupt, "Um . . . no. Not your fault, ever. That jerk. He doesn't want you to succeed. He wants you to be dependent on him. Just wait until you make it big and you're driving your white shiny car around."

"You don't really think that's going to happen, do you? The car?"

I'm taken aback . . . Jake got to her. Man. Or that call today really shook her spirit. "I just want you to shoot for the stars! I really want this for you."

"I know, Em. It's sweet, and I do really enjoy this, and the extra money is nice, but it's just, you know, a side thing. A reason to get out of the house. Just don't take it too seriously, okay? Besides, my guests canceled and I'm kinda glad—I just want the night off."

Yikes. I'm not even sure how to take this. She's glad her guests aren't coming? Vanessa is my best friend; she's seen how seriously I take this. I didn't at first, but I do now. Despite her discouraging words, I know she'll see the light—she will want this more for herself. For now, I'm just glad she got out of the house; tonight will really help her. I'm a believer, and like all truly religious people, I know I can convert her into one, as well!

This "life-changing" narrative tends to be pushed hard in MLM, as if you're a global philanthropist spreading knowledge or wealth. Of course, there is nothing wrong with a job that "changes your life," but putting the sales of creams and supplements on such a pedestal invalidates most other professions, including the ones that actually *do* change lives. It also drives home a deeper message: There is something wrong with the way you are doing things, so you need to always be striving for more within the MLM to really change your life. What is valued is an all-American, upper-middle-class image of success. Making more money is the goal, at any expense.

"Hi, Annie! Hi, Celeste! Nice to see you!" We walk into an event space at a local country club, where I'm guessing one of the consultants is a member. Jamie, yes . . . that's right. She's the one who organized the event and is a pretty high-up consultant who lives in this burg.

"Nice place!" Vanessa says as we walk up to the registration table.

"Ten dollars per consultant, please!" Wait, what? We have to pay for this? I don't remember seeing that on the promo, but I was a little more fixated on how my photo looked, not the content. "But I'm presenting," I mention.

"Yeah, consultants always pay; guests are free, but if you're a consultant, it's ten bucks," the woman behind the table says without cracking a smile. The other registration gal senses the tension and interjects, "Hi! Sorry, consultants host these events themselves, even though a corporate person is here. Jamie actually paid for the event. But if there is enough interest and we eventually get a big enough draw of guests, corporate will sponsor more in the future!"

Well, this is news to me, and to be honest, it seems a little shitty. Even though it's only ten bucks, I know Jamie makes more than I do. I can only imagine how much an event space like this costs, and every consultant has already paid to be part of the company. Seems slimy to make the field "earn" their worth. But what do I know? What I don't realize right now is that as I rise in the ranks, I'll put many of these biz ops on my credit-card bill.

"Pay money to make money," the friendlier woman smiles.

I've heard (and said) that one before, and I'm saying it more frequently these days. I pull out my card, and she hands me a drink ticket (oh yay, one whole drink ticket!). I'm still excited to be speaking, and I suppose $10 is a small price to pay. Forget the fact that I'm doing the work of the company with no actual pay. All of the reps here are taking out time from their evening, as unpaid MLM reps are expected to market constantly but only get paid if they make a sale. Hopefully, my one wine pour is big.

Along with the shitty wine, there is some cheese and a few trays of cookies, but sadly, not a huge crowd. Vanessa and I make small talk with a few other consultants as we fill up our wineglasses, and I scan the room for my guests. I invited three women who said they'd meet me here. They were super interested in Rejuvinat, but I don't see any of them. I check my phone . . . ah, got it. Two texts within the last half hour, which means two people aren't coming. All I have from this evening so far is a shitty glass of wine and ten fewer dollars in my pocket. I'm still holding out for Hannah, my third invitee, but with the clock ticking, it's not looking good.

Vanessa senses my concern. "You know, it's probably better—you can just concentrate on speaking and not worry about entertaining people."

I fight the urge to offer a bland cat poster response, but she's right. I've been working on recruiting all damn week. Maybe what I say will help bring other people into the company! The more the merrier, right? Even if it doesn't benefit me directly, the more people who join our company, the more all of us stand to gain. Or so I've been told. At least it'll be good practice. Still, I get that nagging feeling, once again, that this is eerily similar to sorority rush: the pressure to sell yourself as the "best," and your house as "the place." And no matter how many people there are in the room, you'll always be disappointed, regardless of how much work you put in, because there could always be more/better/best/ pick your own superlative.

"If everyone can take their seats, we'll get started!" Elizabeth, a bubbly young woman from corporate, stands at the front of the room. I'm not totally sure what her role is. She's not a consultant; she works at the corporate company headquarters in Salt Lake City. I think she travels around and speaks at these things. All I know is that I always see her in my email and on social media. She's the one I've been emailing with this week—a liaison between consultants and corporate. I admire how she's dressed to the nines, with designer studded heels. I bite back my envy. After all, she was so sweet to me on the phone and even gave me some insider info about a sale coming up next month, making me feel very special. (Love bombing comes from the corporate level, too!)

Elizabeth chats for a few minutes, thanks everyone for taking the time to come out, and runs through a quick PowerPoint presentation about the company. I'm momentarily distracted when I see Hannah walk in from the side door, and I wave dumbly toward her. She takes a seat in the back and my spirits are lifted again. *Let's hope this works*, I think to myself.

Before I know it, it's my turn. "Next, we have an up-and-coming local consultant who's going to share her story. Emily?"

I'm nervous but this is a pretty small crowd. I walk to the front of the audience as they clap; I grab the microphone, turn around, take a deep breath, and start my masterclass on indoctrination.

"Hi, I'm Emily! I live in Seattle and I'm the mom of five small kids. [Emotional control: I'm so relatable and do so much! You only have two children. Wow, you have so much time on your hands!] I've been with Rejuvinat for about six months. [Thought control: You, too, can succeed in no time at all!] I didn't think I'd ever do something like this, because like many of you probably do, I had plenty of reservations. [Information control: but you'd better ignore that intuition.] I haven't been in the workforce for a long time, and since I'm a stay-at-home mom, this fits so well in the nooks and crannies of my life. [Behavior control: I'll show you how to work ALL THE TIME.] My skin and hair are the best they've ever looked [Information control: They already looked great before Rejuvinat], and all I do is use the products and talk about them. [Behavior control: You'll literally do this all the goddamn time.] The best part is the friendships; I've found my sisterhood with this company. [Emotional control: You need friends, right, you lonely POS?] I have money for a babysitter, and I feel like I have purpose. [Thought control: You also need to want those things!] If you feel like you're missing friendships or money and want a vehicle for change [Emotional control: You need more out of your sad existence], this business is for you. [Behavior control: Join or else your life is going to continue to suck.]"

The room fills with applause, and I bask in the acknowledgment. Wow, that felt good. I was told in college that I was a good public speaker, but it's been so long since I've flexed those muscles. Glad to know I've still got it. And I do feel good about everything I said. All of it was true ... er ... true-ish. I have money to pay the babysitter, but it certainly isn't Rejuvinat money, since I spent all that on products. I definitely have had to make more "nooks and crannies" by getting a babysitter more often. But I follow the scripted version of what I was told to talk about, and it seems to have gone well.

Elizabeth winks and takes the mic from me to close up the biz op. I sit down, look around, and see that everyone is feeling the love, the energy, the possibilities. Hannah has a huge smile on her face and gives me a thumbs-up. Elizabeth continues talking, and I spend half my attention on her words and half of it fantasizing about how this opportunity is going to change my life. She plays another short promo video, showing some of the amazing trips and gifts that are available to consultants.

She closes with "The only thing stopping you is *you*. Lean into your fear. Think positively and you cannot fail. Nothing of significance will happen in your comfort zone. Thanks for coming today."

The room erupts in applause, and Vanessa and I smile at each other. I'm suddenly really glad we came. Maybe she's ready to lean into her fears now, too. I can see that some of the magic has rubbed off on her; there is motivation in her eyes once more.

This kind of speech, this whole process, works on so many because it's aspirational. Who doesn't want to believe they own the key to their own success? That if they just change their thinking, they will never fail?

Motivation is a word that gets thrown around in these retention events quite often. *Courage, strength, grit*—all the pseudo-empowerment vocab is employed. Yes, we all need motivation to get out of bed in the morning, do our homework, or make dinner. Yes, those all require strength, courage, or grit to some extent. And yes, all of those things come from within, and we can draw them from others, blah blah blah. But what MLMs ignore is that the circumstances you're in also dictate what you're able to actually accomplish. We don't all have the same twenty-four hours in a day. Wealthier people like Vanessa and me have more space, goods, money, and free time to avoid or mitigate everyday stresses, whereas poorer people do not. Socioeconomic brackets impact every part of day-to-day life and the degree of status, power, and benefits.

According to the American Psychological Association, "Class affects whether someone is going to be accepted into a particular kind of school, their likelihood of succeeding in that school, the kinds of jobs they have access to, and the kinds of friends they make." It isn't all about mindset when you have to work two jobs and don't have a car. It isn't about motivation when you can't make rent.

I was able to "lean into fear" because I have a husband with a stable job and discretionary time and income, even if it's limited. I am able to be "courageous" because I can drive my own car home to my warm 3,500-square-foot house, whose fridge is filled to the brim because I live in a nice neighborhood that isn't considered a food desert; I can access affordable, nutritious food in five different places within a few blocks of my house. I'm able to be "strong" because I have a network of friends and family who support me. I don't need much "grit" to get one of my friends to buy something from me. Again, "pushing through the comfort zone" just refers to ignoring my intuition, which doesn't earn me any brownie points.

As I now know, preying on your friends to buy shit is nothing to write home about. It's easy to believe you are successful because you've worked hard and had a positive mindset when you are already financially stable and have a big network to signal-boost your "success." And it's really easy to ignore your intuition when your lifestyle, intelligence, empathy, and network are things that gain you praise and flattery, as if *you* were the one to make it all happen. This is why very smart and empathetic people fall into the trap of joining MLMs in the first place. Your intentions are so good, and you probably have a quality education and generally make smart financial decisions. Why would you second-guess something you joined with the intention of making a positive impact, especially when you've been successful in the past, and receive praise and accolades the whole way? It feels good, even when it doesn't.

Pushing through discomfort applies when you're training for a race and need to get from mile two to three to improve. Leaning into fear applies when you are performing a concerto and need to put in extra hours on the difficult passages to meet a goal. It does *not* mean denying your own inner knowing that something is indeed not okay and telling yourself your intuition is wrong. It does not mean that if you repeat mantras, share positive social media messages, read more personal development books, or "fake it till you make it," any of those MLM goals will come true. You can't manifest your own destiny when socio-economic differences stack the cards against you.

But that night after my speech, all of my lies of omission feel okay. In fact, as I'm being patted on the back and congratulated, and my star is shining, it feels more than fine. *I deserve this.* I've been at home with kids for years with no accolades, no trophies, nothing. No wonder everyone who has joined my team so far has been a SAHM who misses a paycheck or a working mom who misses time with her kids. The MLM is sold as the solution to everything.

"Emily, that was awesome—you're a natural up there!" Elizabeth gushes. "Thank you so much for doing this." I introduce her to Vanessa, and we chitchat a bit. I look more closely at her studded shoes; they really are fancy—Valentino, I think. I should put those on my vision board, but first I need to figure out what a vision board is—I think she said something about it during the PowerPoint. She glances around the room. "This was a pretty decent-sized crowd! Did you have any guests tonight? Have a good turnout from your team?"

A little caught off guard, I reply, "Uh, yeah. I mean, Vanessa came with me, and I have one guest, but no other teammates came."

I laugh and shrug because I suddenly feel guilty for some reason.

"Ah, it happens," she says. "You know what, though? Leaders show up. Good for you two." She wags a finger at me and Vanessa. "You know who you can rely on!"

She's right. I have a bunch of consultants, but most of them didn't even make an effort to come. How much do they *really* want this? Sure, they complain that they aren't making much money, but coming to a biz op could've been so easy. Of course, they would have had to invite other people, which is uncomfortable, but like Elizabeth said in her speech, how much growth happens in your comfort zone?

It's easy to start victim blaming. Because if you don't succeed in MLM, or complain that you should be seeing more success, you will be told that you just need to work harder. It's your mindset. Show up. Read more. Watch videos. Anytime I've had a concern—I'm not closing many recruits, people complain about the high prices, a consultant quits—my upline has told me something positive to spin it around. "Schedule more three-ways!" "Read a self-help book!" "Show up for a power hour this evening!"

If your business isn't doing what you'd hoped and you still aren't making money despite doing all the things you're supposed to do, instead of saying, "Well, shoot, you tried" or "Well, maybe you'll just be someone who sells a little bit" or "You can just use it for the discount" or some other frame of reference that makes logical sense, you're basically told that you suck. That it's your fault for not making the money you want to make. Instead of questioning these paradigms, you will continue to try harder and spend more money, more time, and more effort to make this work, because it's up to you, after all! The negative talk drives you further and further into the MLM, because it's sold as the solution to your problems. Need more money? Sell more. Already spent too much? Sunk cost fallacy: You're already in so deep, so just keep going, even if quitting now would make the most financial sense! Feel like you're not doing well? Get on more Zoom training calls. And because there is an endless stream of personal development material and a supposedly endless ladder upon which to climb up the ranks, no matter how high you are in the MLM hierarchy, you could always be making more money, hitting a better title, recruiting more people, selling more product. Be superior at any cost, even if it only makes a very small number of people at the top even richer.

The expectations are dizzying, and with all these new imperatives on how to be a better rep, people might forget they were probably drawn into the MLM in the first place because of a popular tactic: the bait and switch. This happens when your reasons for joining don't match what you actually end up getting. Many people join "just for the discount," since it's a tactic to get current customers who are already spending money to sign up as consultants. They are told from the beginning that they can work as much or as little as they want, in their own spare time. But eventually, if they don't make the MLM their number-one focus (something they likely hadn't initially intended to do), they are shamed for not working hard enough. Capitalism at its finest: People are promised freedom, but they end up in the rat race.

A 2019 study reported that people with more free time are happier, healthier, and more productive than people who work all the time and make more money. MLM reps are promised the same utopia from hard work and constant hustle, but unlike in a capitalist structure that would pay them per hour, they may never actually make a dime.

So far, my team is pretty new, so I'm not sure who is going to make it or not, but looking at effort, Vanessa is definitely my workhorse. I just need to find more people like her. If you follow the system, this is *supposed* to work. And it's definitely working for me!

I remember Elizabeth's words. Leaders show up. I am a leader! Vanessa is a leader. We just need to find more consultants like us. Maybe Hannah will be a leader, too.

"Great job up there!" Hannah says as she gives me a hug.

"Thanks! What did you think?"

"I think it sounds cool. I really want to try the products. I have to head home but I'll catch up with you tomorrow?"

"I'd love to get you on the phone with Becky; she's been doing this longer and has a very similar background. We're free tomorrow at two and three. What works for you?" I offer.

After scheduling a three-way with my usual scripts, I drop Vanessa off and head back to my home. It's dark and quiet, and I have an adrenaline rush from the evening. I pay the babysitter, warm up some pizza rolls, and (why not?) fill another glass of wine. I glance around the kitchen; the dishes need to be done, the highchair is out . . . Shit, I'll be up for a while. I guess it's good that I'm on a bit of a high. Plus, this is the only time I get *me* time.

I sit down with my wine and rolls, and open Facebook. A notification from Kimberly! I read her response to my digital thank-you note on her wall: "No, thank *you*, Emily. This is a team effort. A rising tide lifts all boats." A nod to the trickle-down economics of MLM, except you're constantly working to levitate the upline with the hopes of lifting yourself.

I get caught up in Kimberly's feed and scroll through some of her photos. Look at that house: so much gorgeous shiplap and brass, a kitchen island that looks the size of our entire living room. Those clothes—all designer brands—not a hair out of place, always in heels. Her life looks like perfection. I scroll and see her at the big company convention last year, being inducted into the coveted million-dollar club, reserved only for reps who have earned over a million dollars. It looks like a dream. *My* dream.

Behavior, information, thought, and emotional control are all being exercised in this moment. I want to make that much money and earn those accolades, so I need to do what she's doing (behavior control), and I believe in the picture she's putting out there, whether or not it's real (information control). I'm falling for platitudinous buzzwords like "time freedom" and "full-time income in part-time hours," instead of reality (thought control). Finally, I'm made to feel less than for not having such a great house or great outfits or taking great trips with my kids (emotional control). All of this is working on me—just from a Facebook feed.

I take a swig of my wine and wistfully tell myself, "I'm going to be up there someday. I know I am."

The Ladybosses

I "earned" a cruise from my upline; however, after qualifying I realized it was only partially paid. My husband and I figured it was an investment in my business and a fun getaway for ourselves. It was fine, but we had the smallest cabin, terrible flights, and everything cost more than we anticipated. The worst part? Come tax time, I was slapped with a $10,000 fine from the IRS because I was supposed to file quarterly taxes. My income was inflated thanks to that "free trip" being tacked on as earnings. It was devastating. I had to borrow money from my parents, and I am still paying them back. I would have never worked so hard to "earn" the trip had I known it would be so detrimental.

—KELSEY, former MLM rep

I look around our bedroom and can't believe I'm actually leaving. It has been almost a decade since I've been away from my children—all five of them—for an entire weekend. A lot of people have asked us, "Why five children?" And I wish I could give a better answer than "We're really bad with birth control." But we are, leaving me knee-deep in dirty diapers and screaming babies and bottle warmers and raw nipples for years on end. But those days are now behind me. I am starting over. I am reclaiming *me*.

"Babe, where's the pink carry-on bag?" I call to my husband as he tries to prepare himself for three days without Mom. "Remember, the one with the monogram?"

I've laid out all my clothes, even throwing in a pair of fancy heels I haven't worn in five years because this is the weekend to impress, to show the ladies of Rejuvinat that there's a new girlboss in town. It's only been a year since Becky invited me to join her team, and I have already hit the coveted top 3 percent, earning a free trip to an upscale resort in Colorado.

Kale brings in the luggage and looks across all the folded and neatly organized clothes on our bed.

"It's just three days," he teases, but what he doesn't realize is that it isn't *just* three days. It's the first taste of freedom I've had in years. Kale travels for work, escaping our crowded home filled with temper tantrums and Pokémon cards for corporate retreats and business class. Now, I get to be the one flying away on a jet plane.

I affix the Kate Spade luggage tag I earned from Rejuvinat to my carry-on. I turn to Kale. "What? I'm excited."

He kisses me on the forehead. "Then I'm excited for you."

I understand why husbands like Kale want to support Rejuvinat. For years, he has watched me struggle under the onerous weight of motherhood. While he gets up early to go to work, I'm the one who stays up all night with the kids. We have taken on the traditional roles of working dad and stay-at-home mom, and he knows that I crave something more, something that connects me to other women, that isn't just another "mommy and me" playgroup or hanging out with the parents of our kids' friends.

And now I've proven to him that I can be successful, too. I am being shouted out in team newsletters, gaining so much attention that my Instagram is blowing up. In fact, the day they announced I had achieved the 3 percent status, my followers increased by 3,000 people in twenty-four hours; they were mostly other Rejuvinat consultants, but still! I know I'm not making anything close to Kale's salary, but after years of sharing a joint account, I've opened my own checking account.

It feels good to pay for things and know that I've earned extra perks, like this trip.

Through the distorted lens of social media, team retreats and other MLM incentive trips *seem* like they're all expenses paid, but that isn't exactly true. Generally, retreats are planned by someone's, or several someones', upline; this person then reserves a big house, cabin, or block of rooms (thanks, Becky!). Consultants pay their own way. There are usually ways to reduce the cost, all tied to a list of activities that increase your upline's paycheck: sell more, recruit more, join power hours or Zoom calls. And there are incentives thrown in (like my new Hunter boots and Kate Spade luggage tag and $200 cash back), but they are definitely *not* free. In the case of an incentive trip, Rejuvinat gives you a travel stipend to cover your airline ticket and some other expenses, though the stipend doesn't quite cut it. I realize that the cost of this trip is already eating up my commission from the previous month, and that my upline is getting the benefit of the promotion and the commission, but I laugh it off. It is, after all, an investment in my business. And truth be told, Kale and I can afford the investment.

I GUESS, if I had been paying attention, that might have been a red flag. Because you can only build a business with Rejuvinat if you have the resources to invest in Rejuvinat. I have noticed the slew of luxury handbags on the social media feeds of my fellow consultants. Rejuvinat promises women the opportunity to become financially independent, and chatter quickly moves through the company about women who "retire" their husbands with their business—failing to mention that most of these women had already attained some level of financial independence before being recruited into Rejuvinat.

Most of us are SAHMs because we can afford to be SAHMs; it's why we're such great bait. MLMs and their many incentives are sold as empowering women, but what is female empowerment, anyway? And who is it actually empowering? SAHMs don't have many other external sources of power—I certainly don't. We tell our kids what to do and maybe we're on a committee or two at school, but compared to the lives of women working in finance or law or medicine or real estate or anything with real pay and power, we feel pretty powerless. But in an MLM, we are given that "power" we lack, and we each inflate the egos of other women in the MLM to make all of it seem more important than it really is. In fact, we're coached to reach out to affluent women with good networks. They can afford the products, after all, and they know others who can.

As I begin to grow my network, "recruiting up" is not only something I do all the time—it's something I do well. This faux empowerment isn't about feminism or structural changes, but about buoying the lifestyles of people who already have a lot of privileges. I've heard rags-to-riches stories in MLM of women who had $40 in their bank account and spent it on a business kit in a last-ditch effort to find financial freedom—the "hunger" Becky told me about the first night I joined. However, a year into this venture, I've never actually met anyone with that story.

In fact, not once in my entire tenure at Rejuvinat did I *ever* meet someone who went from poor to Porsche. Because everyone who joins an MLM already has the inherent privilege of an internet connection, cell phone, and money or someone to borrow money from. The idea that "anyone can be successful" couldn't be further from the truth. You need to have money, and you need to know people who have money. The only ones being empowered through MLMs are those who already have inherent privilege, and the more wealth you have access to, the more money you make.

These incentive trips and retreats are all about reifying existing power, which they reframe as empowerment, through information control. And it is bossbabe suicide to sit them out. They promise secrets to success and insider looks at product road maps. *What classified information will they share? What groundbreaking leadership information will I miss? I need personal development to level up!* Qualifications and rules to "earn a spot" are arbitrary and filled with caveats, but are *always* tied to sales and recruiting, so the upline *always* benefits. They are packaged as "be here or else" events meant to fortify your "She-EO status." Photos are posted on social media the entire time, cementing the fact that you *must* be there, and if you aren't, you should try harder next time. They denote success to the onlookers who are foaming at the mouth to get in on them.

These love bombing weekends are effective and expensive, and I am here for all of it.

The commercialization of female empowerment is nothing new, from tampon ads of women running marathons to makeup campaigns with women in business suits. It's simply a story of marketers telling women they are strong in order for them to buy products. This faux connection can be found in alcohol ads, Photoshopped beauty commercials, diet products, and other items that are not empowering (be more beautiful and thinner!) in and of themselves, and often, are lethal (alcohol/cigarettes) or sell a standard of female "strength" that only the models in the ads can achieve. Marketers are skilled at leveraging social causes to piggyback on already established women's movements (International Women's Day, for example), and all of it makes us feel like we need to buy things in order to be strong and powerful. And now they all come with a hashtag, snaking across social media and right into our everyday decisions, choices, and behaviors, making young women even more hooked on the "movement," which is actually just a brand.

According to research, while women drive 70 to 80 percent of all purchasing, 91 percent of them feel misunderstood; it's not enough to make a mainstream product "for her" or simply "paint it pink." Women respond to storytelling and emotion, but brands make outdated assumptions, possibly because only 3 percent of ad agency directors are women, according to Kat Gordon, founder of The 3% Movement, an organization devoted to increasing the number of women and people of color in creative director roles. In the 1920s, women were targeted as homemakers, then in the 1930s and 1940s, Rosie the Riveter became a marketing icon. Things took a step back in the 1950s, when women were portrayed as housewives in ads once again. The 1960s and 1970s brought a wave of feminism, which led to marketing in the 1980s portraying women in powerful roles, while still making them look pristine for their man. And this is where marketing has typically stayed for the past forty years. You're strong, but make sure you're the perfect mother and wife, and stay wrinkle-free and fuckable.

THE NIGHT BEFORE THE BIG RETREAT, I sleep like one of my kids the night before Christmas. I toss and turn with images of sparkling wine and crackling fireplaces in my head. I imagine laughing with other women without waiting for an inevitable "Mom!" It has been years since I've been on a trip without a diaper bag or a stroller, and the next morning, I walk out of the house with only my new Michael Kors purse, courtesy of Rejuvinat, and that pink carry-on, which I haven't had the luxury of carrying in years.

"So, what happens at these retreats?" Kale asked me last night, trying not to betray his concern. My drinking has already been a source of anxiety in our home, and Kale is no dummy. A bunch of women, no spouses or kids, and a lot of booze. What could go wrong?

I told him what I knew and what I'd seen. The team retreats are about fun, sure, but they also include lectures and workshops. They are as much about personal development as they are about sales. And Rejuvinat is all about personal development. Because I have been actively drinking the Kool-Aid, I truly believe that Rejuvinat is helping to make me a better person! Anytime I feel weird about cold-messaging someone, I remember that I just need to dig deep, read some inspirational quotes, throw back a glass of wine, and hit Send. If I'm not hitting the recruiting numbers I want (we are supposed to recruit at least two new people per month), my upline sends me another personal development book so I can do some mindset work. I need to read more about how I'm in control of my destiny, how I need to make this business my priority, and I need to block out the naysayers. After all, Becky wants me to hit the numbers, too, because it only benefits her, and if my downline hits their numbers, it benefits me. I am learning that success comes from within, and if something isn't working for me, I just need to figure out my "why."

We head to the airport—Kale, me, and all five of our kids packed into the minivan. Even as we drive, I am attached to my phone, checking the notifications, the reshares, the followers, and watching as the announcement continues to drive up my numbers. Though my kids are all vying for my attention, I feel justified in the distraction, ignoring how it has become my de facto response to everything. I am connected to Rejuvinat 24/7, arguing that it is for my "job," but the truth is, it's about something much bigger. Yes, it's freedom, it's community, but it's also an escape, a rebellion, and a supply of attention I've been craving and wholly lacking for years.

Once again, my momentary worries about my lack of "time freedom" are allayed as I scroll through my emails. I am on the front page of another team newsletter. Before Rejuvinat, I hadn't been on the front page of anything since, well, ever. I am experiencing the first highs of

MLM success, and it's refreshing to be acknowledged for something that doesn't involve Crayola artwork my kids made for Mother's Day.

We pull up to the airport. All the kids are in the car saying goodbye, and I get out on the curb to make rounds with hugs and kisses. I end with Kale, who tells me, "Have a great weekend, hon. You deserve it. Don't do anything I wouldn't do!"

I bristle at the comment, since we both know full well that I've done plenty of things he wouldn't (I could fill a book with the things I've done—in fact, I have; it's a memoir called *Highlight Real*). This is why I need to get the hell away from this house, my family, our issues. Never have I needed an escape from the people I love most in the world the same way I do now. Two of the five kids start whining and crying, which sets off the whole brood; suddenly, they're all pleading with me not to go. I resist the urge to hop back in the car and rescue them.

"Bye, guys, love you!" I call as I hurry into the airport, practically gasping for air. I need this. Every woman at that retreat needs it. And this is the one thing Rejuvinat gets right. We have been suffocated by our roles as mothers and wives—sacrificing previous careers, dreams, and freedom on the altar of motherhood. But without a good excuse to get away, most of us would have never dreamed of leaving our families for the weekend. Modern motherhood can be so disempowering, all while the weight of the world feels like it's resting on our shoulders. Beth Berry, author of *Motherwhelmed*, describes a "master list" of why modern-day motherhood feels so frustrating, which includes more than thirty different points, such as: having no village, rising workload, being exhausted and spread thin, feeling like we need to buy tons of stuff, and feeling the pressure to bounce back to a pre-baby body after pregnancy, among others. "Motherhood is meant to overwhelm us," she concludes.

Rejuvinat is the best excuse most of us have been offered since our first labor pains, because it seemingly offers solutions to all these pain points. And we all feel intensely grateful for it, even if it's fake. MLMs don't offer a village to help with any of this; they offer an escape and another burden on an already full plate.

As I walk to the departures area, I see some of the other Seattle region Rejuvinat acolytes/indoctrinates, mouthing to them, "See you at the B-A-R." After checking in for my flight, I belly up to the airport bar with a few of the other gals. They shower me with affection and attention for my recent promotion.

"I can't wait to be where you are! How'd you do it?" Shelly gushes.

I pause for a second, surprised that Shelly hasn't reached the 3 percent circle yet. She's been doing Rejuvinat for five years and she's still a Station Zero? I don't have to question this too much; Rejuvinat has conveniently trained us to understand why some don't succeed.

She must not be working hard enough, I think to myself. After all, I'm in the top 3 percent after only one year. Again, had I been paying any kind of attention to the red flags, I would have seen I was a rare three-percenter in a world of Station Zeros. I might have even wondered how consultants like Shelly were paying for this trip without the hard-earned stipend or the commission money to cover the additional costs. I might have wondered what their investment looked like in comparison to my investment (or compared to their income).

Instead, I order another drink and gloat to my audience, who are all hanging on my words, desperate to glean how I have achieved such hallowed status in such a short time.

"I mean, I do what I can," I explain. "I attend all my new recruit business launches. I help them enroll their customers . . . just leading by example, you know?"

The other women nod as I take another large swig of my drink. I am working hard for the money. Always. And unknowingly distorting information to make it more acceptable.

I close out my tab and pick up the tabs of the other ladies on my team who "earned" this trip, including my bestie, Vanessa. I feel obligated to help pay their way, since I know that if I could only "kinda" afford this trip, they definitely can't. I throw in a few incentives for them. Becky offered incentives for me, so how can I not do the same? I fail to see how this isn't bribery, but again, I want them to experience the "taste of the top" with me so they can strive to get there themselves someday. It's the least I can do as a leader: selling the dream, one bar tab at a time.

They announce the boarding of Flight 155, and we all cheer in response, already three drinks deep, and the flight hasn't even taken off. But even more powerful than the alcohol is the freedom, and the adoration. That was the piece I didn't know about when I signed up. What did it even mean to be the popular girl? Sure, I've always been well liked, but I have never been in the position before of having women hang on my every word, love bomb me on social media, and consistently tell me how amazing I am. This is bigger payment than any Michael Kors bag or commission check.

This sense of being part of the in-group might seem innocuous enough, but it's the basis of social supremacy, whereby one group is exalted and honored over all others. White supremacy is about the indoctrination into an ideal of whiteness that the majority of people in the world don't fit into. It works because it hinges on the unconscious acceptance of this ideal, even by those who do not fulfill it. Policies in our country (segregation, mass incarceration, environmental racism) have consistently inhibited Black and Brown Americans from achieving the American dream, even the façade of the American dream as sold by companies like Rejuvinat.

We might laugh about mean girls and ladybosses, but their collective history is far more sinister: Mean girls wouldn't exist without white supremacy, and most MLMs are founded by white men. Look at the corporate leadership of any MLM in the United States. An alarming number of (white, conservative) politicians have their hands and finances tied up with MLMs, and this has been true since the beginning. Take one of the very first and longest-standing MLMs, Amway, founded by two white dudes, Jay Van Andel and Richard DeVos (yes, as in Betsy DeVos's father-in-law, which will be important later). They were devout Christians who met during World War II, eventually became distributors for a door-to-door sales company called Nutrilite, which became quite successful. They saw the potential in direct sales, so they took their five thousand–plus distributors and formed their own company, the American Way Association, or Amway, in April 1959. They acquired Nutrilite, and in addition to vitamins and mineral products, they started selling personal-care and household products, as well as makeup, and developed their own multilevel marketing plan, with the potential to earn bonuses, free merchandise, and trips on top of commissions.

Amway encouraged masculine salesmanship, with spouses joining their husbands in their business venture, to maintain the "head of household" appearance. While Tupperware, Avon, and many other companies sold their opportunities as feminine-empowerment projects, they still assumed, albeit indirectly, a stable, masculine income in the household; after all, the rise in women working outside the home didn't happen until the 1960s and 1970s. Like Amway, most direct-sales organizations founded during this time were done so by someone with experience in another company, where they gained an understanding that the actual sales force was more important than the products they were offering. The leaders at Amway refined the process and found a recipe that stuck. Amway essentially created the culture of rituals and celebrations that all modern MLMs continue to replicate, keeping people engaged in the community rather than invested in sales. And thanks to numerous investigations of Amway by the FTC (Amway v. FTC), to which Amway has established certain policies in response, all MLMs tend to follow in Amway's footsteps to stay legal enough to remain in operation.

Gary Langan Goodenow, a former senior trial attorney in the Securities and Exchange Commission (SEC) enforcement division, states, "Every time I prosecuted a pyramid or Ponzi for the SEC, the first words out of the founder's mouth were: 'I set this up just like Amway.' The fact that Amway has been allowed to operate the way they have for so long has created a breeding ground for MLMs to prosper."

Amway has been the blueprint for the entire MLM industry.

Not surprisingly, the board membership of most MLMs is comprised of primarily white men, while the majority of the sales force in modern direct-sales companies is made up of women. While more than 75 percent of sellers are women, only 5 percent of CEOs in MLMs are women. Though women like me join with the promise of sisterhood and female empowerment, the girlboss myth is intentionally staged by the patriarchy. And just as the patriarchy assumes that masculinity is the norm, white feminism assumes that the lived experiences of white, cis, heterosexual women are the default. Empowering women may or may not entail encouraging them to also buy products to make them thinner, richer, or less wrinkled, but it certainly shouldn't require stepping on other women, or ignoring Black and Brown or LGBTQ+ women in order to achieve that goal.

There is zero regard for intersectional feminism within these faux empowerment messages. Race, sexual orientation, economics, and many other factors influence our lives, yet they are absent in the MLM space. This is no mistake; men didn't start MLMs to truly empower women of all backgrounds—they only branded them as feminist movements to get rich. Because white women aren't actually being empowered with this ladyboss rhetoric, which convinces them that they are the hunter, when actually, they are the prey.

In the MLM world, feminism is redefined as women "having it all," so it's no surprise MLMs specifically target mothers, taking advantage of their already underpaid and undervalued work. This is only exacerbated among women of color, because they aren't even being considered in the MLM demographic. Ijeoma Oluo, author of *So You Want to Talk About Race*, describes white supremacy as the nation's original pyramid scheme: "The system of capitalism is a brutal system that exploits almost everyone.... The promise was that you were going to get something out of it, that you were going to be better off than Black people, that if you worked hard enough you were going to rise to the top in a way that people of color never would, because it was your birthright, not theirs."

What kind of choice is that?

And even though most direct-sales companies have had international expansion, the characteristics needed to participate in MLMs are very similar. According to research, the typical MLM member is a married, forty-three-year-old white woman who has completed some college courses, has no temporary or permanent disabilities, and speaks English at home. Not exactly a wide umbrella of diversity, even internationally.

But dress a capitalist, patriarchal, anti-woman business model in a *Vogue* magazine–style photoshoot with blown-out hair and a bossbabe hashtag, and you have the makings of the perfect wolf in sheep's clothing. It's the ultimate hypocrisy in MLM culture that it seeks to elevate a few rich, Instagram-worthy white women, as well as the largely invisible men at the pinnacle of their corporate structures, at the expense of all others.

While I'm not yet aware of any of this as I'm readying myself for the retreat, I'm starting to feel a little . . . well, prickly. I buckle my seat belt and press the flight-attendant call button for a drink before the wheels have picked up off the runway. I'm already grabbing my planner and taking out the agenda for the weekend. I immediately notice that the "retreat" is the very opposite of "retreating." Not only is there *no* time for relaxing, but there is a full lineup of trainings, outings, a Zoom call with a top earner (which they'll tell us we earned, most likely), and several other personal development activities, like goal setting and time management. The Zoom call with a million-dollar earner is a bit of a slap in the face, to be honest. When you join an MLM, you're told that your team is there to help you anytime. But then, you have to "qualify" to talk to them. It doesn't make sense to me, but again, I chalk it up to personal development. Though I worry that I've traded my already sleepless schedule for a sleepless weekend, I figure it makes sense. We need to make the most of our time together.

Still, it feels a little strange that we would be *that* busy. Later, I will recognize that the faster you spin people, the less capable they become of asking: "Why all the spin?" I and so many others are caught in a system of stay busy and hustle and fake it till you make it, not realizing that the more time and effort we put into the system, the less likely we are to question why the system is only working for a few—and those few all seem to wear the same uniform of success, in that they look, dress, and "invest" in the business the same way. The fancy designer clothing, the runway-ready stilettos, and the perfect hair extensions. Even their loungewear is top of the line, which is why I made sure to load up on Lululemon before this "relaxing" retreat.

After a short flight and a shorter shuttle to the cabin (with champagne flowing and social media posts the whole way), we are greeted by Becky and several other upline leaders, including the queen bee, Kimberly, and team members from all over the country.

Becky immediately throws her arms around me. This is only the second time we've met in person since reuniting, the first being the day I signed on the dotted line.

"Emily! You made it!" she cries, handing me my swag bag. Attention, hugs, and conversation fill the room. Praise is issued for putting business first, gifts are given, and there's empowerment all around. A few years later, I will watch a Trump rally and realize why there are so many die-hard fans. Because when you are routinely forgotten and ignored, all it takes is one person with power to legitimize your existence. This is the heart of the MLM structure. The upline legitimizes the downline through attention, keeping people hooked even when the commissions aren't coming in, even when they have spent five years of their life, money, and time to still be a Station Zero. It's easy to ignore this when the bill of goods you're being sold is a sisterhood you've never really had before. Leaving and being lonely is worse than losing money.

In her book *Terror, Love and Brainwashing: Attachment in Cults and Totalitarian Systems*, Alexandra Stein explains that this is not unusual; in fact, it's expected. Because there is a system of control in any group, companies like Rejuvinat and the women in them form "trauma bonds," which deem everything outside of the group threatening. No matter what the consequences, staying in the "known" feels safer than leaving to face the "unknown." This doesn't just happen in isolated communes or abusive relationships; it happens in situations like this weekend retreat, and it's easy to ignore the warning signs of manipulation, love bombing being just one of them.

After years of being relegated to playgrounds and preschools, I am floored to be spoiled like this. *What great friends I have!* I think as we gather in the great room and jump in with a few ice breakers, putting many Facebook avatars to actual people, since so much of our MLM activity takes place online. This has only amplified the reach of MLMs, of course, because you can hop on a Zoom "power hour" or "training session" from anywhere, anytime. No excuses.

"Congrats on hitting Station Five, Em!" Kristy tells me. "I can't believe how quickly you've grown!"

What I can't believe is that the woman saying this is the same Kristy I know from Facebook, because she looks nothing like her profile photo.

"Thanks, Kristy! It's been an awesome ride!" I say as I finally figure out who she is. As I look around, I realize how heavily filtered most people's photos must be on social media, because they look nothing like themselves, and frankly, their appearances look nothing like the "before" and "after" photos they use to help sell the products. Rather than question the products or the deception, I make a mental note that I should probably be doing more filtering and Photoshopping.

"Glasses up, bossbabes!" Allison opens our rewards dinner with the first of many toasts. Allison is one of the women in my upline, and though I have never met her before today, she's tagged me in social media many times. She's the woman who recruited Becky into Rejuvinat, and I know she makes a ton of money off me. She starts with some awards, and I'm delighted that most of them go to me or the people on my team. In fact, I've had almost enough champagne with each toast to ignore how painful my "fancy" shoes have become. Our awards are gift cards (oooh, Nordstrom!) and more branded swag. You have to be a walking billboard, after all. How can we promote our life-changing opportunity if we don't have it plastered all over our clothes and accessories?

Allison raises her drink again. "You should be proud of yourselves! We should all strive for this level of achievement!"

I see some smiles and whispers, and a few jealous sneers directed our way. Ouch, so much for lifting each other up. This was listed on the retreat agenda as a team celebration event, yet instead of cheering each other on, our accomplishments are pitted against each other, strategically, by the company and the members themselves. This is no different from our monthly "top-ten" leaderboards that I've been striving to achieve this whole year. Female empowerment has turned into a competition, and there can only be one top leader. But in a model with a 99.7 percent failure rate, that's a lot of hair pulling and elbowing to the top.

Rivalry, envy, and betrayal often pervade female relationships. According to a study by *Psych Central*, a mental-health and wellness publication, confidence and competition are encouraged in young boys but are often seen as "catty" traits in young girls. Men generally grow up feeling more comfortable with competition, and women learn that they are not supposed to be competitive; instead, we turn envious and jealous, qualities that are rooted in shame, unlike men, who use it to fuel friendlier competition. Despite the efforts of the feminist movement, we are conditioned to whip our claws out and go for blood when it comes to jobs, money, social approval, and men. Healthy competition is fine, but female rivalry can be toxic.

Less than a century ago, women lacked many of the rights we take for granted today. They couldn't work, they couldn't vote, they couldn't even get divorced. And female rivalry only reinforced women's oppression, so even as our options have grown, so has our rivalry. There are still fewer spots for women in the corporate world, which leaves other women feeling threatened. According to research by Susan Shapiro Barash, author and professor of gender studies at Marymount Manhattan College, 90 percent of women in various jobs report that competition in the workplace is between women, rather than between women and men; in fact, women bully other women up to 80 percent of the time in the workplace. And the top dog is simultaneously praised and hated, like an evil queen whom others secretly want to take down. None of this bothers me at this moment in my life. The way I justify it is, if I'm going to be compared to anyone, at least I'm the three-percenter being used as an example of what to do. I finish my champagne and order another, choosing to ignore the jealousy.

Later, we go to the bar, where for once, I'm not the drunkest woman in the bunch. There are a few rogue groups of men hanging out. It isn't *Girls Gone Wild*, but it isn't exactly tame, either. Though I can certainly relate to wanting to escape the mundane, I've done my fair share of letting loose the past few years, and I don't need any more trouble.

As we order another round of drinks, Becky complains to Allison, "Doesn't she realize she's wasting her time at a desk all day?"

"Who? What are we talking about?" I ask.

Allison explains, "Oh, Tori, you know, in Bianca's downline. She hates her job, yet she doesn't put her *all* into this. I mean, does she want this or not? Why would she want to work so hard when she could be her own boss?"

Ah yes, job shaming. A common conversation topic. For those who come to Rejuvinat with other jobs, there is a thick line in the sand between us (the people who make Rejuvinat their main priority) and them (those who don't). It's not surprising, as many of the complaints echo the same chasm between working moms and stay-at-home moms. The SAHMs judge the working moms for not caring enough, for not giving parenting their all, while the working moms judge the SAHMs for being spoiled or privileged, or simply not qualified for professional life.

The only difference is that this dispute gets weaponized here with money and sales, uplines and downlines. When the SAHMs have a working woman in their downline, she is always judged. And, predictably, shamed. She is pressured to spend more time on the MLM so she can inevitably walk away from her day job. Because there is a very specific idea that makes up the "mompreneur" label, and it's the image of a capable mother available to her children at all times, yet hustling 24/7, which is impossible. Despite the empowerment speak, I would venture to guess that many MLM reps feel discouraged, but this discouragement becomes more bearable when there's someone else, typically an "outsider" who doesn't fit into the accepted business model and rep image, to project the shame onto.

MLM reps are further isolated by their seeming inability to attain the success that they've been conditioned to strive for, but this frustration never goes anywhere. Because they're being love bombed and "personally developed," they still have hope they can rise to the top and be the best. But if you don't have enough money to fill all your orders, or a big enough network to sell to, or enough women to recruit, you fall short and risk losing the network you paid good money for, and possibly, left your job for.

Damned if you do, damned if you don't.

Despite the fact that we constantly punish each other with the expectations of a world that doesn't seem to ultimately want us to succeed, I love that women want it all. But how much do we have to spend to make it? Moreover, sisterhood and personal development shouldn't be at odds with liberation. We are constantly told that we need to transform through personal development because we are ultimately "not enough." In the documentary *LuLaRich*, about the MLM LuLaRoe, this phenomenon is shown in how the founder of the company encourages (and some would say, coerces) weight-loss surgery among her reps. It's evident in the beautiful, thin women who are chosen as speakers and in marketing materials. LuLaRoe and other companies fortify this behavior by using luxury items and shopping sprees as incentives. Liberation is actually realizing that we are enough, just as we are, instead of always being spoon-fed the lie that we must change everything about ourselves in order to succeed. But we've already established that MLMs are not liberating. So here I am, at a retreat teaching me how to change my language, behavior, and thoughts so I can be a better bossbabe.

"It's so crazy to me," Allison continues. "Why wouldn't you *want* to join our team? MLM is a scam? Corporate America is the real scam!"

I don't see it at the time, but much of what I hear in the world of Rejuvinat marks a movement away from mainstream media, science, or economics. I can't yet see how the women of Rejuvinat are already beginning to align with the same conspiracy theorists who believe in the Illuminati, and later, the so-called "plandemic," but it's part of the core argument for the company. The real world is bad and mean and won't actually take care of you. Rejuvinat is the one and only future.

"Yeah, CEO, managers, supervisors, employees . . . and *we're* the pyramid scheme?" Becky gives an exasperated chuckle.

In a legit company (even, gasp, corporate America), every managerial layer above you does not earn commissions from your sales while you work for free. And that's what we are doing, even if I don't realize it at this point. MLM "consultants" are unpaid sales reps with no guaranteed income or employee benefits. And despite what bossbabes and She-EOs will parrot on social media, MLM reps are not business owners. Bossbabes love to bash corporate America, even though every single MLM is a corporation. Let me say that again: Every MLM is a corporation.

Thinking of Becky's words, I remember a saying from a cute graphic that is floating around social media but it couldn't be more inaccurate. It's this graphic that MLMers love to share: "CEO, manager, supervisor, employee. Sorry, looks like a pyramid scheme to me!"

You are not the CEO of a company if that company already has a CEO. As an MLM ladyboss, I couldn't choose my own products, shop suppliers, set my own prices, or have any say in marketing. My commission level was decided for me. I was told what and how often I could post on social media, with a laundry list of things I could and couldn't say. Though I touted this "opportunity" as a "virtual franchise" on the regular, it was anything but, since it guaranteed no exclusive rights to sell in a particular area; instead, I was competing with any number of reps, many of whom were on my own team, selling identical products at identical prices in a saturated market.

It's the reason Josie Naikoi, former MLM rep and host of *Not the Good Girl* on YouTube, calls an MLM "a house of cards built on sand." It takes very little to bring it down.

"Tori is just dead weight at this point," Becky declares. "Her *why* just isn't strong enough."

I have another drink, someone hands me a shot, and the last thing I remember thinking is *My* why *is strong*.

But what is my why, and what is it for?

"WAKE UP, LADIES!" Becky bangs on our door like an annoying camp counselor. "Session starts in ten minutes!"

Shit, I slept in. I try to get up, but my head quickly falls back on the pillow. "I really need some sleep," I groan to myself. "At this rate, I'm going to need a vacation after this retreat."

But who am I kidding? As soon as I get home, I know I'll be back to five kids. At least at home, I would have managed to stay in bed a bit longer, but I know what's at stake this weekend, so I drag myself up and get dressed, putting on enough makeup to mimic an Instagram filter.

By the time I make it to the kitchen, Becky is busy whipping up pancakes for everyone. I shuffle right past her to pop open another bottle of bubbly. Mimosas, that's what's for breakfast! I see a strange truck pull up.

"Who's that?" Becky asks, as we all move over to the window, only to see Allison stumble out. Allison of the happy marriage with two kids. Allison with her contempt for corporate life and all the working moms who "don't care enough."

"Wait, she didn't come back with us last night?" Vanessa asks.

Becky presses her face to the glass. "And who is that guy dropping her off?"

We all gasp. It's radio silence when she walks in the door. She glances at us sheepishly and heads right upstairs. We all look around at each other, then burst into laughter.

"I guess she won't be joining us this morning," Vanessa smirks.

From a livestream on the television in the great room, our top leader, Kimberly, is gracing us with her presence. She is also here in Colorado but is staying at a local resort and apparently isn't going to make the thirty-minute drive to our cabin to hang with the downline. In a way, this move is absolutely brilliant. We hang on every word as though this Zoom chat is a live audience with the queen, and Kimberly is definitely the queen.

I snuggle up under a blanket with my mimosa, prepared for a long day.

The queen speaks, giving the title of her session: "Feel, felt, found. Ladies, those are words to remember."

This lecture is all about how to address the "but what about?" objections when selling the business opportunity to someone. Of course, we all have the files on our Facebook team pages in the form of copious laundry lists of things to say when someone objects.

"Feel, felt, found" was a familiar language I used with my kids.

"I know how you feel—math was hard for me at first, also. I felt frustrated, too. But I found that the more I did it, the easier it got!"

Simple, to the point. Except this time, it was being used to dispel legitimate concerns people had about our "business in a box."

"Don't feel you'll have enough time for this business? I felt that way, too! But I've found that this fits perfectly into our nooks and crannies."

"Don't feel like you know enough people? I felt that way, too! But I found that I can cannibalize any network and recruit the shit out of anyone, anywhere!"

Kimberly asks, "Does anyone have any questions on how to help address objections with this language? Would someone like to do a mock three-way about it?"

After some dialogue with the other ladies, I raise my hand. "What do you do when someone asks how much you make?"

"Don't talk about that," she responds flatly. "It's in poor taste." Convenient way to shut down questioning, and for the "sisterhood" to stay divided by ignorance.

The only problem is that all I'm seeing on social media is the promise of "financial freedom," of "retiring my husband," and "my business blessed me with this and that." I am certain that most people I try to sell on the MLM idea will want these "stats" to be corroborated with details.

As I look at Kimberly, I am reminded of the pictures of her shiplap-heavy kitchen and her Chanel logo–laden attire that she attributes to her "Glory to God" business venture. Because Kimberly wears her Christianity like another icon next to the connected *C*'s of her Chanel tote, and if you haven't figured it out yet, she is #blessed as she laughs, loves, lives her way to church . . . and to the bank.

"So," I pipe up, "we can post about how our business has blessed us, but we can't advertise the actual dollar amount?"

Maybe it's the mimosa talking, or maybe I just can't stand Kimberly as she sits in her hotel room, livestreaming to us from down the road. For the first time, I see a crack in the shiny veneer. Kimberly is over there with her white Mercedes, and Tori is working all day and hustling Rejuvinat at night, wondering why the Kimberlys of the world seem to have it so easy. And in a way, though my life looks a lot like Kimberly's, I am wondering the same.

Kimberly glares at me through the livestream. "Because it's against policy and procedures."

It is the first time I realize you're never actually allowed to talk about how much you make, even with each other. It's not dissimilar to the corporate American structure so many of the women here malign. Because if you knew how much the upline was making compared to the downline, someone might break out the guillotines. The point is to keep you either unaware on the bottom by deliberately withholding information or so well paid at the top, you're willing to overlook the inequity. MLMs are actually a funhouse mirror of American capitalism, exploiting these disproportions through popularity contests, bullying, and silence. What are you giving up in order to be on top? Kimberly is giving up actual connection, sitting alone in her hotel room. We are all giving up little bits of ourselves for the unsubstantiated promise of a piece of the pie.

At this point, I am making $3,000 to $4,000 per month, which is nothing compared to what Kimberly makes, in the hundreds of thousands per month. Still, it's thousands more than anyone in my downline makes. Not bad for a SAHM after a year of slinging eye cream. And while I understood that we can't make claims of what other people could potentially earn, I don't understand why I can't share what I am personally earning with the people I am recruiting, let alone the people around me. Plus, I see bossbabes all over the internet posting photos of their paychecks with the numbers blurred out, bragging about them consistently but not actually showing the number, which seems to defeat the point. Why the secrecy?

But I don't let up, swigging the champagne before I challenge Kimberly again: "Fine, but what can I actually say about how much I make? People wonder. Because we say shit like 'This is the best job I've ever had,' but at the same time, when you take a job, you usually find out the salary."

Silence.

"Oh, shit," Vanessa whispers behind me. "You've pissed off the queen!" Finally, Kimberly breaks the silence with a psychotic smile and glassy eyes. "What you *can* do," she says in an unnaturally high pitch, "is talk about what the money is allowing you to do, as long as you reference the IDS. But do *not* link to it. Just mention it."

Ahhh, the IDS: the income disclosure statement. As an independent consultant, you are supposed to link to the corporate IDS in any and every post or graphic that refers to potential earnings or gifts. This is to safeguard the company against income claims.

Income disclosure statements are made to be complicated for a reason—so we won't dig into them too much. The particular IDS I was meant to link to showed that only 2 percent of paid consultants earned more than $20,000 that year, which is a lot less than you could earn with a regular job. With a field of 400,000 consultants, 99.5 percent are earning less than minimum wage.

Oh, but there's more.

The problem with the income disclosures from MLMs is that they are not accurate or substantiated, and there is no formal standard for what they must disclose regarding making income claims. No IDS that is currently publicly available from any MLM includes reasonable expenses. So much money is spent on the initial product kit and required recurring purchases, but there are also all the hidden costs of participating in an MLM, especially among their target market: moms. These include obtaining childcare for meetings, transportation costs to get to those meetings, sales aids and office supplies, postage, hosting parties, travel expenses for conferences and conventions, outfits for elaborate parties, additional costs to attend, and possibly time off from your "real" job. Basically, all the things you're told you need in this business to be successful. These should be listed as reasonable expenses to consider in the income disclosure, but they aren't.

Another factor that isn't included in an IDS is churn, which is huge in MLM. It's common for more than half of MLM indoctrinates to quit within a year. For those who don't stay a year, their income is *not* included in these figures. Imagine how much worse it would be!

And the biggest cherry on top: This is all before taxes. Cut these figures in half, and it looks bad. Really bad.

Breaking down the income disclosures of sixty-one MLMs' compensation plans from 2019 (there were 106 companies on my list that I could not find an IDS for, which says something), the range of MLM members who lose money is between 73 and 99.9 percent, with an industry-wide average of 92.3 percent. The number of reps who make more than $30,000 per year (again, before taxes and expenses) is an abysmal 0.5 percent.

As a rep, you're led to believe and told to share that the IDS doesn't really matter, because so many people join for the discount. That means, if five out of ten reps join for the discount alone and don't intend to sell, the "sales" numbers are going to be low on average. That factor is used to dispel concerns when potential recruits question the abysmal numbers in the IDS. "Don't worry, Susan, it's not accurate because so many women join for the discount!" Companies do not break down this segment of reps in the income disclosure. But the company could easily supply these numbers, since they know how many reps they have at any given time, and how many reps are actually selling at any given time. Why don't they? One can only assume that supplying these numbers doesn't help the IDS, or else they could make the numbers look much better by excluding the "join for the discount" reps.

However, when you see how many people don't even earn money, it's no wonder nobody is supposed to talk about their actual personal earnings. Being an MLM rep isn't a job. It's a huge financial risk for almost everyone who joins. And despite what Kimberly says, you're actually not supposed to say what the income is allowing you to do, because that in and of itself is an income claim. So are the blurred-out photos of paychecks, and photos of luxury trips and designer purses. No bueno, according to the FTC. It's a constant contradiction.

But on that wintry, mimosa-filled day in Colorado, none of this applies to me because I'm in the top 3 percent. Vanessa and I are still new to this, so in many ways, our line of questioning comes as much from naivete as it does from snark. We have questions and concerns, and we honestly believe that Kimberly, who functions as our supreme leader, might have the answers. We don't yet realize that transparency is maligned and that logic is strongly discouraged.

Much to Kimberly's dismay, Vanessa jumps in after me, asking the best question of all: "What about when someone asks if this is a pyramid scheme?"

All the blood in the room runs cold. I hold back laughter, whispering to her, "Oh my God, she hates you worse than me now! How is that even possible?"

With the burning fire of ten thousand dying suns in her eyes, Kimberly spits, "Pyramid schemes are illegal. What other questions do you have?"

"I get that," Vanessa presses. "But what makes it *not* a pyramid? That is my question."

Kimberly sighs, tired of our antics. "We exchange goods for money. That's just selling. Pyramid schemes are illegal."

But even the most loyal among us know she's wrong. Just because pyramid schemes are illegal doesn't mean that MLMs aren't pyramid schemes. Plenty of things are illegal, and plenty of people break the law every single day. Because of this, the FTC advises people to be very wary of MLMs. They published an article with multiple questions to ask yourself before joining an MLM, warning of the financial risks. Still, Kimberly's "we exchange goods for money" is a valid point, to some degree. As I said, there are many people who "join for the discount on products." Yet the discount in itself is deceiving because the products are horribly inflated compared to retail products of the same caliber. The equivalent of a skincare regimen that sells for $40 at Target may be $150 or more in an MLM. The discounted price to a rep may be $50, which sounds huge! But it's still $60 more than the same stuff you can get at your local big-box store. The discounted price is still far more than you'd pay for similar products sold at retail. It's simply a ruse to get people to join the pyramid underneath the consultant; it benefits the consultant, but not the new recruit.

That isn't to say there aren't plenty of consultants who don't focus on recruiting—there are!

Vanessa got an award for the most customers. She has fun with this, and people trust her. I have plenty of women on my team who just sell a little bit and don't take this too seriously. However, even consultants who just "sell products" are part of the team who recruited them. Even someone who never recruits a human being, who only sells products to customers, is still part of a bigger system that makes money off collecting people to buy into the MLM. "But I'm not recruiting people" is a logical fallacy. If I'm buying drugs from the local drug dealer and not reselling them, I'm still supporting the industry. And you cannot make it to the upper echelons, or even the lower-middle ranks, of any MLM without recruiting humans. Promotions depend on it. And faux female empowerment is the secret sauce to these sales. Language couched in feminism (but practices that are decidedly anti-feminist) and this much-needed promise of community are used to exploit women, both emotionally and financially.

MLMs stand behind their products, but if you have to pay money to join as a consultant and the product comes with it, you are simply buying your place in the pyramid. There are no guarantees, no protections. We are all part of Becky's pyramid, which is part of Allison's pyramid, which is part of Kimberly's pyramid, and many others in between.

At that point in the session, Kimberly establishes her place at the top of the pyramid by ending the call and saying goodbye. I know I will hear about it later, and in many ways, I am just as shocked by the audacity that Vanessa and I displayed in this conversation. We asked the questions that no one else was willing to, partly out of naivete, partly out of curiosity. More telling than the answers Kimberly gave was her reaction to us asking. Questioning the system did not go over well.

Just as Kimberly signs off, Allison comes down the stairs. Someone breaks the awkward silence: "Did you have a late-night three-way or what?"

People start to snicker. See? The innuendo never gets old.

"Okay, ladies." Becky hurries to break up the laughter, trying to ignore what has just happened with the queen. "Next up, our goal-setting session!"

Goal setting is big in MLM. You always need to keep your eyes on the prize! Now that I have "arrived" at the top 3 percent, the next step is to help those I recruit to arrive at their own titles. We get up to stretch and refill our drinks.

Vanessa leans over to me in the kitchen and asks, "Do you ever feel weird about reaching out to strangers? What if this doesn't work for someone?"

Becky overhears her and replies, "It'll work for some and not others. Who cares? It's a numbers game. Next." Again, we're being reminded that the strong ones who want to work will survive. And you can't find them if you don't keep reaching out and talking to more people.

I shrug, nod in agreement, and pour a vodka soda. My Instagram dings: more new followers.

"Who cares if it's a pyramid scheme?" I tell Vanessa, backtracking on my earlier rebellion. Because though I can see the cracks in the façade, I am also benefiting from it; behavior, information, thought, and emotional control all have a hold on my ego, my hopes, but also the belief that, despite those cracks, this is the first taste of freedom or power I have experienced in years. I shrug in acceptance. "It works."

Whether it's the alcohol, day of indoctrination, or rejection of critical analysis, I start realizing that there's a reason Kimberly is at the top. If you can't beat 'em, join 'em.

That Time of the Month

I hosted a "virtual party" to get some free products. Of course, my friend talked me into joining as a consultant once the party was over with promises of making great money, flexible hours, friendships, fun, discounts, and tons of support. At the end of every month, my friend (now upline) would reach out to "check on" me and pressure me to have more parties and sell more items. I didn't hear from her any other time. I started realizing that she didn't care about my sales—it was all about her title. After a few months of that, I decided to terminate my account. The whole exchange basically told me I was just a number being recruited.

—ABBIE, former MLM rep

Why isn't this damn program updating?" I ask under my breath.
"What, Mommy?" a little Minnie Mouse looks up and asks me.
"Nothing, honey, talking to myself!" It's Halloween evening and I'm walking around with my kids, trick-or-treating. My phone is in one hand, and I have a coffee mug filled with wine in the other. My youngest is already passed out in the baby backpack, and I'm hoping the rest get worn out with their fill of candy so I can get back home and to work. In addition to drinking far too much, my usual remedy for anxiety and escape, I am also doing my usual month-end push.

It really sucks that Halloween is at month's end. And New Year's Eve. Christmas and Thanksgiving are pretty close, too. Holidays take on a new meaning during month-end madness.

Every month ends the same way: We rush to fill month-end quotas, spamming our friends, families, and network to sell products or recruit new reps, and purchase massive amounts of product to meet minimum sales numbers, keep our titles, and earn incentives. Titles and paychecks are based on the sales and structure obtained during any given month, and all titles start over monthly. Yes, every single month. Even the tippity-top-of-the-pyramid leaders start at zero on the first. Although once you're at the top, most of your sales are made up of the people under you, so while you still have to make sure those sales happen, as long as your team makes their numbers and the right number of people on your team make those numbers, you retain your spot on the top. It's like playing a game of mathematical Tetris every month. Many of these sales are made last minute, many times through deep discounts, flash sales, bulk purchases, and sometimes (gasp) fraudulent orders.

I am striving to hit another title because next month is the big company convention and I am hoping to earn the special perks. Unfortunately, I am not quite there. It's not on account of my own personal effort, of course—I mean, I'm the bossiest bossbabe around. But if my downline isn't selling and recruiting, then I'm not ranking up. I could have a million customers, and while the money would still be great, as far as titles and bonuses go, it wouldn't matter; my team members need to have their *own* team members for this to work. This particular title, Premier Star, requires three of my direct recruits to achieve a certain title and volume, Station Five, the title I achieved before the Colorado retreat. Only one of them is there so far: Vanessa. Bless her heart! Forever my bestie. It helps that we both have a very similar network, so since our friends don't care whom they buy from, I was able to move some of my customers to her downline (I'll talk more about this practice of "stacking" later) and it was a win-win!

She's qualified, and I'm happy and on my way. Meanwhile, I shift my gaze to my two other potentials: June and Hannah.

June should be set . . . I hope. She's been with me for a while and almost always hits her goals at month end. I had a long chat with her when she wasn't showing up for Zoom calls and biz ops, explaining to her that "leaders always show up," as the corporate mouthpiece told me. June's loyalty to me is strong. She wants to be where I am, and she appreciates what she needs to do to get there.

Hannah is my newest recruit, the one who came to my first biz op almost a year ago. Although she still wasn't sure enough to join that day, or during our three-way, I kept reaching out and didn't give up on her. She saw some of my posts and photos from the retreat a few months ago and finally became intrigued enough to ask more questions. See, the social media fear of missing out (FOMO) and "never take no for an answer" persistence are effective! The promise of sisterhood leads to a sale, but a network is required in order to grow. In a sense, you already need to come prepped with a sisterhood, which is complicated when it's the reason many women join. Have an old sorority network, or a large family structure? You might do okay. Coming in alone? Good luck.

Hannah's only worry is that she was in a different MLM before and felt burned by it, but I knew she would be a shoo-in at this. And that company? Bleh. Of course, we're the real deal—we're different. Better products, better opportunity. Plus, Hannah is gorgeous, is sweet, and has a great network, meaning she knows a ton of people who have deep pockets. I persuaded her to host a party for me with an offer she couldn't refuse: Anyone who signed up or purchased could either be my customers or part of my team, and I'd give her products in return—or they could be *her* instant downline. Either way, I would walk away with

PREMIER STAR

ME

HANNAH

JUNE

VANESSA

**NEEDS ONE
MORE RECRUIT!**

**NEEDS A LITTLE
HELP FROM ME, JUST
A FEW ORDERS!**

**NEEDS 4 MORE OF
AND ONE OF HE
CONSULTANTS NE
2 MORE ORDE**

more customers and consultants. Win-win! The party went great, she
decided to join, and she had enough orders to get her to the firs
promotion. She's just new enough that she hasn't gotten down or
herself yet and hasn't been exposed to any haters. That means she'
still motivated to make this work. She could very well be the next m
in Rejuvinat! I feel like Becky must have felt when she landed me
Hannah is perfect for my downline, and I have no doubt she'll help
bring up her recruitment.

But first I have to get home in order to make sure everyone is hitting
their minimum sales numbers and titles. Convention depends on it.

"Trick-or-treat!" my kids say in unison.

"Oh, don't you look cute!" a woman gushes as she fills the kids' plastic pumpkins with candy. I have to admit, she's right. Damn, I have some cute kids. But these cute kids need to finish the hell up because Mama's got some quotas to fill, and my wine mug is empty.

"Ready to head home? Wow, look at all that candy!" I cajole. "You're not going to be able to carry it much longer!" I'm suddenly regretting coming out and walking in the rain instead of handing out candy at the house. Kale lucked out! I could have been doing some work between doorbell rings.

"Yeah, Mama, let's go!" Oh, thank God. We head back toward the house. "Have any Kit Kats in there?" I ask.

"Here you go!" Riley hands me a Twix.

"Em! Over here!" someone calls as I rip open the candy wrapper. "Boo! Happy Halloween!"

I turn around and see someone in a unicorn onesie waving at me. Oh, shit, it's June! Her little unicorn ears must be burning.

"Hey! Cute costume. We're just heading home. Month-end magic happening?"

"Huh?" She cocks her head to one side.

You've got to be kidding me.

"June! It's October 31. Month end? Qualifications for Convention?"

Her eyes get big and her mouth drops. "Oh, duh! Yes! No worries, we are good—plenty of time! I have my aunt and mom on the hook; they told me if I needed anything, they would place some orders. Trust me, we are *good*."

She winks, and I feel slightly relieved. Phew, bullet dodged, at least temporarily, though I'm still a bit miffed that she completely forgot month end. "Awesome! Remember, Station Five gets some cool perks at Convention. You don't want to miss out!"

I rack my brain. What are the perks for that rank? Level Up front-row seats? Ultimate Sparkle party? Why do the names need to be so stupid? Before I can recall, she interjects, clearly fearing disapproval: "Oh yeah, I'm all over the Leaders Lounge perk! I want that bad! Don't worry, I won't let you down!"

MLMs are consistently dangling carrots to convince you to sell just a little more or recruit more people. Every month there's a special offer, bundle, discount, or other gimmicky marketing tactic to sell to your already burned-out network of friends and customers. We're supposed to be a luxury product, but how many sales do you see actual luxury products having? Louis Vuitton and Maserati certainly don't offer discounts. It's more like a Groundhog Day going-out-of-business sale for a furniture store, except the store never seems to close. These consistent marketing tactics become a way to target your downline and guilt them into achieving more. When companies want to increase numbers, they just toss in a stupid "Leaders Lounge" perk, which is basically a glorified hotel room with a few bags of chips and some sparkling water. But add the word *leader*, aka power, and these women will run for it! And I am one of those women.

I walk up the steps to my house. Kale is handing out candy and, oh no, bringing in boxes. Shit. I know what these are: orders from the last incentive trip I earned. I was so close to making my own numbers for that trip. I just needed to place some orders under my team in order to get them to rank up. These boxes were supposed to show up *during* the week! Damn that two-day shipping.

"Daddy!" Our little monsters reach up for Kale with sticky fingers.

"Hey, kids!" He quickly turns to me, a stern look on his face. "Why are there so many Rejuvinat boxes?"

Front-loading, or inventory loading, is the practice of buying a ton of stock so that customers can purchase directly from you . . . supposedly. The reason it's done in many instances is to make ranks and titles because you are financially rewarded for doing so. Distributors order items to qualify for something, not because they need it for sales. It's a huge benefit to the company and uplines. They earn commission and sales, so while the policies and procedures might discourage this type of behavior, it is never discouraged by my uplines.

Of course, it's fine that consumers (consultants) purchase products and use them. The issue is when you get rewarded under the compensation plan for your own personal consumption. The more the company ties rewards to your own consumption, the more pressure you're under to buy products, and the more pressure to use the company's products. All MLM compensation plans have inventory purchase qualifications, even if you aren't technically *required* to purchase, and the only way to maintain your position is by the volume of (you guessed it) purchased products. This creates an incentive to front-load. The starter-kit, or initial consultant "join" package in itself, if large enough, is front-loading, because it's more product than one person needs. Plus, your uplines encourage you to be a "product of the products," meaning: Use all the products the company offers, all the time. Whether people buy because they want to use the products or because they want to meet qualifications doesn't matter. They are now consumers, regardless.

The FTC rules that front-loading is not proper activity: "Front-loading or inventorying of product in which excessive product purchases are viewed as prohibited consideration for the requirement that individuals make an initial investment of product purchased to engage in the company." In modern MLMs, you don't need to have inventory; after all, orders are shipped from the company fulfillment center. These product purchases are for me to make rank and earn trips, nothing more. I just convinced myself they were necessary to the tune of hundreds, sometimes thousands, of dollars.

I think for a minute . . . I could fib and say they are all incentives? Gifts? I get a shit ton of gifts from the company. But he knows—there are too many of them. I need to come clean.

"Okay, you know that trip to Hawaii I earned for us (picture yourself on a beach, Kale!)? Hannah needed some help making her numbers last month. I wouldn't have earned the trip without her. You know how new she is."

"But shouldn't she be the one placing the orders? How much did you spend? What are you going to do with all of this product?"

All valid questions. Luckily, my uplines have prepared me for this line of questioning. We have scripts for spouses, too, to help compartmentalize insider versus outsider information. "Kale, this is my business, and buying product is the rent on my business! I can't sell what I don't use. I can use all this stuff for gifts, stocking stuffers, giveaways—"

He interrupts, "Yeah, yeah, spend money to make money. But seriously, how many people are you giving Christmas gifts to? This is too much, Emmy. We don't need all this shit. Nobody needs all this shit. How much are you really making if you're buying all this?"

I wonder for a second if that is a rhetorical question before snapping back, "Well, I got a trip to Hawaii! How much is that worth? Doesn't it make sense to invest that in my business?"

Thank God my uplines give me talking points for this.

"That's not how investing works, babe. You're *buying* your title. I mean, I'm not telling you what to do, but this isn't sustainable. You can't do this every month and not burn out."

I know that he's right, but my hope is that Hannah will get herself there eventually. Right now, she doesn't have the disposable income, so she can't place these orders herself, and she doesn't quite have the network buy-in yet, either. Plus, she's so grateful I helped her out. Once she gets a taste of her new title and her Convention perks, I know she will do anything to keep them. It's certainly what I'm doing; my pride is just a little too strong to let my title drop or miss out on any incentive trips, and the company and my upline make sure of that. It's one of the reasons they plaster your name everywhere when you earn a title, to guarantee you feel ashamed if you don't make that leaderboard or rank. Just one more month—that's all I need.

"It won't always be like this, I promise. Just be excited for our Hawaii vacay in the spring, okay?" I turn on the charm by batting my eyelashes and handing him a Heath bar I confiscated from one of the kids' candy buckets. His favorite.

He rolls his eyes but can't contain his smirk. "Okay, I'll get these little trick-or-treaters to bed so you can finish up."

"Thanks, babe."

I peel off my boots and sit down with my phone. Time to strategize.

In order to hit Premier Star, I need three more people to hit Station Five (and yes, this is the language of our promotions). Vanessa is already there, so I can check her off the list; June needs four more orders, but she has enough people to manage that; and Hannah needs to recruit one more consultant. That's a big one, and I know Hannah has really been struggling with recruitment.

My mind is a blur of month-end madness, qualifications, and incentive trips. Have you ever seen your favorite direct-sales friend post a "flash sale" or a "bulk order"? She's probably trying to get rid of product from this type of situation, loading inventory to boost numbers artificially, or attempting to inflate sales to hit a promotion or qualification.

Consultants will justify this activity by ordering products "I'll use, anyway" under family accounts. I know I did. Everyone I knew made accounts for their kids (bonus that I had five of them), their spouses, their relatives, even their pets. Just ask Robyn Paulson, my daughter's former hamster (RIP), who often ordered a few items at month end to make my numbers look good. This was definitely a gray area, because while it was perfectly acceptable to have more than one account in your household as long as you were purchasing a reasonable amount of product, who decides what is reasonable? There were dollar limits per person, but all you needed to do was order more under someone else, and voilà!

Ever notice the piles of products showcased in some of your MLM friends' social media feeds? Come on, Stacy! Nobody needs that many essential oils. But you get caught up because the carrot is being dangled in front of you—that next promotion comes with a $500 bonus. So what if you spend $500 in order to make it happen? It's not actually about the cash. If it were, you wouldn't be doing it. It's about the accolades! And your upline will likely look the other way, if not outright encourage it.

Eventually, Rejuvinat did catch on to this type of behavior and began to only allow a certain dollar amount of purchases per credit card. But one of my uplines found a loophole: buy prepaid gift cards. I remember Allison buying thousands of dollars in prepaid gift cards for a title she bought—er, achieved—one month. I emulated her strategy about six months later. There was always a way to game the system to benefit your title.

But once you go down this rabbit hole, you need to order more and more to hit these sales or titles. You've raised the bar. You've set a precedent. And month end becomes this painful push to do it all again, plus some. Because if you sell $1,000 worth of product one month, you're going to have to do the same thing the next just to maintain, let alone grow. And there is always attrition—customers canceling or consultants quitting—so you need to replace them to stay in your upline's good graces. This doesn't even include your own required product purchases, which can be several hundred dollars. Kale is right; it isn't sustainable. But there is so much pride tied up in these titles because they are publicly shouted out on team pages and corporate emails, so it feels defeating to let the field at large see you drop rank. Thus, it perpetuates the behavior.

I spent so many holidays focused on month end, trip qualifications, Convention ranks, bonuses, and leaderboards. All the while, I kept dismissing that nagging feeling that what I was doing was less than ethical, while training my team to do the same, because my upline and the field of consultants around me were doing it. I was spending a lot of time alone in the name of sisterhood, locked in my office in the name of time freedom. Again, pride and white supremacy go hand-in-hand here. You have to do what it takes to be the best, because they don't notice the people at the bottom, and after all this work, if you don't hit the top, what was the point?

Although sales goals and promotional trips aren't exclusive to MLMs, the downline requirement makes it sketchy, to put it mildly. In a traditional job, there are checks and balances through the hiring process; you need qualifications, diplomas, or previous experience in any sales role other than entry level. But most MLM contractors are offered no real business training (personal development activities and Zoom vision boarding are *not* business seminars), no vetting, no background checks. At a real job, you might work late nights, but on a finite project with a definitive end. You get insurance, benefits, and a paycheck, even if you don't hit those goals and that extra bonus. MLMs encourage members to employ a sunk cost fallacy. In case you forgot, this is when you are so committed to seeing results—the title, the trip, the paycheck—that you feel compelled to continue spending money, time, and effort, even when it's obvious the investment is not going to pay off.

I refill my wineglass, open my laptop, log in to the consultant platform, and see that June hit Station Five! Oh, thank goodness. Two out of three. I tag her in a photo on Facebook: "Awesome job, Rockstar! Can't wait to celebrate you at Convention!"

Now, just one left. I'd better call Hannah to see where she's at.

She answers the phone immediately, probably anticipating my desperate call to action, confessing, "I don't know if I'm going to make it, Em. My sister was going to sign up, but now she's flaking."

Shit. Hannah is my only hope at this point. She needs this, and so do I. Actually, *I* need this, and I need to convince her that she needs it, too. I cannot come this far only to come this far . . . another mantra I've seen floating around social media. Time to pull out the big guns: a late-night three-way.

"Let's get her on the phone. I'm free now!" I offer.

"It's eleven thirty p.m."

"Is she up? Why not?"

Desperate times call for desperate measures. I need Hannah to make it to the finish line in the next thirty minutes, and this is my last chance. It has to be the three-way of my life. I have to show Hannah's sister that she can't pass up such an opportunity. All I need is a credit card, a Social Security number, and a heartbeat. That's literally it.

"Okay!" Hannah relents. "I'll get her on!"

I fumble with my phone and duck into a quiet corner so I don't wake my kids. "Anika, it's Emily. Hannah has told me so much about you! You have some questions about Rejuvinat?"

"Um, I suppose," she stutters, startled by the call. "It's a little late for this, isn't it? I don't know that I have questions; I'm just not totally convinced that this is for me."

Lucky for her, I'm very convincing. It's time to turn on the charm. I launch into a diatribe that feels like an out-of-body experience. "Anika, I couldn't go to sleep tonight without sharing this with you, and neither could your sister. What if you had twelve extra paychecks a year? How about a community of friends to work alongside you? What if you could just buy the shoes, take the trip, or give back like you want to? We help people do that. Your sister helps people do that. She can help *you* do that. She has one spot left tonight. She's saving it for you! I know you want to find an exit strategy for your job and spend more time with your kids. I know it's hard to make this decision, but it's not as hard as leaving your daughter every day, right? What do you say?"

Damn, I'm both impressed and disgusted with myself. The perfect combination of charming and predatory, and all from the arsenal of scripts I have memorized. (And, as I'll discover later, my speech contains all the elements of the BITE Model.) I know Anika's vulnerabilities because Hannah has shared them with me, and they seem to revolve around working-mom guilt. It's a bit of a stretch already, with the potential false income claims (twelve paychecks a year, but hey, I didn't say they'd be more than zero dollars!), but the lifestyle claims are more painful and emotional. Mom guilt already comes from the unrealistic ideal of being a perfect mom, so guilting and shaming a working mom into a business opportunity is as predatory as it gets. And telling her that there's "one spot left" is absolute bullshit. There are always unlimited spots, on every team, in every MLM, *everywhere*. That's the literal business model, but for some reason, this sense of urgency works. They don't call it FOMO for nothing.

The reality? The magic I'm selling her, this "opportunity," will likely be a burden. And I can't help but notice the irony and hypocrisy, as I'm sitting here selling "opportunities" for freedom at almost midnight on an evening I spent rushing to finish with my kids. How much am I with my kids when I'm trapped in my office at month end? When I'm going to retreats? Sitting on my phone? Maybe women in MLMs target vulnerable people because we are the vulnerable people. After all, Becky wouldn't have recruited me unless she thought it was the best thing for me, right? Why can't this be the best thing for Anika, too? I make peace with my cognitive dissonance by reminding myself that I'm exercising empathy. I take another swig of wine and sit through a bit of silence. All I need is for her to sign up, and I have a feeling I'm close.

Anika relents, albeit with a bit of hesitation. "Why not? There's a return policy, right?"

Thank God.

"Sure is, Anika. You're making a great decision. And I suggest buying the biggest product kit to make sure you start out as successfully as possible! Welcome to the team." Again, it's bullshit. The bigger the kit, the more volume Hannah (and I and our entire upline) gets. The only thing Anika will successfully do is empty her pocketbook. But I'm not lying about the return policy, which always temporarily allays my guilt for pressuring people into spending as much money as possible.

I'm sure the folks at Rejuvinat knew this when they designed the selling system. How can you feel bad about forcing someone into a decision that is absolutely reversible? Sort of. It's reversible in the sense that she can absolutely return the kit, but it will come at the price of disappointing her sister and having a team of Rejuvinat reps on her ass trying to convince her not to. MLMs recognize that the more time that passes after a sale is made, the higher the likelihood that they can keep you invested. People think, *Well, shoot, I bought the starter kit. I might as well keep at it for a bit.* This mental pause offers an opportunity for the upline to step in, making you more indoctrinated, and more influenced.

The fact that it benefits me to have Hannah recruit someone leads to a common behavior in MLM called *stacking.* Stacking refers to enrolling distributors in your genealogy tree (pyramid) to add levels of commission payout, and to amplify sales. I could have spent that time on the phone with Anika to enroll her directly with me, so why wouldn't I? I'm rewarded for the structure of the pyramid; if Anika enrolls with Hannah, she ranks up, and so do I. Hannah achieves Station Five, and I hit Premier Star! I make money either way. Stacking isn't illegal in and of itself, but it opens the door to potential illegality when people enroll "fake" distributors in their downline in order to benefit. I knew many distributors who enrolled their children using their Social Security numbers, then enrolled women underneath them: boom! Instant promotion. It's another loophole that leads women desperate to make rank and save face to do things that are less than ethical.

But I don't need to worry about that; Hannah and I have done this fair and square. Despite the begging, pleading, and guilt-tripping at ten minutes to midnight on Halloween.

After we hang up, a text pops up from Hannah: "YOU ARE MAGICAL, thank you!" with six unicorn emojis. Phew, another month complete. I'm safe. I decide to stay up another hour to do my month-end shoutout posts to my amazing team. Gotta capitalize on this and keep the momentum flowing. I take to Facebook: "I'm so blessed with my team! This is the best job ever. Personal development with a paycheck! I loved watching that month-end hustle! Cannot wait to spoil you ladies at Convention next month!" I tag Vanessa, June, and Hannah, and a few other consultants who earned bonuses this month. I also welcome Anika to our ever-growing team. I wonder for a second if she's being tagged against her will, as I reflect on my surprise business announcement on Facebook my first day, but I hit Post anyway.

"Personal development with a paycheck!" I roll my eyes at myself. As I head upstairs to (finally) go to bed, I briefly wonder, *What am I becoming? And at what cost?*

Lots of Dollars and Absolutely No Sense

✦ ✦
✦

I thought Convention sounded super fun, and I had some frequent-flier miles, so I decided to opt in, even though I was a new consultant. The tickets were expensive, and the hotel blocks weren't cheap either, but my upline told me it was a good investment in my new business. The entire experience was exhausting. It was a popularity contest, with the top earners parading around sharing their "wisdom," sessions and parties all weekend long. At the end, I was expected to spend more money on new products and workouts, and I learned absolutely nothing. I thought it would be motivating, but it made me realize that I wanted no part in it.

—SARA, former MLM rep

I 'm in the food court at Concourse G, meet you here!" Becky texts me during a layover on our way to another bossbabe trip, except this one is *the* bossbabe trip of all bossbabe trips: Convention! It's the ultimate test of MLM success. No matter what MLM you are in, Convention is the annual gathering of ladybosses to celebrate, receive personal development, and renew excitement and passion for the company. Leaders show up. Be there or be square. The FOMO is strong, and so is the guilt-tripping if you abstain.

Conventions are the largest retention events and are extremely important in MLM culture. As Robert L. FitzPatrick describes in his book, *Ponzinomics*: "Holding ceremonial spectacles in enormous stadiums and posing on stage as high priests possessing sacred secrets, MLM promoters tout their schemes as the fulfillment of the mythic American Dream. They flaunt their own wealth as proof that they can align the stars, so to speak, to deliver success and happiness to followers."

Conventions allow the company to indoctrinate the attendees, and the added bonus is that it's the attendees who pay to be there, so the overhead for the company is extremely low. Even the majority of the training sessions are led by consultants who present for free because they believe being asked to speak at Convention is an honor. And Conventions are not cheap for consultants. They typically cost a few hundred dollars to a thousand dollars just for a ticket, and that does not include hotel rooms, airfare, meals, or any product purchases. But the culture of constant education and personal development makes these Conventions profitable for the company and popular with consultants. I'd already spent weeks (months, actually) preparing outfits for what was supposed to be a fun and enjoyable trip, and the outfits were important because we were going to be taking lots of staged photos.

This will be my first Convention. Last year, I had to choose between the retreat and Convention, and I told myself I couldn't miss out again. I had so much FOMO! It looked so cool, with concerts, glitz and glam, and parties galore. With such a big team watching me now, I can't not go—plus, this year, I'm getting stage recognition for my new title, Premier Star! The extra bonus is that Vanessa is with me, since her ex will be taking the kids the whole weekend.

We stop for a layover in Salt Lake City to meet up with Becky before our last leg. This is the first time I've seen her since my recent promotion, which means she's hit another bonus, too, but this time, I've actually surpassed her in title. She's only had one direct consultant level up past Station Five (me!), and now I have three (Vanessa, June, and Hannah). I've wondered how this would go down. She's not the jealous type, but I've seen this dynamic play out with other consultants, and it can get ugly.

"We're on our way! Is there a bar in that concourse?"

In MLMs, it's absolutely possible to rank up past your upline, the person who recruited you into the company. This is actually another argument to the "it's a pyramid scheme" objection, and one I've used time and time again. "It's not a pyramid if you can outrank your upline!"

In reality, the pyramid is still very much intact. Though my title (based on a very manufactured and manipulated structure) is technically a higher rank than Becky, she still earns money on *everything* I buy and sell, and everything my team buys and sells, as well as bonuses on all of those promotions. The only rub is the fact that I will earn more accolades, be featured in more promotional material and biz ops, and even walk the stage at Convention, while she watches from the sidelines. Depending on the type of person your upline is, that FOMO can be hard to stomach and can further ignite the desire to do whatever it takes to make rank.

But Becky has always been so kind and gracious, and the spotlight has never really been her thing. I'm lucky in that sense, as there has never been any jealous competition between us, but when we meet at the bar (yay!), I realize this new promotion has rubbed her a different way.

"I was surprised that you brought Vanessa as your plus one. Hannah and June are showing so much promise. Vanessa is just coasting. You basically carry her," she says in a whisper while Vanessa stops at the ladies room.

As part of my Convention swag, I qualified for a super-posh bling package in my suite, with a spot for a plus one. It includes some spa items and other goodies, but the real benefit is the public recognition that I earned it. It's as ridiculous as it sounds, but I'm going with it, and it will make great social media material for potential recruits.

The company allows you to bring a spouse or another consultant for some incentives, including this one. Kale has to juggle the kids and work, so obviously, my plus one is my best friend, who happens to be a consultant. I still don't love the idea of people needing to earn my friendship, and I wouldn't want to room with anyone else. But it makes me wonder: *What happens if Vanessa doesn't qualify next time?* She *has* dropped below her rank a few times recently, and I've helped her out because that's what friends do.

Becky is making me question the future of this arrangement, or maybe she's annoyed that I didn't assign *her* as my plus one.

"Becky, I know what you mean, and I'm super proud of Hannah and June, but Vanessa's been with me from the beginning, two years now, and she's been pretty solid the last few months. With everything going on with her ex, she deserves to be here. Friends help friends out."

Why is this any of her business, anyway?

"No, I get it, I do—you're right," she relents, but she's not done with the upline advice. "The other thing, though—I noticed at month end that you were up posting after midnight. You have to get an assistant. You're getting up there!"

She sits back and swigs her beer. "You can't be fiddling around with all the busywork, doing all your own swag bags and social media posts. First, how long is this shit taking you? And second, how do you think that looks to your team? Do you think they're going to want to be fiddling around with all that stuff? Get an auto-posting program, or someone to help you with social media. You're just the face of the business, so talk the talk and walk the walk."

I am torn between nodding and shaking my head, which makes me glare and tilt my head to the side like a dog who just heard something it didn't understand. I mean, she's the one who *taught me* to do this!

And at the same time, she's right—I *have* been bogged down with busywork lately. The bigger my team gets, the more social media I need to do and the more incentives I need to send out. It's a lot. And now that I've outranked her, I know I need to continue to "sell the dream," and it's nobody's dream to do this shit. But then, I think about finances. Yeah, I'm bringing in some extra cash, about $6,000 per month at this point, but every month there's also something extra I need to pay for. Here I am, heading to the "investing in my business" Convention trip, and now I'm looking at yet another investment.

I haven't even boarded the plane yet and Convention is already exhausting me, but I know Becky is right—I have to walk the walk if I want to be a leader. Kimberly once told us that she refused to work with anyone in her downline who didn't attend Convention. A far cry from the "work with anyone from anywhere" rhetoric that she would spin when someone was considering joining.

"I'll consider it," I tell Becky. "I know what I'm doing isn't sustainable."

I need to crunch the numbers and decide how I'm going to swing it, but I'm burning the candle at both ends and am unsure how much longer I can keep up with this. At the same time, I can't *not* keep up with this—the money is too good. Or at least it appears that way, if I'm just looking at my revenue and not my expenses, and especially if I ignore that very few other people in the company have paychecks that resemble mine.

"Well, we don't need to worry about that this weekend," Becky says as Vanessa returns to the table. "Cheers to Texas!" I change the subject back to how much freaking fun we're going to have in Austin this weekend.

"Cheers!" Becky, Vanessa, and I clink our mimosa glasses.

Just then, Kale texts me. "Where are the lunch bags?"

"Ugh, hang on, ladies. I need to call home."

"Hey, babe, I actually made the lunches already; they're in the small fridge," I tell him when he picks up.

"I saw those, but Riley doesn't want what you made her. I can't find the extra bags." I can hear him digging through the pantry.

"Hon, who's the parent, you or her?" I'm annoyed that he's calling me with something this trivial. We bicker back and forth until I see Vanessa signal for the check. "Kale, I have to go—my flight is boarding."

I hang up and head back to the bar, swig my mimosa, and grab my purse before we rush to the gate.

The bigger my team gets and the more traveling I do, the more strained my family and marriage seem to become. I know I'm the one taxing the system, but for years, I stayed home, while Kale was the one who worked. And now, I'm bringing in pretty good money (minus those pesky expenses), but we don't have a ton of help to fall back on. We have our babysitter and friends whom we can pass off the kids to, but it's a scheduling nightmare week to week, especially when I travel. Dividing and conquering isn't working as well as I'd hoped it would, because it's not like Kale's job became more flexible. The workload and stress are higher than ever, and so are the childcare costs.

I know it's too much to put on his shoulders, but still, when is it going to be *my* turn? I stayed up last night and got lists ready for him, made the lunches, and did so much prep work that I barely slept; instead, I caffeinated and am now powering through. Why can't I just leave and check out completely? It's the mental load of motherhood I can't escape from, no matter how many states away I am, no matter how many glasses of wine I have. Celeste Yvonne, author of *It's Not about the Wine*, sums this up well: "The wine memes that jam our social media feeds are only communicating what women have been trying to convey for years: we are exhausted, overwhelmed, overworked, and in serious need of help, above all else."

Becky, Vanessa, and I board the plane. Becky goes to first class, and we cram ourselves into our coach seats. I wonder, *Now that I've ranked up, do I need to start buying first-class tickets to "walk the walk"?* Not sure that's going to be in the budget. Becky makes double what I'm making now, so that will be an expense for another day.

First order of business, as I load my carry-on and continue to have a text argument with Kale, is figuring out this childcare business. Actually, first order of business is ordering vodka sodas. Vanessa and I "cheers" each other, and as the plane takes off, we both open our laptops. No rest for the weary. I peruse a website about childcare and see info about au pairs. Hmm. That could actually work. Someone living with us to offer up another set of hands? It's spendy, but I'm already paying a ton in babysitter costs. More flexibility and even more resources to spend time with Kale might be exactly what we need. It's unfortunate that childcare costs are so high and that I feel I need to justify it financially, but isn't that why many of us SAHMs fall for MLMs in the first place? The promise of a job without the need for childcare? And ironically, now I need childcare.

I start filling out information and begin applying with au-pair companies for interviews. I glance over to see what Vanessa is working on. I do a double take. She's looking at job ads, *real* job ads. What is this? Blasphemy!

"Why are you looking at jobs?" I ask, horrified. I can't even imagine how someone could go back to a nine-to-five after being in their own business. Didn't we cover all of this in our retreat last year? She looks at me like I have three heads.

"Dude, you know I'm single now," she explains emphatically. "Jake doesn't pay child support every month. What do you expect me to do?"

I know all of this, of course, better than most people. I've been by her side the whole time, through her ugly divorce. But I'm still baffled. And clearly brainwashed.

"Why not just put more effort into Rejuvinat?" I ask.

"Seriously?" she deadpans. "I need health insurance. I need stability. There is no guarantee or stability with this, Em. Yes, it's fun, and yes,

I'm glad I'm here. Yes, the extra money is great, and I appreciate you sharing your perks with me, but for the love of God, I'm talking about my family here. I don't have a husband holding down the finances like you do."

I've never heard her talk this way, and it's a little jarring to realize that my bestie is suggesting we're from different worlds. I begin to soften; after all, I might feel differently if I were single, too. But then, I think back to my scripts: Or, maybe instead of giving up, I'd put *everything* into this. Yes, that's what a *real* bossbabe would do.

"No, I get it. Let me know if you need a reference or anything," I sulk.

Maybe Becky's right. Maybe I should have brought June or Hannah as my plus one. I can't help but feel disappointed in Vanessa for not wanting to put her all into this, and in myself for wanting this more than she does and making her feel bad about it.

After many more vodka sodas, a short nap, and about thirteen au-pair applications, we arrive at the Austin airport. At the baggage claim, I lug along the three suitcases I brought for one weekend. One is outfits, one is product, and one is gifts for my team: books, monogrammed water bottles, necklaces. Vanessa laughs as I maneuver the huge luggage cart. Last year, Becky and several other women in my upline spoiled everyone on the team, as did leaders across the company. I can't *not* show my appreciation and be totally upstaged by everyone else. I have to make sure everyone's happy, motivated, and excited to come back again next year.

But I also have to play the part of "top leader who makes a crap ton of money" so they can all strive for that dream themselves, so they can know it's actually realistic (even if it isn't). Gifts keep even the lowest-ranking recruit engaged. Maybe you're spending a little too much each month on product, but look at the cute bracelet you received! It's enough to keep you from doing a profit and loss statement and realizing that you're losing money, for just one more month. The longer you can keep someone hooked on the MLM and on your team, the longer you can use them for rank and numbers. Yes, it's bribery, and it's encouraging dependency on something that isn't even viable. But it's also effective marketing, because those recruits then post photos of their cute gifts, tag you, and talk about how grateful they are for the business. That makes other people think, *Wow, cool, that looks easy and fun!* That's the magic of the FOMO campaign.

FOMO marketing is done across the board, and it has consumers purchasing products before the offer passes them by all the time. And it works because humans are risk averse. We don't want to miss out on the buy one, get one (BOGO) or the kids-eat-free, which is happening ... this weekend only! In an MLM, the potential results are only based on what MLM reps show on social media, and the more sensational, the more consumers are afraid to lose. Yet what they don't know is that they will likely lose their entire investment. But the photos from the beach and the brand-new purse can be tempting enough for the next potential recruit to take the risk.

We have just a few minutes to haul our bags to the hotel, check in and get our badges, drop off swag bags to my entire team, and rush to our first Convention sessions. Once again, every single second of the agenda is packed. But I'm not arguing, because I paid thousands of dollars to be here, so I may as well get my money's worth!

Although we have good perks, we don't have the major VIP perks like the very tippity-top leaders have: shorter lines, express check-in, front-row seating, valet service. *Next year, Emily, next year*, I think to myself as I walk through the crowded convention center, shoulder-to-shoulder with other tired and sweaty consultants, all of us checking out nametags, ranks, and outfits for a quick comparison to see where we stand relative to each other.

The last session is with our CFO; it's the closing session for the day in the big arena. We have crummy seats, but they aren't quite nosebleed, so that's something. There are professional lights, loud music, and an emcee, and the crowd goes absolutely wild when the CFO walks out. It's pretty incredible how they make this arena feel like a Taylor Swift concert. The adrenaline rush is palpable. We are part of something important.

The CFO, a white male who has worked for decades in corporate finance, talks for about thirty minutes about the background of the company—all super-inspirational stuff that warms the heart and drums up excitement for the coming year. It's Motivation and Inspiration 101. At the end of his speech, he closes with "I'm a believer. I believe in Rejuvinat. I believe that you've all been put in this arena for a reason, to do something bigger than just yourself. This business is the vehicle to do that. To do whatever you want. This is your assignment from the Lord!"

Vanessa and I look at each other. We were with him until that last line.

"What the actual fuck?" Vanessa whispers.

There is more thunderous applause. I open my eyes wide and shake my head in response, and I clap once, to be nice. I believe in God and everything, but our assignment from the Lord? Really? Vanessa does a sign of the cross; we're both laughing and shaking our heads at this nonsense.

Many MLMs use religious connotations in their messaging with the inference (or outright statement) that their business is a gift from God. It offers people a purpose bigger than themselves, a way to fulfill their destiny. And some take it to the extreme, saying that it's a true calling and the way to have spiritual and financial fulfillment.

The strong religious undertone in many MLMs is no surprise, since Utah, the stomping grounds of the Church of Jesus Christ of Latter-Day Saints (aka the Mormons), is the direct-sales capital of the world; it has more MLM headquarters than any other state per capita.

Preaching the gospel is an easy tie-in with selling products. Whether you're changing lives with wellness products or religion, who cares? The goal is to spread the message and get lots of people on board. And Utah is also prime recruiting grounds for young, white, middle-class SAHMs. In fact, according to a study by Trinity College, "Mormon women remain twice as likely to be homemakers as non-Mormons, regardless of income levels."

Several MLMs are faith-based, such as Thirty-One Gifts, as described on their own website:

> Thirty-One's name is derived from Proverbs 31 of the Bible which describes a virtuous woman who exhibits hard work, wisdom, encouragement & care for others. Because of these qualities, she is worthy of reward, honor & praise.... Through God's strength, we've built a family of individuals who feel women deserve to treat themselves to something special.

There are many others that don't market themselves publicly as Christian-based yet still use strong religious language in their sales and marketing. For example, Young Living Essential Oils was founded by Gary Young, who blended his own devout Mormon faith with a passion for alternative remedies. The company even published a book for its members, *My Word Made Flesh*. According to a rep who received it, it encouraged Young Living members to repeat things like "I am the resurrection and the life of my lineage," and essentially do what she described as "seances with oils." The book was scrubbed from Young Living's website after some public backlash.

Obviously, even the hashtag #blessed has roots in religion. The prosperity gospel is all about capitalism infiltrating faith. Amanda Montell describes this phenomenon in her book *Cultish*: "So much capitalist vernacular—from the sacred stock market bell to the almighty dollar—continues to have religious overtones. And again, this feeds into Meritocracy; that with God and a lot of hustle, you can achieve whatever you want."

There's nothing wrong with being Mormon or Christian or religious in general, but MLMs exploit strong faith, community, and family values to encourage sales. It's no wonder MLMs run thick in church communities, since they are their own closed environments in which people tend to believe the same thing. Religion in its worst manifestation also discourages critical thinking and questioning of authority, so it makes sense that employing religious language would be so effective, in that it mimics a lot of people's early models of unquestioned authority. Sometimes, MLMs even replace church communities by creating a "sisterhood" that many women are looking for. Using Jesus to legitimize your business opportunity is an easy next step.

As everyone around us applauds the CFO's callout to JC, I'm not totally on board with tying face cream products into religion, but I'm also too tired to be completely creeped out.

"Yeah, this is weird," I admit to Vanessa as we file out of the convention center with hordes of other exhausted and slightly inebriated women (some of us more inebriated than others).

We finally retreat to our room, kick off our uncomfortable shoes, and check out our bling-suite perks: a box with two glittery robes and eye masks. *Really? That's* the bling-suite swag? Sure, it's cute and all, but this is what we worked our asses off for? I'm annoyed, but no matter how cheesy it is, I can't pass up the opportunity to inspire social media FOMO, especially since I already told the whole Facebook world that I earned this. So, we gussy up and find good lighting to take a photo.

"Thank you, Rejuvinat, for the awesome Bling Suite perks! We are so #blessed!" Or something like that. Filter, tag, post, done.

"Gawd, this is itchy—what is it made out of, aluminum foil?" Vanessa cringes as she throws the robe on the floor.

"I'm sure we have a cream for that," I shoot back, making light of how ridiculous this entire situation is.

"Dang, we have an hour to get ready!" Vanessa realizes as she looks at the clock.

This day has been a whirlwind. I'm still on zero sleep, and my buzz from the plane has all but worn off. Tonight is a big one, the Sparkle Party! It's yet another perk we qualified for, another glorified celebration/worship session of Kimberly and the few other million-dollar earners at the top. And again, while we "qualified," we still had to pay for the tickets ($350) and buy sparkly shoes and dresses ($250—for items I am definitely never going to wear again).

Vanessa and I get all blinged out; she's in head-to-toe gold and I'm matching in silver. We split a $50 Uber ride to the venue. I have to admit we look damn good, even if the occasion is over-the-top ridiculous.

"I'm absolutely starving," Vanessa groans. So am I. We barely had time to eat the pretzels on the plane, and we walked a trillion miles through the convention center. Luckily, there will be food and a bar at the event!

We walk into an amazingly decorated and packed venue. Apparently, the qualifications for this weren't as stringent as I thought. We chat with June and Hannah and a few of the other ladies on the team while we get checked in and proceed to stand in the mile-long drink line.

"Good luck getting anything to eat," June complains. "It's cupcakes and cookies—no real food."

"Seriously, I may die of starvation; today was brutal," Hannah adds. "I can't believe I busted my ass for this!"

I'm feeling the pain, big time, and I'm feeling guilty that I pushed them so much to "earn" their right to be at what is quickly turning into an exhausting echo chamber with no food, and certainly not enough to drink, especially since they spent so much money to be here. Maybe we are in the top 3 percent, but we are still the bottom of the barrel at this party. Still, we can't show our disappointment publicly. I need to put a positive spin on this. Damage control.

"Okay, maybe this party is lame, but look at us, we're all dolled up! Let's take a photo in front of the dance floor to post on social media, and then get the heck out of here, grab some Tex-Mex, and go dancing. My treat."

"Yeah! Screw this place," June says.

"You're the best leader ever, Em!" Hannah concurs.

This is going to be spendy, but then again, it's an investment in my business. Along with Vanessa, Hannah, and June, I foot the bill for Carly, Annie, and Mandy, too. But at least it will be more fun than standing in line and sucking up to the million-dollar earners. Anyway, Vanessa is single, and there's nothing that married moms love more than living vicariously through their single friends, right?

I know putting more on the credit card is a little dangerous. Even though we can basically afford it, it also makes me realize how inaccessible this is for others. There is no way Vanessa could spring for her team like this, even if she grew her business. Same for June and Hannah. How long can I keep spending like this? I hope that by next year, my team will be able to get here on their own.

We cram into pedicabs in our ridiculous outfits and land in a western-themed bar with a dance floor and amazing food. After eating approximately six hundred baskets of chips and devouring more rounds of tacos and tequila shots than we can handle, we end up joining someone's bachelorette party. I'm guessing we start conversing with them for recruitment purposes. The rest of the night is a bit of a blur. Somewhere over the course of the evening, Carly and Annie head out, as do Mandy, Hannah, and June, while Vanessa and I stay the course, line dancing and taking shots. Vanessa is dancing with a super cute local (from what I can tell, since I'm now seeing double), and I sidle up to the bar and order a water from the bartender.

"Slowing down?" he smiles.

"Attempting to!" I raise my glass. My drinking has been a concern for a while, as have my social outings, for both myself and my husband. The more I drink to escape, the more things I have to escape from. But happy hours and playdates with wine have become so commonplace, and who doesn't need to drink to cope? I just seem to need it a lot more these days. Now, with more events on the calendar thanks to Rejuvinat, there are more reasons to be concerned. But tonight, I'm trying to keep a low profile . . . in head-to-toe silver sequins.

"What are you ladies celebrating tonight? Your sparkly outfits are . . . fun!" He seems amused.

Oh good, it's a chance to give my elevator pitch. I perk up. "Actually, we're in town for a convention for Rejuvinat—have you heard of it? It's one of the top wellness brands in the country!" I take another swig of water, and it's dawning on me how dehydrated I am.

Mouth. Is. A. Desert.

"Oh, Lord, is it like one of those pyramid-scheme things?"

Ugh. I don't have the energy for this. I contemplate a response and glance down at my phone, realizing how late it is. "Omg, V! It's four in the morning!"

I have to be up in three hours. Fuck.

"Have a good one!" I throw a few crumpled dollars on the counter for the bartender and grab Vanessa by the arm. "We have to go!"

"Oh, got it! Hey, can you give us a ride?" Vanessa asks the dude she's been dancing with.

"Oh, noooo, we're good, we can just take an Uber!" I offer. Please no, Vanessa, step away from the cute dude.

"Nah, I'd love to take you girls home. But it's gonna cost you . . . your phone number." He winks at Vanessa.

Even I'm not buzzed enough to be fooled by this douchebag.

Vanessa obliges and barters a ride in exchange for her number, and we climb into his (wow, pretty damn nice) car. He drives us to our hotel, where instead of pulling up to the front entrance, he drives up to the valet. Vanessa and I glance at each other and realize what's happening. This isn't just a ride home—he thinks he's invited in! Vanessa's eyes dart around, and while the car hasn't even come to a complete stop, she yells, "Run!"

She opens the door and we both rush inside, and definitely not in straight lines.

"I. Think. We. Lost. Him." Vanessa breaks down in laughter in the elevator.

"I'm going to pee myself." I'm laughing so hard I can't even breathe.

We make it back to our room, and our heads hit the pillow at approximately five in the morning. After what feels like five minutes, the sun is up and the alarm goes off. I'm running on caffeine and minutes of sleep.

"Vanessa, I think I'm dead. Am I dead? If I'm not dead, will you please kill me?"

"If you're dead, I'm dead, too. Maybe we're in heaven?" she grumbles.

"Feels like hell!"

I giggle. Ouch, my head. I sit up. I'm somehow still drunk and hungover at the same time. I don't know how I'm going to get through this day.

"Will you be pissed if I don't go to your stage-walk thingy?" Vanessa begs.

"No! *I* don't even want to go!" That's only partially true. I want to strut my stuff across that stage, because it'll make for great footage for social media. But my head is pounding. Good on Vanessa for staying; I would, too, if it weren't me doing the walking. Need the Advil. Where's my phone? Shit.

"V, where's my phone?"

"Ugh, I don't know. Where's *mine*? Wait, here." She hands me her iPhone. "Call yourself."

I pick it up, turn it on, and erupt in laughter. Even my headache can't keep this inside.

"What? What is it? What's so funny?"

I drop to the floor, not able to contain myself. "It's. A. Dick. Pic," I practically scream as I hand her the phone, still gasping for breath from laughing so hard. I'm too old for this shit.

"Ahhhh. Yeah, I made the right choice not letting him come in last night." Vanessa rolls over to go back to bed. "I love you! Rock that stage!"

I pump my fist in the air and grab the half-drunk bottle of champagne on the counter. I chug three Advil with it and do my best to put on more makeup and re-curl my hair. I finally find my phone under a pile of gold and silver sequins, and glance at myself in the mirror. I am a far cry from the woman I was just a few years ago—packing lunches, scheduling camp, and showing up for my children. It's not that I don't still do all those things, but now I'm also polishing off day-old bottles of champagne in a hotel room and my bloodshot eyes show it.

In a way, it helps that I wasn't asleep very long and my makeup and hair are pretty much intact. My cognitive function? Not so much. I riffled through the eight different dresses I brought, assess how bloated I am, and decide that red is a good choice.

"Vanessa, how do I look?"

But Vanessa is passed back out. I opt to carry my heels and wear my sneakers for the walk to the convention center in an attempt to work off some of this alcohol and also refrain from breaking my ankles. In the elevator, I run into another consultant who looks familiar. I see from her badge that she's from Seattle, too. She's also carrying her shoes, so I guess she must have had a similar evening.

"Hey, have we met? You look familiar!" I ask her.

"Yeah, I know you. I'm Serena. I'm in Jamie's downline. We're somewhere on the same team." She gesticulates playfully with her hands and smiles. "I saw you at the Sparkle Party last night. How lame was that?"

"*So* lame!"

I remember Serena. We're "crossline," which means we're on the same team with the same upline, but that upline splits off at some point, so we don't have any financial ties to each other. It's like being second cousins. I notice that we have the same title. "You're walking the stage this morning?"

"Yeah, are you?" she asks, eyes open wide. "Want to sit together?"

Great, I've found someone to walk with today, since Vanessa is under the weather; plus, it'll be so nice to have a conversation with someone who doesn't make money off me and who I don't make money off. It's a different dynamic when you don't have to keep up the whole positive "leaders always show up" bullshit.

We arrive in the arena, which is filled with consultants. The music is blaring, and the production is over the top. We sit in an assigned area toward the front and listen to the morning keynote speaker (more motivation and grit and courage and blah blah blah). Serena removes a flask from her bag and takes a swig, offering me some. Oh, Serena, we are going to get along great. It helps that so many people in MLMs are carbon copies of each other, creating a sense of proximity even if the friendship and sisterhood are functioning at a superficial level. In reality, you're working in an echo chamber. But at this moment, I don't mind the echo chamber, as I take a long swig from the flask.

After some more empowerment speak, it's time for us to walk the stage! Finally. An assistant guides a group of us through the back of the arena. I follow Serena, and someone instructs us to walk across the stage when our name is called. It feels so fancy and official. Serena is up first, and then I hear my name on the loudspeaker. I'm handed a white rose, and I wave as I walk across the stage. There is thunderous applause, lights, cameras flashing. Wow, look at that crowd! I shake hands with the CEO, our field leader Elizabeth, and a few other people from corporate I don't know yet but I'm pretty sure are important. My heart is beating so fast. I'm flushed with adrenaline. I could get used to this. Serena and I hug before we walk back to our seats.

"Congrats, Emily!" Serena offers once we're offstage.

"Same to you!"

I wish we had champagne. To celebrate, yes, but also, this hangover needs a remedy. As we walk down the aisle, Becky flags me down. "Congrats, Em! I got photos!"

"Tag me in one?"

Because did it even happen if there's no proof on social media?

Allison pops up behind her. "Where's Vanessa?"

Shit.

I pretend I don't hear her question and wave goodbye as I'm ushered down the aisle. I don't need more guilt trips about how leaders show up.

As Serena and I walk back to our seats, I see envious consultants eyeing us with our lanyards and roses. We aren't the million-dollar earners yet, but we are certainly higher in rank than most of the women here. We've helped so many others level up in this business, and this is our reward. In turn, we only have to ignore the fact that hundreds of other women haven't leveled up, or that it took our bribery to get them there. Right now, though, I have to admit, it feels good to be envied.

I sit back down in the audience and dig through my purse for some Advil. I'm *so* exhausted. But I have to stay to be one of the first (fifteen thousand people) to find out what the new product is! Again, the company has us by the proverbial balls by enticing us with another flashy new thing to peddle to our customers and our downline (who are also just glorified customers).

New products are power for the consultants and the company, but not in the way you may think. The real commodity in an MLM is the people: people who join, and people who buy products. Money is only ever transferred in one direction: up the pyramid. The actual products? You can get them anywhere, over the counter or online. The skincare, haircare, collagen, and vitamins are truly nothing special. If you peruse the ingredient list, even the most proprietary items shilled by an MLM have virtually identical counterparts at a lower cost. There are plenty of websites that offer "dupes" of any MLM product. The company leads you to believe they are the best, and of course, because you're only given their studies, their marketing material, and their pricing information, and the sales benefit *you*, why would you question them? Plus, whether you're an MLM customer or consultant, you are locked into a VIP or preferred auto-shipment program that almost always includes a minimum purchase and a fee. These can be extremely difficult to change or cancel, leaving consumers using products they don't want, or using them longer than they intend to. But the products are just the bait for the prey: potential recruits and customers.

When people are the commodity, consultants want to sell the dream to everyone, even if it's not technically possible for that dream to be fulfilled. This is why you see and hear so much about the "income opportunity." As Robert L. FitzPatrick describes in *Ponzinomics*, "The market has been drawing in more people since MLM started in 1945, and then grew tremendously since the mid 1970s. Today, it includes students with college debt, seniors facing mountains of medical bills and disappearing savings, families with unbearable rents, people already working jobs, immigrants trying to survive, and military spouses facing multiple deployments, among others. The income-opportunity market is exploding!"

And the real opportunity is the vulnerable people at the heart of these companies, many of whom I know are right here with me at the convention center, dreaming of the moment they, too, might grace the stage to the tune of a white rose and the audience's envy.

"Oh, I'm excited!" I say to Serena. "Last year, people were all over the undereye patches. What do you think it is this year?"

"You mean, you don't know yet? It's a hair serum. Supposed to be awesome!" she whispers.

"Wait, how do you know that already?" I ask her.

"Oh, my upline has loose lips. So many of the top earners can't keep their mouths shut because they want their teams to have an edge." She laughs and rolls her eyes.

"Interesting," I mutter. I'm a little miffed that I don't get any insider info, but Kimberly would never threaten her queen status by giving her lowly court an edge. I'm growing more grateful that I ran into Serena this morning.

The stage erupts into more lights and music. The CEO and president grace the stage, and the new product is unveiled. You can feel the energy in the air, and I'm still on that adrenaline high! Being buzzed and sick isn't a great combo, but I'm here for it. The curtain parts, and the product is unveiled. There it is . . . the new hair serum! It's greeted with thunderous applause and a smattering of confetti; it's like an upper-crust gender reveal on steroids.

Honestly, it probably wouldn't even matter what the product actually was—people would be jacked, no matter what.

"A telephone book, OH MY GAWD! Sign me up!"

"A plastic ruler! My future is set!"

There's something about the recipe of exhaustion, obligation, and financial pressure that makes us all believe the unveiled object is a winner, even if it's legitimately a dud. Finally, the price is announced: "Hurry, get your Convention special package with five serums and a free carrying bag, only available here, for only $695!"

"Cha-ching!" Serena sings.

Every year at Convention, there is a new product that's touted as a "game changer." And every MLM does the same thing by unveiling a new groundbreaking product. I notice that they coincidentally retire products every couple of years. One of the game-changing products that was out on the table in the wine bar when I signed up? It's already been retired. I know that products get upgraded and improved, but it's hard to take any of them seriously when they're "the best thing ever invented" one day and obsolete two years later. But it's common practice in most MLMs because it only works to further drive the FOMO.

I wonder how long this hyped-up hair serum will be around. Long enough to make the company some money before it moves on to the next thing. And it benefits the company in either instance. When a product is discontinued, it causes the consultants to panic purchase for their loyal customers. When new products come out, they tend to "sell out," probably by design, so consultants and customers are prepped with credit cards, ready to purchase as many as possible to avoid missing out. Coming up empty-handed after a product launch is a no-no. MLMs depend on consumerism, the obsession around acquiring stuff. That's what draws people in. Your current sales force and customer base need to consistently be remade into new customers. Tweak a serum, retire an old product, and make a new one. Or throw out a promotional item or BOGO with purchase—whatever it takes to keep customers spending, joining, and thinking they're getting the latest, greatest thing.

The *only* people who will be allowed to purchase the new product in the next few weeks will be current reps. It's one of the big draws that makes so many of us open our wallets to come to Convention in the first place, and a huge recruiting tool to get new consultants on board. Commission-wise, Convention months are always the biggest months; paychecks are sky high. So, who is the customer? Purchases are all coming from people already enrolled in the MLM. And sure, it's a way to entice interested people to join ("Hey, you can only get this amazing phone book if you're a consultant!"), but at the end of the day, the *cha-ching* is coming from consultants, not retail customers. And consultants buy it because they are told, "You can't sell what you aren't using!" and shamed for not investing in their business if they don't buy the hot new product. I should know—it's something I was told and something I repeated.

But dang—$695? The only option, of course, is a huge bundle, so I am going to have to put this on a credit card. I feel like I should get more than one, since the people at home who didn't come to Convention won't be able to get them for a while. And some of the million-dollar earners have had this in their hands for months, so they're way ahead of the game. Serena and I race to the expo to purchase this shit, and I feel dizzy. It's so hot, and the crowds are almost suffocating. I don't know how I'm going to stay up for the gala tonight.

We elbow through more crowds, stand in line for our products, and finally, *finally* make it to the front. Serena and I hand our credit cards over at checkout, and I see June.

"Leaders Lounge!" she yells at me.

Oh, that's right! Another perk! Maybe this one won't suck. Serena overhears and adds, "Oh yeah, I think they have champagne."

Sold.

We gather our bags, find our way to the Leaders Lounge, and wait in line again, though this one isn't quite as miserably long as the others. We grab champagne (we take two apiece) from the tray and find a spot to sit.

"I'm exhausted," June says. Mandy and Carly nod in agreement. "But I can't wait to try this serum! I should take a before picture!"

Good point, I think to myself. Time to look at my social media feed and update some things. From the scroll, this looks like the life. There are tagged and filtered photos of me in the Bling Suite, at the Sparkle Party, in a pedicab, and walking the stage. I add a quick snap of my feet up in the Leaders Lounge. I can't help but giggle at what you can't see in the pictures: the long lines, the exhaustion, the early mornings trying to get my makeup perfect in order to walk the walk and talk the talk, the rogue dick pic, the credit-card bills, the pounding headache, and the stress of planning how to get my team to purchase this expensive-ass product. I scroll past a picture of Hannah, whom I haven't seen yet today, and my heart sinks when I realize she isn't going to be able to afford this. Convention practically broke the bank for her. Maybe I'll purchase an extra one for her, too. After all, you can't sell what you don't use.

Before-and-after pics are already being posted, probably from the ladies who had advance access. These same people have been touting the benefits of our products from day one, and now this has suddenly changed their hair? Smoke. And. Mirrors. But I oblige and dig out the crappiest picture of my hair I can find so I can make my own before-and-after. I need to make sure everyone on the team is doing the same and prepping their wallets for this product. I take to my team Facebook page:

> The new product is here, ladies! For those of you who didn't make the investment in Convention, you'll have to wait until next week, but MAKE A PLAN to invest in yourself and your business! In the meantime, here's your homework for the week:
>
> 1. Post an inspirational quote or photo.
> 2. Take your before photo.
> 3. Add ten Facebook friends.
> 4. Send five messages.
> 5. Post a product photo and a lifestyle photo.
> 6. Do one hour of personal development reading!

You've got this, ladies! Remember, this is more than a business—this is a vehicle of change, for whatever you want in your life. You were given this opportunity for a reason.

No shame in passing along some inspiration. I consider adding "from God," but even I can't go there. I take another swig of champagne, then grab my bag and attempt to quietly head toward the exit.

"Where are you going?" Serena asks.

"Can't sell what you don't use! I'm going to head back to the expo to purchase more Convention specials."

She nods and joins me.

She gets it, I think to myself, feeling pride in this recent addition to my sisterhood.

"Licking" Things to Claim Them as Your Own

✦ ✦
✦

I joined an MLM for books because I didn't think it was as "bad" as all the others. Once I actually got into it, I realized I wasn't making much money because I wasn't recruiting anyone. I tried but it made me feel icky, and I was competing with my upline since our social circles overlapped and she'd already gotten to everyone before I could! I also was made to feel guilty when I bought books from any other company. It made no sense to me. I just hated how black and white it was. I quit before the year was up, and it really strained my relationship with the friend who recruited me.

—ALANA, former MLM rep

S itting on the most uncomfortable, crunchy examination-table paper, I flip through my phone and browse my long prospects list. Of course, I work during a doctor's appointment! Can't let a little doc follow-up get in the way of my bossbabe game. Plus, my doctor also happens to be one of my prospects, so I'm killing several birds with one stone here.

My prospect list is more of a running scan of Facebook Messenger: Check who has ignored my message, send a quick "making sure you saw this" nudge, push to schedule a call with those who've responded, and follow up with those who have expressed even the remotest interest. Easy peasy! Copy and paste, copy and paste.

Something stops my scroll immediately—a notification about a new post from a locally famous hairstylist I follow. She's a dream-teamer, for sure. I hop over to her page to see what she posted. My jaw drops when I read: "Hi, all! Want to learn more about Rejuvinat! If I have any followers who are reps, please message me!"

OMG, SHUT UP. I practically leap off the table. This is *huge*. I need to think of a good in here; she has over 100K followers, so she's gonna get so many messages. How do I stand out? Phew, I'll have to think about this. Too much pressure in the doctor's office. In the meantime, I decide it's a perfect opportunity to showcase how I can work from anywhere and lean back to take a selfie, when the doctor walks in. Awkward.

"Hi! Sorry to keep you waiting," she stammers. She looks serious.

"No worries, I was just catching up on a little work." Here we go—never pass up an opportunity to show . . . the opportunity. Shit, maybe that's why she called me in today! Who knows?

She doesn't waste any time before telling me, "Unfortunately, I have some bad news, Emily. Your results came back, and they show malignancy."

Wait. What? I stare blankly. She looks down at her chart and looks back at me, waiting for what she said to register, though I'm not quite allowing it to sink in. Um, we were looking for malignancy? My mind is still stuck on her being my newest business partner.

"Are you saying it's . . . cancer?" I ask, hoping she will correct me and say, "Nooooo, not that," but she simply nods.

"Yes, I'm sorry. Luckily, we caught it very early and it should be an easy surgery. I'm going to refer you to a specialist, an oncologist, so I can't say anything for certain, but in my experience, I don't think you should expect any additional treatment, chemo, or anything. You're very lucky."

She just said *oncologist* and *surgery* and *chemo* and *lucky* in the same sentence. How did we get here? A few weeks ago, I came in for a flu shot and she mentioned it had been a while since my last pap, and now I'm sitting here being diagnosed with cervical cancer?

This has really taken a turn. I can't process the enormity of what I've just been given, and I'm still thinking of how to spin it to ask if I can put a display of my products in her office.

After some more conversation, paperwork, and phone calls, I leave the office, stunned. I start to make preparations for who I'm going to tell first and how I'm going to juggle all the things. Luckily, with our new au pair, who joined the family in the last year, it will be much easier. It's been extremely helpful since my team has grown and my workload has increased. I also got an assistant, thanks to Becky's (albeit unsolicited) recommendation, so I can focus on being the face of the business and spend less time on the busywork. Doesn't stop me from needing to be on my phone as much, unfortunately. And now, I wonder how I can be the face of the business from a hospital bed. This will be the true test of how "flexible" this business actually is.

In an MLM, you are expected to work from anywhere because that's part of the draw, sold as a perk when you join, but working from anywhere actually means working from *everywhere*. Sitting at home with the kids? Send some messages! Have a lunch break? Do some recruiting! I can't tell you the number of times I saw photos of people proudly "working" from doctors' offices, like the selfie I just took, but also hospital beds while in labor, at weddings (sometimes, their own), in traffic, even at funerals! The allure of being able to work from anywhere becomes the burden of being required to be on call 24/7.

And the "work" is generally referred to by the company and our uplines in MLM as "income-producing activity," which is comical, because very little of it actually produces income. Sometimes, it includes phone calls or text messages making *actual* sales, getting credit-card information, selling products, or doing content marketing. The rest? Sitting on pointless Zoom "trainings" with uplines or corporate, and either being bullied for not doing enough or having sunshine blown up your ass for how amazing this business is and being told why you need to stay plugged in. Other "business activities" include sending messages, posting selfies and self-congratulatory motivational missives, adding friends on social media, watching a so-called training video, or reading a personal development book. Maybe the behavior will eventually lead to a sale, or maybe not, but it certainly should not be called income-producing because it's completely unpaid activity.

And it makes sense, because just like the time spent at Convention and other retention events, the more time you spin, doing busywork that makes you feel like you're making a real impact, the less time you have to question the system. The more indoctrination and time spent in proximity with people who you come to believe are your friends, the less likely you are to want to leave. Spending every waking minute on work (paid or not) benefits the organization as well, because it's a marketing tactic that enables them to use reps to amplify their message.

It should be no surprise, given the importance of my business, that the next person I call, just a few short days after talking with my family and my oncologist, is Becky.

"Oh, Em. I'm so sorry," Becky sobs over the phone before her voice quickly turns high-pitched as she tries, per usual, to put a positive spin on things. "You know Kayla, remember her, on Allison's team? She had cervical cancer, and she's totally fine now!"

"I know." I appreciate the vote of confidence. I actually feel much more at ease after talking with my oncologist. I have a pretty simple surgery scheduled next month, and I am cautiously optimistic that I will put it all behind me.

"Plus, think about the downtime. I mean, you're just sitting there, right? You can still message and make phone calls!" she sings through the phone.

There it is! My first instinct is to tell her to go fuck herself, because again, my intuition is right—work should be the last thing on my mind. But instead, I actually think, *Good point.*

"You know," Becky continues before I can respond, "this could be really good for your business."

"What? How so?" I am trying to figure out how cancer, surgery, or a little downtime for phone calls can be good for anything.

"Remember last year when that one lady's husband died—what was her name . . . Jessa? Lives in Louisiana."

I vaguely remember. Although I don't know Jessa, everyone in Rejuvinat sent their love and posted about her.

"I mean, her business blew *up* after," Becky continues. "So many people purchased out of sympathy. And not just from her—tons of people in the company were able to capitalize on it!"

Sympathy? Capitalize? Yikes. My initial feeling is *cringe.* It feels a little . . . exploitative, maybe. I don't know if I'm comfortable with that. But Becky hasn't led me astray yet. And I do remember how much love and support surrounded Jessa. It couldn't hurt, right? My wheels start turning . . . Maybe I can do some sort of fundraiser?

"Actually," I offer, noticing a header on some of my hospital paper-work, "January is Cervical Cancer Awareness Month. What if I donated a portion of every sale to cancer research or something?"

"Genius!" Becky squeals. "I'll throw in some donations, too!"

Obviously, it's an added bonus for her, since she gets a cut of all those sales, anyway; she's no dummy.

If you look around Facebook before/during/after any holiday, national disaster, pandemic, social injustice, you're guaranteed to see it: an MLM promo or party that "benefits" a charity or nonprofit, with a percentage of commission or cash donation that is attached to a product's sale.

"Buy my essential oil and I'll donate $20 to the victims of the hurricane!"

"Sign up as a customer and I'll give 10 percent of your sale to the Red Cross!"

"For every ten sales of self-tanner, I'll give $50 to the Christian Children's Fund!"

Now, the intention of rolling charity into MLM parties or promotions is not a bad one, but the implementation is where things get questionable. It's not like the women in MLMs don't care about hurricane relief or Christian funds; they do, with all their bossbabe hearts. And it's not to say that these donations are fraudulent; I'm sure many of the reps who offer these fundraisers make good on them. However, forcing someone to buy a product in order to contribute to a charitable cause sets up a host of moral and ethical issues. Ask any nonprofit and they'll tell you they prefer direct financial donations. If a purchase of a non-donatable item is required, there is always an ulterior motive at play. And even if reps claim to be donating their commission, portions of every single sale will still move upline, to the sponsor above them, the one above them, and the company itself.

Not to mention, all sales help a rep "rank up" in the company. Even the good intentions aren't that good; the fact that they are usually self-serving is hidden in the claim of charity. Every time a customer or a rep buys a product, whether they buy it with their own money or donated money, the MLM still gets publicity by advertising the fundraiser in the first place.

William Keep, a professor of marketing at The College of New Jersey who has studied MLMs extensively, believes donation pushes are used as a marketing tool by distributors to maintain purchase volume. "The carrot that's being held out here is that we're helping people who need to be helped," he says. "When a person donates money for someone to make a purchase from an MLM, they are actually supporting the profits of the parent firm, not the charity organization."

Even though most companies will say they look down on using natural disasters or states of emergency as a means to promote businesses or sales, reps consistently continue to hide behind fundraisers to line their own pockets, as long as they state that their parent company doesn't endorse it. After all, reps are independent contractors, not employees, so there is no oversight or guidance on how they should or should not take advantage of crisis situations under the guise of a "generous spirit."

The reality is, if I wanted $20 to go to cervical-cancer research, I could ask people to donate directly to organizations that support it. But by requiring a purchase and attaching a donation to it (not to mention my own personal story to *really* pull at the heartstrings), I was helping myself, Becky, and the company. I saw it as a win-win-win—but in hindsight, it was duplicitous as fuck.

"Okay, Becky, I'll work out the details. Talk to you soon."

Though I've had enough cancer talk for the last few weeks, the call with Becky actually gives me something to look forward to—I'm going to turn these cancer cells into a selling point! But between doctors' appointments, meal trains, worst-case scenarios, it's been a lot, and I haven't even told my customers or the rest of my team yet. All that can wait. Next on the agenda: I need to formulate my *very* thought-out response to Madison, the fabulously famous hairdresser on Facebook. Quite some time has gone by, and I see hundreds of comments on her post (even though she said for people to message her—can't they read?), so I hope she hasn't already moved on from the topic. Maybe I can use the reason for my delay as part of my message. Hmm. I rack my brain before referencing some scripts, editing for a while, and finally, clicking Send on the following message:

Hi Madison. I couldn't help but notice your post. I have followed you for a long time and love your work. I saw your photoshoot in *Seattle Bride Magazine*, and it was incredible. I live in Seattle, too! I'd love to have a phone conversation with you if possible, or perhaps coffee? I also wanted to apologize for getting back to you a few days after I intended. I saw your message in the doctor's office just as I got an unfortunate cancer diagnosis! But it's one reason I'm so grateful that I run my own business and can work from anywhere! Our product launch from last Convention was incredible (perhaps you saw it), and with a network like yours, I can only imagine how far you could take this! A captive audience of people who love hair and makeup? I'm sure you've received tons of messages, but if mine resonates with you, let me know, I'd love to chat. Emily

Smart? Maybe. Too much? Probably. Manipulative? Definitely.

But like my upline always told me, do whatever it takes; if they can join anyone, make them want to join you. And this is based in science: the dopamine hit that comes with the thrill of the chase. Lisa Earle McLeod writes in the *Forbes* article "Is Your Sales Team Addicted to Dopamine?" that dopamine, the neurotransmitter controlling your brain's reward and pleasure center, is associated with chasing a desired object, which in this case is Madison. But it fades quickly, leaving you wanting more. In fact, too much dopamine can make you frantic. So when you prioritize getting a dopamine hit over lasting purpose and impact (actually making a difference and connecting with people), you're more likely to have transactional relationships, lack of strategic thinking, and ethical lapses. Which is why, in that moment, I'm okay with this tacky message for the sake of the sale.

Holy shit, I can see she's typing already! I sit up with anticipation as the little bubbles pop up on the screen.

"Emily, I'd love to chat. I have received tons of messages, but I was drawn to yours. I'm so sorry about your diagnosis. Let me know when you're free."

Damn! Becky was right. When you're recruiting from the same pool of people, you have to stand out. This could be a gold mine!

Celebrities or high-profile people who join MLMs have an easy in. They already have a captive audience of devoted fans—an automatic dirt list—who will likely purchase anything and everything they recommend. A very famous celebrity joined Rejuvinat shortly after I did and she hit the top of the pyramid almost immediately, earning the company car and every trip, seemingly without lifting a finger. The reason for this is a sad one: People simply wanted to join her team so they could be closer to her, to say they worked with and knew her. And they would pay anything to do it. "Buy a $2,000 kit? Spend money on a retreat I can't afford? Well, as long as I get to hang out with [XYZ celebrity]!" It's influencer culture at its most exploitative because you aren't just buying a recommended product so they get a cut; you're joining a commercial cult. This is truly the cannibalization of a current business, following, or fan base.

But as I've discussed, the real money is made in recruiting. If someone thinks they know you, and they like and trust you, your endorsement likely won't need much fact-checking on their part. After all, why would you buy some eye cream from a superstar celebrity when you could *be on her team* and directly associate with her? Celebrities are used to legitimize the business opportunity for people in the system, and often, they are misquoted. It's easier to share a meme than it is to fact-check.

I set up a coffee date with Madison and check my to-do list. I've been so consumed with the cancer diagnosis that I've been putting things on the back burner, remembering that I need to return a call from our regional manager, Seth. Even without Madison (yet), my numbers are *big.* Thankfully, my entire team bought the Convention offers, so my volume has almost doubled, and my paychecks have grown yet again. Seattle has become such a hot Rejuvinat growth area, thanks to my team and Serena's team, that corporate is putting on another biz op—this time, footing the bill—and I am being asked to speak at it again!

I make sure the kids are quiet and put my new headset on to get CEO-ready.

"Hi, Seth, Emily returning your call."

"Emily, great to hear from you. How are you?" the smooth-talking fellow from corporate responds.

"I'm great. You?" Damn, I sound like a boss.

"Well, I'm awesome, and I have to say, huge congratulations on the growth we're seeing in Seattle! Since we're hosting the biz op in Woodinville on Saturday morning, as an extra bonus, we're flying some of the top leaders in for a fun wine-tasting tour afterward. We want to showcase the up-and-coming growth areas. You should be proud!"

"Thank you so much. I'm flattered!"

Wow. This is huge. I get to sell the dream on a much larger scale. And some of the bigger higher-ups are going to be there, too, including Kimberly. The best part? My new bud, Serena, has also been chosen to speak. *We* are being showcased as the up-and-coming area of growth.

"We'll even cover your hotel that evening, so you can get a night away! You earned it!" he shares, enthused, as though he's giving me a $10,000 raise.

"Thank you, Seth, I cannot wait. See you soon."

I hang up the phone and am beaming. I still can't believe what I've been able to accomplish in a couple short years. Seattle was barely on the map when I joined, and now it's a hot spot!

The phrase *high-growth area* is something I've heard many times in the past few years. "Los Angeles is booming! Join during this huge growth phase!" "Detroit is up and coming!" "There are hardly any consultants in North Carolina—be part of the huge growth potential!" And, of course, "We are opening in a new country—unlimited growth potential!" Saturation drives this marketing tactic, from one town to another, and then one country to another. While MLMs will say saturation isn't a thing, it is.

This is directly connected to the *I* in the BITE Model: information control, or using facts and statements out of context to prove a misleading point. (And I should know, since I once led a company-wide training on saturation. Cringe.) I used the example that there are always people being born, with 385,000 babies born per day—all potential future customers. Yes, I did. Of course, my unpaid "training" included no actual statistics, and if I'd done the math, I'd know that those "future customers" (aka babies) were still far fewer in number than the consultants who are preying on them. And they also wouldn't be aging into potential MLM reps for decades to come, but hey, I was thinking long-term! Clearly, not logically.

In real-world franchises and distributorships, there are protections—contracts that define territories and markets so there aren't too many sellers or stores in a given area. Even the most successful stores or products have a finite market share. But an MLM will eventually "hire" too many people who cannot compete because their networks are already targeted by other reps. They obscure the statistics on growth by simply promoting in areas of the country with fewer consultants, until there aren't any areas for new growth. And if there aren't any areas of growth in the United States, they launch in a new country! Rejuvinat went big in the United States, and now that most cities are full, we are expanding into Canada, Australia, and Japan. What a lot of people don't know is that it's necessary because the United States has become saturated.

Follow the trajectory of any MLM and you will see the same thing: Opening one country after another is meant to keep you believing that the company is actually growing. But growth potential doesn't mean the same thing as it does with a traditional franchise or company; it just means there are fewer consultants than in the most saturated areas. Because, in the MLM industry, nobody is managing the number of consultants, inventory, or market penetration to make sure there is success for all involved.

A "normal" company will quit hiring when there are enough people. In MLMs, the more people who are involved, the more successful the company is, regardless of how successful the consultant is. When Suzy Q buys her business kit, the company already has her money; they never need her to sell another thing, and she's doing free advertising for them. It doesn't matter if she goes broke or loses money. The more people who join an MLM, the more money the MLM makes, *regardless* of how many people in the MLM lose money. And the indoctrination is so solid that even when people are losing money, there are enough people singing the company's praises to drown them out.

Before Serena and Jamie and me, there weren't too many consultants in Seattle, so now our area is experiencing "huge growth," but only because the other previously "hot" markets are all saturated. Eventually, the same thing will happen in Seattle.

MLMs will tell you that saturation doesn't matter, because they don't draw a distinction between total saturation and market saturation. In a city as small as 100,000 people, market saturation can be reached with only a handful of distributors. And even if total saturation may not be reached with that handful, the town could still reach market saturation from distributors from *other* MLMs, since so many have overlapping recruitment campaigns and product lineups. For example, there are thirty MLMs that sell cosmetics alone, so if you already have a Mary Kay lady on your block, how well are the Avon lady, Younique presenter, Beautycounter rep, and Seint consultant going to fare? Nobody needs that much blush.

Consumer Fraud reporting gives a great example—and yes, this is a real example:

> The population of the United States is about 300,000,000. Let's say you want to sell a new type of bra; obviously not everyone will want to buy one. That means, out of 300 million people, there are about 110 million who are adult women, your target market. If you sell the bra at $45 each, you can eliminate most women who are in the lower income groups; so now you are down to 50 million potential customers. Then there is the style. Even with a wildly popular style, it still won't appeal to everyone, so of the remaining 50 million potential customers, probably only half will want it enough to buy one. Therefore, we can reasonably say that the potential maximum size of our market for designer bras will be no more than 25 million women, out of a total population of 300 million people in the United States. That's about 1/10 of the population, even for something as basic and necessary as a bra.

MLMs skirt around the saturation question because they have such high turnover; many people quit and don't return, which requires replacement. Robert L. FitzPatrick states in *The Myth of MLM Income Opportunity* that when it comes to MLMs, "the very term 'growth' is a lie." In MLM parlance, growth does not mean enlargement of a customer base, but rather, replacement of a customer base. Every several years, each MLM's entire so-called sales force, and whatever "customers" they may have, quit and never return, usually after losing money. They must be entirely replaced, so "growth" simply means recruiting more people than the number who quit year over year. Those who quit likely won't come back, while new consultants will join on the promise of "unlimited income" and "business opportunity." MLMs are exempt from federal disclosure rules that apply to other businesses, so they do not disclose dropout rates, and thus, the collective replacement of consultants is considered growth, regardless of the larger number of people who are succeeding, failing, or quitting.

But in that moment, I am the queen bee of the hot market, and I'm taking advantage of this situation and getting an overnight stay out of it. Though Kale's early warning that it's not sustainable still rings in my ear from time to time, my paychecks have only been increasing ($8,000 last month!), and I have my perks (more purses, jewelry, and trips). Since Vanessa has started her new job—an awesome sales position in a pharmaceutical company with travel and an actual paycheck—I can't include my bestie in these things anymore. But thankfully, I've been happy to have Serena to pal around with. Serena joined for many of the same reasons I did: She wanted connection, hoped to get results from the products, and wanted an outlet from her husband and two kids. She was a former marketing star and, since having babies, had dabbled in a few nonprofits, but had never really found anything that gave her a sense of purpose. Now, she I and are dominating Seattle. We are two of a kind.

While it always looks like amicable girl time on social media, there are people who actually hate everyone on their team. On my Hawaii trip, other reps shared terrible stories of their uplines pressuring them to do things like produce events they didn't want to host, shaming them by canceling their hotel reservations at retreats to let them know they were no longer welcome, and even pressuring them to pray more or attend church. The stories I heard constantly made me feel gratitude for Becky and solidified the belief that I treated my own downline pretty well. The gossip spreads far and wide, and while the truth probably lies somewhere in the middle, all I know is that I'm lucky I care about the women I'm working with. They're my friends.

Before I leave, I make the usual lists for the au pair. It's becoming easier to get away now that I have her, but I'm also spending less time with my kids and my husband, and I really don't need to talk much about logistics anymore, which is both a good thing and a bad thing, especially if we don't have anything else to talk about. Luckily, the more money I bring home, the less strain we have on our finances and the calmer the household. My drinking is still a common topic, which will make explaining this wine-tasting weekend difficult, but it's for business! I'm sure Kale will be proud that I'm being showcased.

Serena and I decide to make an entire day of it on our way to Woodinville, taking an early morning Uber. One hour and two bottles of wine later, we've strategized, compared notes and downlines, and figured out how, between the two of us, we can continue to take Seattle by storm. It's so nice to have a friend who understands the business (and is ambitious in it!) but doesn't have a financial link to me since she's not in my upline or downline, so I don't have to worry about faking it all the time.

We settle in for our biz op, and if I do say so myself, Serena and I dazzle, even after the early morning wine "tasting." This is the biggest group of guests we've ever had—more than 250 women in the audience! People are eating this stuff up, and both of our teams are growing like gangbusters. We entertain and answer questions as our celeb status grows bigger by the day. Both of our teams add several team members and dozens of customers.

After the biz op ends, it's time for fun! We check into our rooms, which are over the top: crystal chandeliers, full mini bars, huge soaking tubs. I text Serena from my room: "THIS IS AMAZING!" There are gifts and cards; Becky, Allison, and a few of my other upline leaders sent me chocolate-covered strawberries, and the corporate office gave me a passport holder that reads, "Going Places," attached to the Rejuvinat logo. I don't waste any time taking a photo with my new gifts and posting it on social media: "I love getting spoiled by corporate!"

I post it and see that Serena has posted a very similar one. Great minds.

We load into the tour bus and meet the other leaders, who were flown in for the celebration. We spend the day wine tasting and rubbing elbows with million-dollar earners, admiring their shoes and jewelry. More studded heels, diamonds, and lots, I mean lots, of Chanel. I feel like this is a vision board come to life. We mingle with corporate and chat with the other consultants, who are all gushing about our "growing market" and asking for tips and tricks. Wait, the million-dollar earners are asking *us* for advice? Pinch me! The only one who is seemingly not impressed is Kimberly. You'd think she'd be happier, considering she makes money off both me and Serena, but it's clear that she doesn't like the spotlight being taken away from her. She barely talks to us the entire day.

After the third or fourth winery (who can keep count?), we all gather around a table at the final stop for dinner. The dining room is beautifully decorated, with nametags on every place setting. A small designer makeup bag with each of our initials sits on the plate. So sweet! I'm a little fuzzy at this point. Serena and I look at each other across the room, and I see that she's fading a bit, too. We just need to get through the evening. I give her a thumbs-up, and she feigns a smile and blinks widely.

Seth from corporate gives a speech around the table and introduces a few of the other corporate VPs in attendance. After some more talking, introducing, ass-kissing, and (finally) eating, the VP of sales stands and clinks his champagne glass as the waitress pours another round. Ho boy. I don't need any more, but who am I to turn down a toast?

"We are letting you all know first, because you are the top leaders in the company—" At this point, I'm blushing . . . or am I just having a hot flash from drinking so much? Not sure. "We just found out today that after being number two for the last three years, we are now the number-one wellness company in the United States!" The room erupts in applause. High-fives, screams, cackles—these chicks go absolutely nuts. I stand up and wobble, so I immediately sit back down again and clap from my seat. I see Serena is doing the same. She puts her index finger in the air and mouths, "We're number one!" I laugh, realizing I can see two of her.

You will often see MLMs tout their status as number one.

"We are the number-one skincare line!"

"We are number one in the premium haircare industry!"

"We are the number-one leisure apparel company!"

Sounds impressive, right? Especially since they're generally stacked up against national department-store brands. But it isn't as impressive as it sounds, since those "number-one" figures are *revenue,* not *profit.* And when a company has hundreds of thousands of consultants, who are *required* to buy product monthly to stay commissionable, and are hyped and pressured to buy the newest "game changer" at every turn, and are required to buy products to join, then no shit! Of course revenue is going to be through the roof! As my organization grew, of course there were new customers, but the huge majority of sales were from the team of previously enrolled consultants. The reality is, the consultants *are* the customers in an MLM. I remember why I'm here in the first place, because of the Convention product that my entire team purchased, pushing my commission (and Serena's) into overdrive and helping to make Seattle a "hot market." I am skeptical of number-one status, but it sounds good, and it's certainly something with which to gild my posts and make them pop. I raise my glass and think, *This could be what gets me my car.*

Serena and I might be going places, but the next place we need to go is bed.

I WAKE UP HORRIDLY HUNGOVER. I expected this, but also, shit. I can't quite remember the end of the night. What happened after the toast? Did we take the bus back to our hotel or walk? This is my hotel, right? Yes. Okay, I guess we got home safely. I look at the bed and there are brown stains everywhere. At first, I wonder if I got so drunk that I shit myself, but thankfully, it's just melted chocolate and strawberries I must have eaten when I got back, whenever that was. I pick up my phone and see a missed call from Becky and one from Allison, probably to hear about how amazing the day was yesterday. I see Facebook notifications—oh, I've been tagged in photos, yay! Let's see! Oh no. Oh God. Drunk photos. FROM KIMBERLY!

Noooo! Why would you post these, Kimberly? The more I scroll, the worse it gets. There's a photo of me sitting on the lap of our VP of sales . . . smoking a cigarette? When did that happen and where did I get a cigarette? And Serena and I with our arms around the COO, doing shots? This is a nightmare. Shit! I text the pictures to Serena and get an immediate phone call.

Serena is panicked, just like me. "We are so screwed."

I try to pass the blame: "They pumped us full of alcohol all day long—what did they expect? Ugh. Why would Kimberly post these?"

"Because she's a jealous bitch and we upstaged her," Serena says without taking a breath. "And look at all these sightseeing photos, and all the other photos at the biz op—she didn't do any of this shit. She was in her hotel room getting her hair and makeup done. She never comes out of her room at these things. It's all for show; she'd never mingle with the help. And now, she's just trying to make us look like drunk assholes. Which we kinda were, but let's be real—everyone knows those aren't the photos you post publicly unless you're trying to humiliate someone. Fuck. Her."

"All right, I'll just ask her to un-tag us or delete the photos. I can't imagine many people have seen them yet." Then, I remember the missed calls from Becky and Allison, and realize why they were probably calling. Damn it.

"Let's just pack up and get out of here before anyone sees us. I'll message her from the car." I hop out of bed and start packing.

"Irish goodbye. I'm on it. I'll meet you in the lobby in ten."

I don't know how I power through the hangover, but I manage to throw my shit in my overnight bag and get out the door in five. I sneak downstairs before anyone else, pouring myself a cup of coffee by the front desk. As I turn around, I see Kimberly sitting with her Gucci suitcase, staring at her phone. I'm not sure if it's the fumes from the Nespresso or the dehydration from the wine, but I feel my cheeks get hot. I march over and stand right in front of her. She looks up, and I can see she forgot to put on one of her fake eyelashes. It's not a good look.

"Why would you post those pictures of me and Serena?" I blurt. "How would you feel if someone plastered photos of you like that all over social media?"

She puts her phone in her ridiculously expensive purse and looks up at me, glassy-eyed. "Emily, let's not make this about me. I would *never* have a photo of me posted like that, because I would never act that way. If you and Serena want to be at the top, you had better learn to control yourselves. So unladylike." She shakes her head like a disappointed parent. "You are representing the company with that behavior."

The fuck? These incentives and trips and biz ops always turn into drinking fests, and while she's sitting here clutching her pearls, plenty of the leaders "at the top" get their party on.

I open my mouth to respond, but she continues, "By the way, I talked to her first."

Wait, what? "Talked to who? About what? You mean, about last night?" I respond, completely confused.

"No. Madison Barker. The hairstylist? I talked to her first. My assistant had a phone call scheduled with her. And yesterday, she canceled it because she said she was already speaking with another consultant. *You.*" She cocks her head to the side and glares at me while she points her ridiculously long fingernail in my direction.

She's pissed about Madison?

I scoff, "Kimberly, how would I know that you were going to talk to her, or that she would meet with me? I'm one of the zillion people who messaged her. That's not my fault."

"Hmm. Well, all I know is that Rejuvinat teammates don't poach people from each other." She picks her phone back up and looks away.

When you work in a business where profit is based on recruiting—and is also more than 75 percent female—you have a breeding ground for turf wars. And jealousy is a weapon that you're taught to employ; after all, if your friends and family won't join you, it can't be because you're annoying—it must be because they are jealous of your success! So, it makes sense that the same jealousy would proliferate within the organization. It was a constant bitch fest in Messenger threads and texts:

"Who talked to that customer first?"

"Who is closer friends with that person?"

"Why did they join that team instead of mine?"

"I can't believe they joined that company instead of ours!"

And this should come as no surprise because *people* are the commodity; they are the thing being bought and sold. As a rep, you are taught to network on every occasion; everything from church to grocery shopping to working out at the gym is all just opportunities to funnel people into your MLM. In this exploitative model, femininity itself is commodified; women are selling things to perpetuate a narrow ideal of womanhood. The celebrity status and hype in an MLM get to your head, so it's easy to take that with you to the "outside world" and assume that other people must want what you have (wine trips, fancy hotels, purses, social media fame), and if they don't, then they're just jealous. Anyone within the organization who steps in your path must also be jealous and trying to get in your way. Not exactly empowering.

When someone signs up with a different consultant, or a different team, or a different company, it feels like a personal insult, because you have put so much effort into getting them in your downline. It becomes a fight over degrees of loyalty, and suddenly, the people you once saw as your collaborators have the potential to become your enemies. Should the customer be loyal to the consultant? The consultant to the company? The consultants to each other? Of course, saturation comes into play in this tug-of-war, because when there are so many consultants in one area, your personal network has likely already been swallowed by someone else's. I had a recent conversation with Hannah, who was complaining about this exact problem; by the time she became a consultant, most of her dream team and dirt list were *already* a part of Rejuvinat. I felt for her but brushed off her concern with some victim blaming; after all, she should have joined sooner!

Regardless of how close you are to someone, or how many times you talk to or message them, you don't own them, and it's their decision who/what/where/why/when/if they join. Still, when someone offers themselves up as an easy potential recruit and dozens of women go after them, there is bound to be a fight. Especially when it's a jackpot like Madison, with already-gorgeous skin and hair and a million friends to sell to.

And there's the rub—whether you're a famous celebrity or not, the friends that you, or anyone in your downline, might end up selling to are not really *your* friends. It didn't take me long to realize that I wasn't in the business of selling supplements or skincare; I was in the practice of collecting "friends." And the better my friends were at sales, the more I was supposed to love them (even if this dynamic was bound to create a few frenemies, since unhealthy competition is inherent in the MLM model). Once you start randomly striking up conversations, adding people on Facebook, and "sharing your opportunity," with the ultimate goal of getting someone into your downline, it becomes second nature. This starts with the innocent dirt list and dream-team list, then cut-and-paste scripts, then three-way calls, and eventually, you see everyone as a walking target. Community (ironically, the very thing I longed for when I signed up for the dream life Rejuvinat was promising me) becomes a commodity.

As I glare at Kimberly, I realize that Serena was right on the money: Kimberly's just jealous. I can't help but feel a little pride that Madison chose me over Kimberly. I have once again pissed off the queen, and damn if I don't like it. She thinks her social media shaming is actually going to work? Like I've never been tagged in a drunk picture before? I almost feel sorry for her now but can't let it go that easily. Though I'm usually great with witty comebacks, my hangover has made me a little slow this morning and all I can muster before I storm away is "Well, you're missing eyelashes."

I walk toward the front desk and see Serena coming down the stairs. Thank God. Get me out of here.

As we open the door to leave, we hear, "Serena? Emily? Can I speak to you for a second?" We turn around and see the COO standing there.

Oh shit.

She opens her mouth, and before she can say anything, Serena blurts out, "Please don't be mad at us—you guys took us wine-tasting all day, and she just found out she has cancer!"

I'm rarely speechless, but right now, there are no words. We all stare blankly at each other until the COO finally breaks the silence: "Just wanted to say we had a lovely time yesterday. Congrats to the both of you."

I recall my earlier conversation with Becky. I guess sympathy *does* work in this business! Or maybe it was the shots.

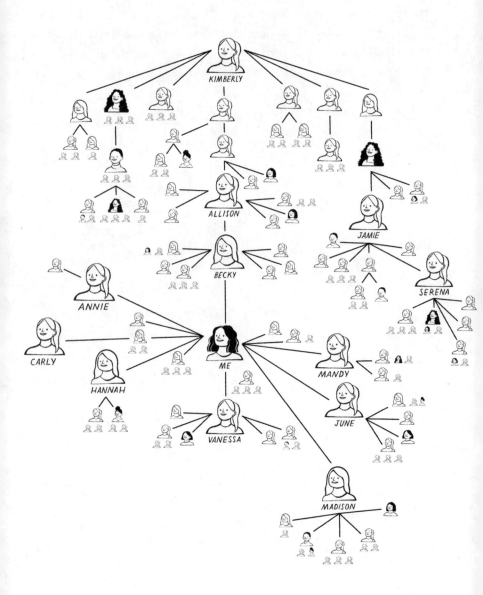

The Party Never Ends, and Neither Does Your Anxiety

+ ✦
✦

I could not handle the constant hustling in my MLM. They told me when I joined that I could do whatever I wanted with it, but then they shamed me when I didn't want to hustle 24/7. On one hand, they would say, "Stay in your own lane; don't worry about what other people are doing," and then in the same breath would say, "Be a team player—this is your family. Be loyal to your company." I realized that the only thing anyone cared about was anything that impacted their paycheck. It wasn't about time freedom; it was about money. It was so stressful for me, I quit and never looked back.
—MONICA, former MLM rep

Bang bang bang!

I don't wake up to the knock on my door right away. Though I hear it loud and clear, it feels like it's just a part of my drunken slumber. You know, when you're still half asleep and the alarm or the bird chirping or the door knocking just becomes integrated into your dream? I am that level of out of it. Finally, the knocking gets louder. Then the doorbell (I have a doorbell?) rouses me awake.

Here I am at another Convention. In Vegas this time. Three years in, and I've reached yet another rank of celebrity. And I'm hurtling my way to rock bottom.

I have crusty contacts plastered to my eyes, and it feels like one of them might be lodged somewhere behind my eyeball. As my eyes finally open, I realize I'm still in my jumpsuit from the night before, with one heel on. I try to get it off so I can open the door, but my hand is shaking too much to undo the small buckle on the strap.

Bang bang bang!

FUUUCK.

"Okay, coming!" I hobble to the door, throw a jacket over myself, and crack the door open.

"Hello?"

"Yes, miss, hi, I'm just checking on you before I leave my shift."

I give him an up-and-down glance (he has a uniform on, so I don't think he's a killer) before I open the door a bit wider.

"Oh, hi, you're checking on me?" I ask, puzzled.

"Yes, uh, you were . . .," he stammers, visibly embarrassed. "The taxi driver and I helped get you to your room last night. You were not well. You weren't totally unconscious or anything. We had the EMT check you out, and we brought you up to your room once you started talking. You said you were fine. But I wanted to check before I left, just to make sure."

What. The. Fuck. Not *totally* unconscious? Taxi driver? EMT?

"Oh, right," I respond as if I have any remote clue what he's talking about. "The taxi driver. Do you know— Sorry . . . what time was that? Was I alone?" I'm struggling for words as my heart races, praying that he can give me more clues.

"Yes, miss, the taxi driver brought you and a friend to a party, but when he got you there, you stayed in the car. She got out and went to the party. You wouldn't get out and you weren't talking, so he brought you back here," he explains, clearly uncomfortable.

Oh my God. That's right. It's all coming back. Jamie and I were at a leader party and left to hit up another one—prom-themed, hence my sequin jumpsuit. I remember being in the hotel room getting ready between parties, but that's it. She *left* me in the car? Passed out, with a *stranger*? My blood runs cold.

My clothes are still intact. I am wearing a jumpsuit and lord knows how hard those are to get off to pee in, so I'm pretty sure nobody assaulted me, but really?

He sees the terror on my face, offering, "The taxi driver, he's a really nice man. I know him. He is a good guy."

"Oh," I reply, truly relieved, trusting this man who is clearly more concerned about my welfare than I have been. "Of course. No, I was just . . . wow. I'm so sorry that happened. And thank you. Really . . . I'm so sorry."

"This is Vegas, ma'am—it is not unusual. Have a better day!" He smiles before tipping his hat and walking away.

It actually makes me feel better. Validated. Even as I close the door and sink to the floor. My mind is racing. Who saw me? What if someone from corporate or in my upline witnessed that moment? This is *bad*.

Unfortunately, this is also becoming frighteningly normal. Corporate gave Serena and me a talking-to after the wine weekend (no actual consequences, just more shaming and guilt). I've been trying to control my intake ever since, but my drinking has only worsened. The pain of my surgery a few months ago (which, thankfully, was a success, and my cancer was fully removed) led to a little bit of a pill problem, which I was able to kick, but only with the help of even more wine. And things like this have been happening more often—blackouts, not remembering where I am, and having to cobble together all the details in the ensuing hours. It's impacting my marriage because my husband is losing trust in me, and I'm dropping the ball with my kids, forgetting to send lunch money or field-trip forms. But at this point, I'm more worried about the repercussions on my business than my home life.

I don't know Jamie that well. We've spent a little time together over the past few years at biz ops; she hosted the first one I spoke at. She's also from Seattle, and at this point I've surpassed her in title and pay many times over. We were only together last night because we happened to qualify for the same party, though I can't remember what we were celebrating. The thing is, anyone in your Rejuvinat family is supposed to look out for you. I certainly wouldn't have buddied up with her if I'd known she'd leave me for dead in the back of a cab. So much for sisterhood.

Like many addictions, what starts out as fun begins to become more dangerous. I always thought that my drinking "helped me"—to have fun, be more outgoing, and be a better salesperson. But I'm finding myself doing things I don't want to be doing and blacking out more of my life, to the point where I no longer recognize who I am. Joining Rejuvinat was supposed to make me a more "whole" person, but it has only made me more fragmented and lost. And more addicted. This whole environment of parties and celebrations encourages it. Though we all claim to be part of the wellness industry, our behavior at the bar is anything but. We host parties to recruit, we drink on trips, and unsurprisingly, many of us drink at home as we're "working," which makes us, and particularly me, feel justified in the behavior.

My drinking is beginning to affect every aspect of my life, but I don't want to stop. I don't know how to stop, and it's such a big part of Rejuvinat, I worry what will happen to my #goals if I do. I know that the wine nights are my best prospecting events. I know I'm more uninhibited and able to make a sale when I drink, even if I don't remember it. And I can play the part of the woman who can celebrate and drink wine and still stay on top. But perhaps by design, I don't have enough downtime to think about it, because there is always another meeting, party, or celebration. It never ends.

I need to pull myself together. I grab my phone and am horrified to see that it's already noon. I was supposed to meet my team for breakfast at nine! Fuck! Becky and Allison will brush it off, but Madison and her entire team were supposed to be there, too. She's going to be pissed. This is her first Convention, and what I have quickly learned from scoring Madison is that she is *demanding*. Or what Rejuvinat calls "high maintenance, high producer."

I attended a training session yesterday morning, and they classified several different types of consultants on a pie chart with categories of "maintenance" and "production"—as in, low-maintenance consultants were those you never heard from, and high-producing consultants were those who got big sales.

According to the training, the best type of consultant is low maintenance *and* high production because they make your numbers big without requiring much help. The worst? High maintenance, low production: the ones who ask a ton of questions, expect a ton of help, but don't make shit in sales. Yes, we had a training ranking the best types of people, followed by ranking our own team members on a spreadsheet. Like in a sorority. Hailee Stegall, a former sorority recruit at Colorado State University, described this phenomenon in her article for the *Rocky Mountain Collegian,* "Sorority Rush Bears Frightening Similarities to Cult Recruitment." The most dedicated women are deemed "special" and love bombed with attention and trinkets, while holding out hope to be deemed worthy of their top-choice house; if they withdraw, or don't get chosen, they feel isolated and alone. It's all about being a certain type of woman: friendly, focused, with the same interests and aspirations. And this ranking within the MLM was no different. We were expected to treat our recruits differently based on how they behaved. What happened to the days of "There's room for everyone, no matter how much or little you sell! I'm your sponsor, I'll help you with anything!"?

The real motto is "Get your shit together, don't bug me, and sell your ass off."

Madison is high maintenance and high producing. She recruited almost her entire salon full of hair stylists within her first couple of months. My sales volume has tripled, my paycheck is over $10,000 per month, and I'm now qualifying for my car because of her. But let me tell you, I *work* for it. She texts or calls me multiple times a day and expects me to be at her beck and call. Last week, she couldn't get a hold of me in a thirty-minute period, so she tagged me on Facebook and asked, "Where are you?"

Seriously.

So, of course, I have six missed calls from her, and I'm terrified to listen to them. But before I can scroll through my texts, there's another knock on the door. Please don't let it be the doorman again.

Thankfully, it's Serena. She lets out a huge sigh and throws her arms around me. "Em, what happened? We were so worried about you! Why didn't you return my calls?" I've told her about my worries around my drinking, and I can tell by her face that she's just glad I'm alive.

"I was so worried when Jamie came in by herself. I knew I should have met you both beforehand." At least *someone* was looking out for me.

"Get a dress on—and here, drink this." She hands me a Pepsi and I give her side eye. Serena decodes my expression and obliges, heading to the fridge. "Okay, hair of the dog. But go get dressed! We have to be at the leader luncheon in fifteen minutes!"

"Oh God . . . *no*! Who are we meeting with again? What's this for? Shit, can you help me with this thing?" I struggle with my jumpsuit zipper. Never again with the jumpsuit. Damn you, Rent the Runway!

"The CEO is going to be there! Something about top sales, blah blah blah, I don't know. Remember the Run to Convention contest last month? Whatever, it's a big deal that we qualified for it. Get your face on!"

Right, I remember now. Madison qualified for this, too, so I can beg for forgiveness. I send her a quick text: "So sorry, will explain later!"

"Kimberly will be there, so let's be sure to act like proper ladies this time." She rolls her eyes and hands me a Yeti mug filled with champagne. "Bottoms up!" I need to take a roadie with me.

MLMs are constantly creating contests within contests. It wasn't enough to pay for Convention; you had to also compete for parties and lounges and "leader luncheons." For any of these addendums, you had to qualify with a certain sales number, recruiting number, or some other very specific metric that would benefit the company. This is not dissimilar to the incentive programs of many non-MLMs. Incentive programs can drive healthy competition, dedication, and loyalty. They can enhance productivity. Who doesn't love a reward? But when you're in a salaried position, you are being paid for the work you do to achieve these incentives. This is not the case with MLM incentives, because as I've mentioned, much of the "work" to achieve these sales is unpaid. With the achievement, you'd be shouted out in an email or on a company flyer, or you'd get an extra sticker on your badge, or extra perks to make you think you actually earned something for yourself. This low- (or no-) value item was simply to increase the company's bottom line.

Worse, it isolated segments of women within a constant hierarchy by perpetuating the fear of being left out; the fear of not being noticed; or the fear of being left off important email threads, Facebook Messenger chats, accountability groups, parties, and celebrations. It didn't matter how low value the "win" actually was; women who were supposedly "on the same team" were consistently pitted against each other for the prize.

This "leader luncheon" I'm about to head to is no different. One leader who is not included, and not happy about it, is Becky, whom we pass in the hallway on the way to the banquet hall.

I take another swig.

"Emily, where were you? Madison is livid," Becky seethes.

Thanks, Captain Obvious. I can't contain my snark. "I'm fine, Becky, thanks for asking!"

Becky softens. "Sorry, we were worried about you. I think I smoothed things over with Madison, but you have some explaining to do."

"Explaining to do?" I was already planning on apologizing, but now I'm just annoyed. "Becky, I missed a breakfast. That's it. She will live."

I continue walking and Becky walks with us, almost manic. "Emily, she is the biggest portion of your paycheck."

Oh, right. And I'm the biggest portion of Becky's paycheck. The more someone works on your team, the more you're supposed to love and spend time with them. But I don't like Madison. She drives me up the wall. We have nothing in common, our personalities clash, I find her snobby, she complains constantly, and she's not someone I would be friends with had we not connected through Rejuvinat. Honestly, despite the money she's bringing in, it would have served me better if Madison had signed up with Kimberly instead, just like Kimberly whined about at the wine event; then, Madison could have driven Kimberly nuts instead of me.

Win-win.

This is the difference between Becky and me: I know where to draw boundaries, and apparently, she is willing to kiss ass no matter what spoiled-brat behavior Madison pulls.

"Just apologize, okay? Leaders show up, Emily," she chides.

Though I've parroted that phrase millions of times, it stings coming from her.

"Got it," I cut her off. "Need to get going. I'll talk to Madison at this leadership thing."

You know, the one you didn't qualify for, Becky? I smirk to myself. Maybe she's playing the game, but I'm earning the bonuses.

Serena and I exchange glances, not needing to repeat what we are both thinking. Then, as if the day could get any worse, the first person we run into as we walk into the banquet hall is Kimberly. I used to be so impressed that she would show up to events for the peons, but now I'm realizing it's because she cannot and will not be left out of anything.

We haven't seen her since the drunken-tags-on-Facebook weekend. (Spoiler: She never removed the photos.)

"Hi, ladies!" she says in the most annoying singsongy voice. I'm suspicious that she's being so nice, and then I realize that corporate is here. We nod and wave to a few people, then turn our attention back to her. Serena and I both fake a smile while we continue to scan the room for our seats.

"Emily! I was so happy to hear that you beat cancer. I was worried!" Kimberly flashes a sympathetic smile at me.

Um, worried? *Really?* Am I being punked? "Thanks . . . K-Kimberly," I stutter. Maybe she does have a conscience, after all.

She steps in front of us, looks to her left and right, and leans in as if to tell us a secret.

"Did you hear about Shelby Frazier?" she whispers.

Serena gasps. "No! What? I saw her at the party last night."

I try to recall who she is . . . someone on Serena's team, I think. The name doesn't sound familiar, but I'm gathering from Serena's reaction that she knows her well.

"Yeah," Kimberly continues. "She had to go to the hospital last night. Someone slipped something into her drink at the bar! She's fine—she left before anything happened, but wow, right?" Her eyes get big, and she puts her hands on her hips.

"Oh my God!" Serena squeals. "Poor thing!"

Serena grabs me by the arm. "Em, I'm sorry, can you cover for me? I need to go see her. She's on my team."

"Of course! Let me know if I can do anything!" I respond as Serena collects herself and leaves the banquet hall, and I'm stuck here with

Kimberly. I glance down and see those heels again—studded, expensive. While I'm gazing, I can't help but think that with the night I had, that same thing could have so easily happened to me.

"Thank God nothing happened to her," I say to Kimberly.

"Well, did you *see* what she was wearing last night?" she scoffs and rolls her eyes. "And she was *all* over the bar, dancing with random, strange men. I mean, what did she expect?"

My jaw drops and my eyes narrow. I almost can't believe these are actual words coming from her mouth, as though she's reading from a textbook on Misogyny 101. "What the hell did you say?" I demand, a little too loudly, as a few women in earshot turn around. The VP of sales begins to walk in our direction.

"Shhhh!" she hisses. "Look, women can't have it both ways. You can't dress however you want and expect men to respect you." She looks me up and down and walks away. I can almost feel steam coming out my ears, I'm so hot with anger.

This rape-culture mentality is, unfortunately, not unusual. In fact, you might say it comes with the territory. As hyped up on girl power as they might purport to be, MLMs are fueled by internalized misogyny. "She was asking for it" is a prevalent mindset in white supremacy culture—one that is often leveled against vulnerable groups of people (women of color, trans women, sex workers, houseless people, and others who are unlikely to have the privilege of institutional support or collective sympathy) to keep them in their place. And why wouldn't this mindset continue when your work strategically employs a "no means not right now" marketing scheme?

I didn't fully realize it at the time, but when you're in the business of telling other women that they need to lose weight; have better skin, longer hair, and more money; or spend more time with their kids, you really don't have their best interests at heart. The name of the game is breaking them down by preying on existing fears and insecurities, then equipping them with a set of unrealistic expectations. But the co-opting of female solidarity to shill products and shame women into compliance is the opposite of feminism.

As Savannah Worley explains in her viral *Medium* article, "Dear White Women: Here's Why It's Hard to Be Friends with You," white women, myself included (knowingly or unknowingly), maintain the patriarchy by relying on white supremacy. Internalized misogyny and racism (subconscious or not) teach us that we should climb over anyone to get to the top of the white-male hierarchy. Because white men will always be at the top. The feminized patriarchal image we've been raised with will make us cling to our own white supremacy and internalized misogyny. I understand in retrospect that the culture of partying and drinking that is so often upheld in MLMs is meant to loosen women's reservations (and their wallets), while unsurprisingly being the perfect setup for victim blamers like Kimberly to pop off.

"Fucking bitch," I whisper under my breath. I turn and see the VP of sales standing in front of me. "Oh . . . hi!" Same guy whose lap I sat on while smoking a cigarette during the disastrous wine-tasting weekend. Awk-ward.

"Everything okay, Emily?"

"Yep, I'm good." My heart is racing.

"Great. Find your seat and we'll get started!"

I'm pissed, embarrassed, and hungover, and now I see Madison coming across the room toward me. Could this morning get any more horrendous? Thank God the champagne tray passes by, since I've already emptied my Yeti.

"Hi, Madison, I'm so sorry about this morning." I grab a champagne and preemptively strike before she guilts me to death.

"Yeah, it was a bummer. I was disappointed. Thankfully, Becky was so sweet and helpful." She pauses, shakes her head, and stands in silence waiting for me to, I don't know, kiss her ass? Apologize some more?

"Yeah, Becky's great. Should we sit?" I walk toward the table and hope that's the end of the reprimand. This is going to be a long lunch.

We sit at round tables with placeholders. Madison and I are at the table with Allison and a few other people I don't know, as well as Stephanie and Christine, whom I recognize from a previous incentive trip. Fortunately, we aren't seated with Kimberly. We say our hellos and check out each other's clothes and badges. I realize I'm the highest rank at the table. Hopefully, I don't get interrogated—my aching head cannot handle it.

After some pastries, mimosas, and speeches from the corporate office ("Congrats, our company is amazing, yay you! God is great, blah blah blah"), we are gifted a special David Yurman bracelet to celebrate earning this luncheon. As the speeches end, we have the chance to chat among ourselves. At first, we keep it simple, talking about who our uplines are, what teams we're on, what we earned at Convention, and stuff like that.

Madison is bragging to Brianna and Christine that she is about to hit Premier Star. I sip my champagne and congratulate her. The bonus of having someone on your team who's a rockstar is the ability to claim some of their success.

(Not their failures, though—those are their fault.)

"I remember when I hit Premier Star," I offer, again demonstrating how we've been trained to turn friendly competition into jealousy. "My next few months are going to be big," I tell the other ladies. "I'm up for Excellence Circle."

"Now, that will be a hard one to get," Christine says, countering me, wide-eyed.

Madison is clearly annoyed that I took the spotlight off her.

The title system is a lot like the gifts, trips, and incentives, and just like this leader luncheon with the bracelets being passed out. It's not about true value; it's about perceived value. Because the true value of a title? Nothing. Literally nothing. Some MLMs get really creative with their titles, offering names like Double Diamond, Managing Market Mentor, Crystal Director, and my favorite, Royal in Waiting. At least Rejuvinat makes it sound like a real promotion and not the title of a Hallmark movie.

"So did you earn the Level Up trip yet?" Christine counters Madison. This is the other secret language of direct sales: business lingo that no one else understands. If you were to ask someone, "Did you hit your numbers this month?" or "Did you meet your quota?" they'd basically understand what you mean even if they didn't work in the same industry. They'd be a little more confused by "Did you hit Platinum Success Circle?" The unnecessarily complex language, endless levels, and even the whimsical names are meant to separate and confuse, creating a distinct boundary between "us" and "them." The connotations of royalty are quite overt, no doubt purposefully cementing the hierarchical structure. Of course, your husband or sister doesn't understand when you're trying to reach Super Elite Crystal Princess in Waiting. They'd be even more confused if they knew what you had to do to earn it.

The currency in the direct-sales economy isn't just collecting people and selling skincare and supplements; it's social media shoutouts. You have to earn love bombs from the people in your upline. You even have to earn time with them, from a phone call to a coveted in-person visit. Though your upline is "at your service" when you join, if you don't make them money, they won't continue to make themselves available to you; it's mentorship with a high-dollar price tag. Top sellers would usually be booked out at Convention to share the secrets to their success, which downline consultants had been awarded for their sales numbers. Again, none of this offers true value, but it *does* drive competition, and MLMs thrive in competition. If you're just a few sales away from being on a top-ten list, you'll do anything to make it happen, even if it's less than ethical.

The worst part is that the cycle of titles, incentives, promotions, awards, and contests never ends. They are designed to lure new converts, and to keep current members committed for the long haul. Companies consistently raise and lower the bar in order to make things look better to the "outside." Lower a car qualification, and behold, you have two hundred "FREE car" achievers. Someone sees that and thinks, *Wow, the company must be doing so well!* But nothing has changed about the company except its marketing strategy. There's always another "reward" trip or "leader luncheon" with arbitrary metrics connected to recruiting: "Highest PSQV in the L1–L6 volume in the month of January!" What the hell does that even mean? Rankings, titles, and prizes motivate the competition, and it's no wonder they push women to poach (steal other reps' recruits), cheat (set up fake accounts to boost their numbers), or inventory-load (order products they don't need to inflate sales) in order to hit the always-moving targets.

We finish up our conversation, exchange Facebook info with the other new bossbabe friends from our table, and of course, take a group picture. At leadership events like this, the MLM posts photos on their social media channels, which the entire company of consultants follows, to really show everyone who's boss. I realize how exhausted I am, wondering how I'm going to make it through another day of this. I'm light-headed and sweaty, and I can't stop thinking about what happened last night and what happened to Serena's friend.

I can't keep doing this. I can't keep googling "Am I an alcoholic?" and then closing the browser because it's confronting. I can't keep confiding in friends who tell me that my drinking doesn't look that bad, when they don't realize how much I'm drinking when I'm not with them. I know I need help, but I don't know how to do that right now. At some point, I know I'm going to hurt myself or my marriage or get arrested . . . maybe all three. But how am I going to sell this dream if I'm not living it? As with the red flags of this business, or my overwhelm as a mother, it's easier to continue to ignore my drinking than to make any actual change.

As a radical act of self-care, I decide to turn off my phone and head back to my room to rest. I know I'll miss the afternoon sessions and I'll probably hear about it from someone, but I need some downtime—plus, Serena is not going to be there. I send a text to Becky: "NEED REST—C YOU AT GALA TONIGHT." I'll sleep and have enough time to get dolled up for yet another walk across the stage. I just can't power through another day.

Before I turn off my phone, I get a call from Hannah. I contemplate not answering. I can't deal with this right now! But Hannah has been losing belief in the company, and I can't lose her. I need to make sure she's still loyal, so I answer.

"Hi, Hannah! So good to hear from you!"

Hannah struggles with this business in so many ways. She didn't come to Convention because she couldn't afford it, and I can't keep dragging her. Of course, I haven't told her that; she already feels horribly guilty.

"Emily, I am having such a hard time with my sister, and I don't know what to do! This business is driving a wedge between us. She keeps sending me negative YouTube videos and cautioning me about all the money I'm spending. And I want to believe you that this may work. But I just don't know!"

I'm torn. I love Hannah, but she's too influenced by others—which is probably why she was such an easy recruit. MLMs chide women for being overly influenced, but it's what makes them easy to recruit in the first place. We want people to believe us, and only us, and not listen to anyone else. Last month, Hannah's sister Anika, whom she recruited last fall thanks to our late-night three way, quit. Now, Anika is on a rampage to dismantle the MLM industry. To make up for the lost business partner, Hannah heeded the advice from my upline to take out another credit card to pay for product. I have two choices here: tell her that she shouldn't have "toxic" people in her life, like the women who trained me have told me to do, or tell her to run the other way. But if she quits, that will impact my rank. I don't feel good about either answer.

"Hannah, don't worry about this right now. So much great stuff is happening here at Convention that I can't wait to fill you in on. Let's pick this up when I get back, all right?"

I hang up the phone and also hang up the idea of resting. I turn around and walk back toward the convention center. The conversation has me rattled. Hannah has done everything I've asked of her, and she continues to lose money and burn bridges. How is that possible? My intuition has been drowned out for so long, I don't know which way is up. And I'm so, so tired.

Elbowing my way through crowds, I end up at my scheduled session: How to Lead Leaders. Yes, that's the actual title. One of the million-dollar earners is teaching. I squint to see who it is. Of course, it's Kimberly!

"Emily! You made it, after all! You decided not to rest?" Becky throws her arms around me.

"Leaders show up," I say, feigning a smile.

She giggles and takes my arm as we find a seat toward the front. I can't believe I have to listen to Kimberly for an hour. I still feel guilty about Serena's friend and conflicted about my conversation with Hannah, and I realize I should have just gone back to lie down. My face gets hot, and tears start welling up in my eyes.

I sniffle and wipe them away, and Becky inhales sharply. "Oh, Em, are you all right?" She puts her arm around me and grabs a tissue from her bag.

"No, I'm not. I'm really not. Becky, this is getting to be too much. I feel . . ."

"Feel what?" Becky asks lovingly after a pause. The room lights start to dim as the presentation is about to start.

I lower my voice to a whisper. "I feel like I really need to step back a bit. From Rejuvinat. From all of this. It's too much right now. I can't balance everything."

"Em," Becky says calmly, withdrawing her arm. "Everything will be fine. Whatever you need. Trust me, we're here for you. But it's not a good idea to back off right now, not when things are at a fever pitch like this. You are *so close* to your car. Please don't give up on yourself now. You'll feel so much better after walking the stage tonight. You inspire people! Then you can go back to your hotel room and sleep."

Of course, Becky wasn't going to encourage me to stop. What would that do to her numbers? She was about to have a car earner on her team! I am beginning to realize that Rejuvinat is committed to keeping its people not because it cares, but because the people *are* its product. The skincare and supplements are just the marketing ploy. The entire structure is built to keep reps ensnared. Just like I've trapped Hannah, and Becky has trapped me, and her upline trapped her, and on and on, up and up the chain. But I'm in too deep at this point. How do I unravel from this?

I nod and get out my pen and notebook. "You're right. I'm just tired. Tonight will be fun." I see a can of wine in my bag and let out an audible sigh of relief. I look up and make eye contact with Kimberly as I take a swig, defeated.

Leaders show up, I think to myself. I showed up blackout drunk. Becky showed up to gaslight. Kimberly showed up to slut-shame. Hannah showed up begging for a life preserver. And I bet each of us is exhausted by all of it.

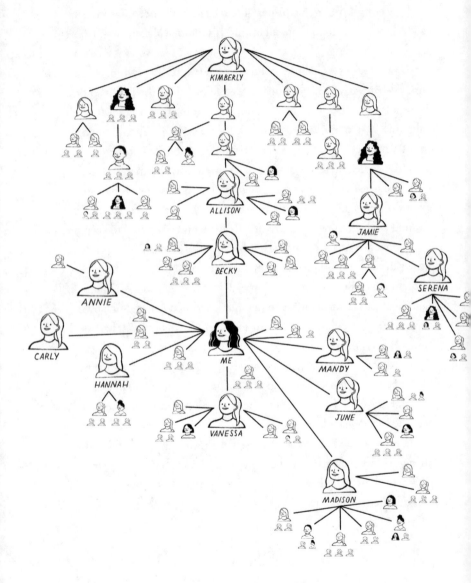

It's Lonely (and Ugly) at the Top

I am a proud Asian/African American woman. I honestly wanted to be the one to change the white MLM world. Now, I realize I was a pawn. I was constantly in the company marketing materials and asked to speak at corporate training. I thought that it was because they considered me "the top," but the reality is, they just wanted the company to look more diverse. They didn't care about me personally. When I sent in my termination form, my uplines blocked me, yet the company still continued to use my photos for months after I quit. Couldn't find another token Black woman, I suppose.

—KHALISTA, former MLM rep

S ee you at the car party tonight?" I text Madison.

You'd think by the fortieth text, I'd be ready to give up, but I know better. Everything depends on tonight. It's my chance to show both my upline and my downline that I've made it, and the one thing that drives sales—er, I mean, recruitment—is showing people you've made it. As you're hopefully beginning to see, the entire structure of MLM is based on those levels; it's about organizing the people below you in order to support the people above. I've been a rising star for a while now, but with this party, I'm showing people that I'm on top.

And the proof? That shiny white SUV, with a personalized "FREECAR" license plate (yes, really).

We all know the free car. I still remember being a kid and seeing one of our neighbors receive her pink Cadillac. I didn't understand at the time how selling makeup could earn you a free car, but it's a gimmick that's been around for ages. Now, I know it's about so much more than that. Because here's the thing about the FREE car (which is always advertised in caps, for some reason): It isn't actually free.

As my husband reads the agreement for the vehicle, reams of paperwork I have to sign before being anointed with a mid-range luxury SUV, he asks me, "So, you have to pay for the insurance, title, registration, *and* the down payment?"

"Yeah," I tell him, so deep into Rejuvinat's marketing that I'm slightly annoyed by the question. "But they're taking care of the payments."

He flips through a few pages, and though a part of me wonders how many people don't actually read this lengthy contract, I try not to think about it. I wave my hand in his direction. "They pay as long as you're working for them."

He laughs. "It's not really free, honey. It's just a company car. Actually, with a company car, you don't pay for the title and registration. And certainly not the down payment. Plus, you have to maintain the rank you have now. Isn't that hard to do?"

I don't know what to say, so I do what I usually do: I reach for my glass of wine that for some reason is frequently sitting on the nightstand by my bedside and take a sip.

"I earned it," I say, putting my glass back down, remembering what they have taught us at Rejuvinat: Ignore the haters.

Because there are a lot of haters out there, sometimes even within your own family. People who will make fun of MLMs; people who will call them pyramid schemes; people who, like my husband, will question their practices. But what they don't understand is that with each insult, they fuel the fire of our defensiveness. If you have seen someone make fun of an MLM online, it's like putting a drop of blood in shark-infested waters. Just watch for the fiery, self-justifying comments from MLM bossbabes, because dissenters' comments diminish our work, and most of us have never worked so hard in our lives.

Plus, isn't it my turn for some success?

I think of all the times we have sacrificed for Kale's job, moving across the country to a city and state where I didn't know a soul. I think of the long nights and what I have gone through raising five kids while my husband escapes on out-of-town trips and late nights at the office. I think of all the dirty diapers and screaming kids and evenings spent in a glider trying to get a baby to sleep so they don't wake up everyone else. I deserve my shiny white Mercedes! So what if it's going to cost us a little more each month? After all, what's considered "women's work" is undervalued, yet the value we are taught to attribute to our contributions is still framed in patriarchal supremacist terms that suggest a particular status.

Women aren't really allowed to have a work/life balance; work and life are supposed to be compartmentalized. It's the reason people would ask me if my husband was "babysitting" when he was home with the kids. No, he's parenting, Sheila. It's the same reason nobody asked if he was a "working dad" or felt guilty leaving his kids when he went on work trips. The "momming" and home duties generally fall on women because labor (domestic and professional) is still gendered. Even though women perform about five times as much unpaid work as men, what's valued is generally the work that brings in the most money. And I'm finally bringing home the bacon.

"It's fine, honey," he says, conciliatory, as he hands me back the agreement. "I'm happy for you. Always. I just didn't think we needed a new car."

What he doesn't understand is that this isn't a new car, it's a FREE (yes, all caps) car. It's a rolling trophy. The one I have earned by making my way to the top. The one I am now going to invite a bunch of people to an expensive party to see. That's right. I am having a car party, and it is going to be perfect.

Thankfully, Kale doesn't ask as many questions about the party. He knows that Rejuvinat offers us a stipend to throw the parties. What he doesn't know is how much more money I am spending than what the stipend offers. But if a Mercedes SUV drives through a forest and no one is there to see it, how do they even know that you got it for FREE?!

I send off the last text and look at the time. I still have to go get my nails done, get my blowout, confirm the donut truck, and pick up the SUV from getting detailed. They're even going to affix the big red bow that Rejuvinat suggested I use. It's like I'm being crowned Miss Rejuvinat, except I'm the one producing the pageant and pretty much paying for all of it.

MLMs entice women because of these parties, the free car, the swag, the travel, and drinks at the bar. These are rewards for work that exists outside of the system of "valued" labor, but they still suggest the value attributed to that labor. And so many of us have come from that place of dirty diapers and uncomfortable rockers that it can feel like an early release from prison. For years, we have been living with our hair in a bun and nails bitten down to the quick. But with MLMs, we can become celebrities. We can go to awards dinners and walk the red carpet. We're given diamond jewelry and Louis Vuitton suitcases. We get so much swag that a lot of women start looking at bigger homes just so they have a place to put their FREE stuff. But that's the hook. Because none of it is actually free.

The parties? Sure, they may give you a stipend. In fact, I've been given $1,000 to throw this party tonight. But I've also been told to invite a hundred people. That's $10 a head, with free drinks, free food, and a location that's going to say, "I made it."

If I shove a bunch of women into a rec-center gym and hand them microwaved hors d'oeuvres with some Two-Buck Chuck, what kind of dream am I selling them? They need to believe; they need to see that Rejuvinat is all about being VIP. And VIP costs way more than $10 a head. The location rental alone costs me $2,000. The booze costs me another $4,000. I actually save some money with the donut truck because I'm hoping the women won't get too hungry, and at least donuts fill you up (and who doesn't love donuts from a truck?). I have to provide swag, too. Sure, the gift bags are filled with Rejuvinat products, but that's the last thing that will ever be free. I have to pay for all of it. In the end, my budget is close to $10,000. So, that FREE car we were just talking about? The one I could have just gone into any Mercedes dealership on the planet to lease? It's already cost me $9,000 more the Rejuvinat way.

But it's not about the SUV; it's about the VIP.

And in the eyes of Rejuvinat, I am announcing to everyone in both my upline and my downline, as well as any potential recruits who attend that night, that I am a very important person, and Rejuvinat is the vehicle that made it happen.

"I can't believe you got the car!" Hannah stands in front of it like it's the only one in the world. A thought flits across my mind—*It's just a car*—but I take another swig of champagne and remind myself why we're really here.

"It's because I *believed*, Hannah," I tell her, my voice resolute and motivational. I know she needs this. Hannah has been working so hard to recruit women, but as she's said many times before, everyone she knows is already in an MLM or has something negative to say about them. And her sister is still on a rampage to get her to quit. I grab her hand in true sisterhood.

"You'll get there. I know you will," I tell her, and she nods. I keep telling her to do whatever it takes. Last week, she took out another credit card to make her end-of-month sales. At least I didn't have to float her again! She didn't tell her husband about that one, but to commiserate, I share my story of my own husband questioning the car.

Questioning MLMs is something that is seemingly happening more often these days, from Hannah's husband to her sister, and many more. When I joined, there were a few naysayers, but by this point, there are multiple YouTube channels and social media feeds dedicated to educating people about MLMs. Specifically, why not to join them. The anti-MLM movement embraced social media just as we bossbabes did, with blogs, Facebook groups, and Reddit pages—but YouTube became the epicenter of this movement, which makes sense, since it has more than two billion users per month. Rejuvinat told us to avoid these pages, of course, like all media that challenged what they were saying, but from what I heard, they mostly contained anecdotal evidence and stories from "women scorned" who didn't make it in their own MLM.

However, that wasn't actually the case. These anti-MLM creators were smart. They used bossbabes' own language, social media posts, and even their private Zoom calls, as evidence. "Leaked" meetings showed MLM team leaders pressuring members or telling them to make false health or income claims. I found this out when I became a topic of one very popular anti-MLM YouTube creator's video, as she debunked my "saturation" training that I did for my team. I hesitated to watch it, because I knew I wasn't supposed to, but as I did, it was the first time that I thought, *You know, maybe these haters aren't completely wrong*. I made sure to use more secure Zoom credentials going forward. Now, I just need to keep Hannah away from videos like that; her belief doesn't need to be shaken any more.

"They just don't get it," I tell her. "I mean, what is that? They don't want us to work? We get to be our own bosses. And maybe it just scares them." I don't know if I really believe any of this. I'm simply trained to gaslight reps' concerns and spout off hyperbole, because I need Hannah to also be a believer.

I go get a donut from the donut truck, which might have just been the whole point of the party, and I start talking with the owner, whom I've become friendly with over my months of planning. After my third or fourth serving of mini donuts, he laughs: "Dang, you white chicks love your shiny white cars!"

I look around at the party. There are close to a hundred women here, and the crowd reflects exactly the model Rejuvinat designed, one that caters to affluent white women and almost no one else. They are carbon copies of each other, with the same well-styled hair, the same skinny jeans and dresses, the same four-inch heels or leather booties. It's like one giant ad for Nordstrom. Rejuvinat likes it this way. Sure, the Black and Latinx and Asian girls are in the marketing, but there is no Diversity, Equity, and Inclusion (DEI) training or recruitment pushes into Black, Indigenous, and people of color (BIPOC) communities. Maybe it's better that way, because even if Rejuvinat could successfully recruit more Black and Brown women, it wouldn't be safe for them there.

If you take a look at the "Direct Selling in the United States" fact sheet put out by the Direct Selling Association (DSA—we will get to them later), it states that "Direct Selling Reflects America!" But when you look more closely, they separate out the Hispanic population to skew the data. In reality, 85 percent of the people in direct selling are white. Based on the US census, the entire US population is only 60 percent white. So, in theory, if "Direct Selling Reflects America" were accurate, I should be looking at a room of sixty white people, eighteen Hispanic people, five Asian people, fifteen Black people, and a couple of Pacific Islanders, Native Hawaiians, or Native Americans. Never, anywhere, have I seen that lineup represented in the direct-sales space. This party is a sea of white women, minus the women in the clearly staged marketing materials. This deception is information control, the distortion of marketing to make it more acceptable. But why would BIPOC women be interested in our company, anyhow? The product shades in our makeup line aren't diverse. There are only a couple that cater to skin tones deeper than *midnight beige*. On the other end of the spectrum are dozens of tones in the "light" category.

Diversity is talked about in MLMs, but it's usually seasonal, during Black History Month or on Martin Luther King Jr. Day. There are committees put together, but they never actually do anything, and they always feel more like they're checking a box instead of truly exploring what diversity, equity, or inclusion could look like. Rejuvinat once put together a Spanish-language biz op, but it was poorly marketed and nobody showed up, especially since none of our other product marketing or packaging was in Spanish. Fast-forward to June 2020, in the wake of the extrajudicial police killing of George Floyd: I would see how MLMs embraced it as a moment to drive sales, some even going so far as to have Black Lives Matter sales.

Anything for a buck.

Of course, I don't know or think about any of that yet. If you asked me that night if Rejuvinat was a racially diverse company, I would have gladly pointed to the banners I had hung at the party, showing light-skinned Black women and Asian women, likely hired models. The only actual "training" I received on diversity was in relation to sales stats: a seminar titled, "The Buying Power of Racial Groups." In it, we learned that "the buying power of the Hispanic community is 1.7 trillion; Black consumers have the buying power of 1.4 trillion, and Asian consumers have the buying power of 1.2 trillion!"

Apparently, being diverse meant taking money from people who fit into these categories, but the push for diversity ended there.

I laugh with the owner of the donut truck: "And we white women love our donuts!"

I find Vanessa, Becky, Madison, June, Serena, and Allison in conversation and quickly join, shaking off the comment with some good old competition.

Becky and Allison already have their cars and Serena is close, but there's always an opportunity for us bossbabes to flex our brag.

"Well, *this* is a very exciting day for you, Emily! And I have some exciting news to add, too!" Becky twirls in her pink sparkly dress.

Oh, here? I mean, couldn't she have waited until, I don't know, tomorrow, to make a personal announcement? I continue to surpass her in title, and she takes it in stride most of the time, but things like this make me wonder if it's starting to grate on her a bit. Though her paycheck is *killer* thanks to my and Madison's huge teams, over $40,000 per month, she doesn't have the strong front line that I do, and unless she recruits more Emilys, she'll likely stay at the same rank, while I continue to skyrocket. I suppose I can throw her a bone and lend her my spotlight for a second.

She inhales and exclaims, "Brady is retiring next week!" She lets out a squeal. "I'm retiring my husband!"

"Congratulations!" Allison, June, and Madison exclaim in creepy unison.

"That's awesome, Becky, I'm happy for you!" I say as Serena grabs me by the arm.

"Donut time!" she says as she pulls me away toward the truck. I know Serena will have a field day with this one. She leans over and shakes her head. "Seriously, Emily, do me a favor, just *kill me* if I ever utter the words 'retiring my husband.' It's so cringey. What is he, a fucking racehorse?"

She grabs a chocolate-covered mini donut and asks, "How do you bang a guy who's mooching off you?"

I erupt in laughter because it's funny and she's right. Frankly, isn't that why so many of us get roped into these MLMs in the first place?

The promise of making something of ourselves? To earn a little to support the family? To have some autonomy and not be so reliant on men? How did this turn into removing those same men from the workforce? On its face, it sounds like a great goal to work toward, but it's just another way MLMs seek to dominate the landscape of their reps' lives.

"Retiring your husband" is not a financial decision; it's a false demonstration of fempowerment to share on social media. "Look at me! I'm making so much money, my husband doesn't have to work!" This is the same control as when we pressure women to leave their "real jobs" and make the MLM their full-time gig, so they won't have anything to fall back on.

But what about the 401K, health benefits, paid time off, and other protections that came with that job? MLMs provide exactly zero of those things. Not to mention, who in their right mind wants to hustle and grind in retirement? Retirement means that you're no longer working, so you can enjoy the rest of your life, golf, go to book club, eat dinner at four in the afternoon, and maybe babysit a few grandkids.

Not so you can continue to cold-message and stroke your pyramid until you die. Absence of employment is not retirement. "Retire your husband" in MLM-speak means your spouse quits their job and works the MLM. Of course, every MLM encourages both partners to be "all in" so they stick with it. Look at Amway and the top tiers of many MLMs, where successful, top-ranking reps are pictured *as couples*. Also, ever wonder why it's always "retire my husband" and not "retire my wife" or "retire my spouse"? The heteronormative speak is *the* MLM language.

The truth is, if you retire your spouse, that means you are now the sole financial provider in your home, reliant entirely on Rejuvinat to cover your mortgage, your kids' school, and your own retirement.

You are more dependent on the network, the support, and the money, making you less likely to leave. You will put your all into it because you have no other income, and now your spouse will be expected to do the same. This economic control is essential, because if you don't have any other financial options—no "real job" to fall back on, or the second income of a spouse—you are at the mercy of the MLM, which is exactly what your upline and the company want.

Serena is making almost as much as I am at this point, over $15,000 per month, but only enough to keep our spending going, not enough for our breadwinner husbands to stop working, even if we want them to. I guess Becky's paycheck is enough to justify taking her husband out of the workforce.

Thankfully, no matter how much I make, Kale will *never* retire. Although I have to admit, the thought has crossed my mind. Yes, this is "my thing," but the idea of him being around more, and both of us spending more time together with the kids, isn't so bad. According to social media, Kimberly and her husband are always together, doing fun things. And if Kale were to retire, it would be fun to have his support. After all, the image of family that is perpetuated by MLMs is a happy household with 2.5 kids, frolicking on beaches without a care in the world, all in the name of "changing lives." It would be nice to have him around more, but then again, our au-pair solution is working out just fine. I'm grateful this business has allowed me to make more money so that I can pay someone to watch my kids so I can make more money. Hmm.

Serena and I head back with our next round of donuts and drinks, and we listen as Becky and Madison talk about titles and trips and who's making it and who's not. Since Hannah isn't producing the way I'd hoped, I've been spending more time grooming—er, training—Madison. Plus, Madison demands it. She annoys me, but she's profitable. I've been meeting prospects with her, doing three-way calls, and singing the praises of Rejuvinat like a good upline should. She keeps me *busy*! And though some of the recruits are duds, it's a numbers game. Like we always say, "Recruit for quantity, train for quality!"

"You're really going places, Madison," I tell her. "Hey, let's take a picture with the car. Let everyone know that you're on your way to your own FREE car." Even my words seem to sing out the all caps of FREE.

"*Am* I on my way?" Madison asks innocently.

Becky laughs and reassures the captive audience of bossbabes, "Honey, you're all on your way."

We take a photo and I immediately post it to Instagram with all the right tags and hashtags, talking up Madison and her team and how she's next in line for the car. Though it's common practice in MLMs, it dawns on me that it's a bit odd to brag about the things your upline has earned that you haven't earned yet—prizes and cars they've achieved on the backs of their downline. Still, Madison, Allison, and Becky share the post, and by the time we're done with our conversation, Madison shows us her phone.

"I've gotten two hundred new follows just from your posts," she tells us. I smile and nod, knowing full well that most of those people are already Rejuvinat indoctrinates, but why not let her have her moment?

Becky finishes her glass of champagne and takes another from the catering tray that magically passes by. "You just gotta put yourself out there. People love a success story."

Becky is right. People *do* love a success story, which is why we project success at any cost. We've all learned to game the system, but the system was built to be gamed. We break up orders into smaller lots to earn incentive bonuses, we sign up potential customers as consultants even if they don't really want to be, we throw in freebies that we have to purchase ourselves, and we pressure people (often family or close friends) into buying things they don't really want based on minimums or strange product-configuration requirements. The company then unloads less-purchased or discontinued items by requiring that you purchase them in a bundle with the more popular items; maybe you don't want the tooth-whitening paste, but you can only get the latest, greatest wrinkle filler if you buy them together, so you're gonna do it. And in the end, the company and reps make more money. While these actions in and of themselves may not be illegal, they are borderline unethical. But it's easy to justify when we experience the dopamine hit of rewards for our "work": earning a prize, being asked to speak at another recruiting event, or being featured on a team leaderboard.

Everyone loves a success story, but everyone also loves success. It is as addictive as the champagne that many of us are swilling that night, and if some of us don't make it, if some of us are taking out second credit cards and begging our sisters for help, we probably just aren't boss enough. Like poor Hannah, bless her heart. She struggles so much with her self-confidence, and it's shaking her ability to build. I keep telling her to read more books! Take more courses! Personal development is key in this business, and in order to excel, one must shift their mindset.

I know my mindset is golden. And that's not to say I'm not aware of and haven't weighed the cost to myself. I know I'm losing friendships over it. Friends are sick of me constantly trying to make a sale, wondering if I'm reaching out because I care or because I need to hit a title that month. I'm beginning to find it's easier to reach out to strangers rather than continue to bark up the same old tree. I usually have a few drinks before the cold texting begins: "Hey, hun, I'm wondering if I could pick your brain about my business opportunity . . ." But after a few exchanges, I find myself getting almost belligerent, as it's hard for me to take no for an answer. I start telling them that I'm super close to a goal, that all they need to do is sign up, that I'll hook them up with free products if they just buy this one package. Or better yet, they should just sign up "for the discount," which benefits me even more. Social Security number and another warm body to sign the dotted line, that's all I need. The next day, I look at my text messages and Facebook posts and groan, embarrassed by the things I am doing and saying, but then again, I'm the one getting the "FREE" car. If I'm paying for it with my integrity and dignity, oh well. That's just the price of doing business.

Although those cold texts came with some costly side effects, they admittedly garnered results, as I kept signing more women to my downline. I kept getting more shoutouts on social media, more features in team newsletters, more accolades from corporate via email to the whole field. Graphics and leaderboards would be sent out to other consultants as a "nah nah nah nah naaaah naaaah" comparison trap. Sometimes, I would wonder whether people on the "outside" were getting sick of hearing about my "accomplishments." I noticed that my Facebook posts were receiving fewer comments and likes, and that people had expressed annoyance with my constant posts about Rejuvinat.

A good friend of mine, Amanda, started distancing herself from me when I joined Rejuvinat, yet I continued to bug her to join. Every conversation we had became about the MLM. No wonder she stopped calling back. My own brother told me to never talk about my "Ponzi scheme" with him. I was unfriended by many people. I just couldn't understand how they could watch me become so successful and not want this for themselves. This falls in line with the strong "us versus them" mentality, with MLM reps in general viewing a prospect's choices as being: join the MLM, sit on the fence to decide to join the MLM, or be a hater. I personally echoed this sentiment across social media:

> "How long are you going to sit on the sidelines and watch me before you join?"
>
> "Why are you scared? Don't limit yourself!"
>
> "Stop making excuses and start making money."

But it's not that people are scared, limiting themselves, sitting on the sidelines, making excuses, or whatever stupid assumptions we have about them; it's just they just don't fucking want to. Problem is, MLM reps never assume that people might just not want to be bossbabes, which is odd, given that this doesn't happen with other kinds of jobs. "What? You don't want to be a fireman? It's amazing! You're just going to sit there and watch me fight fires and post about it and not join me? What's wrong with you!?" Can you imagine? Not everyone wants to do the same thing! But the levels of superiority (and white supremacy) that are engendered in an MLM, all because you're constantly told you're amazing, make you believe that everyone outside the MLM wants to be where you are. It's easy to presume that everyone would want to give this their *all*, by quitting jobs and retiring husbands and being at the top of the pyramid with a sparkly pink dress on at a car party—because where the hell else would you want to be?

I could only imagine how worn out my non-MLM network was with my constant posting and accolades. Yet, at the same time, it was those same accolades that were helping me to recruit. As much as I was pushing some people away, I was bringing in those who saw and believed in the dream I was selling, even if I was starting to alienate the people I really cared about. I couldn't let them stand in the way of my success!

I get another glass of champagne, as it's almost time for my coronation speech. I don't remember much of what I say, because I've had more glasses of Veuve than I've had donuts, and I've had a lot of donuts, but I'm pretty sure it's a stock hashtag speech about being blessed (as though God had bestowed this white SUV upon me) and about how hard I've worked (which is true, because I've never done so much busywork in my life) and how everyone in the room can one day achieve the same prize (even if, when I pause long enough to ruminate on what I'm doing, I doubt that's actually true). I remember wanting to be inspirational, as this is my big cheerleader moment—"Sell, sell, sell!"—but instead, I use the personal development language we have been taught: "Dream, dream, dream!"

I am living the dream, so why, when I look out at the audience and see Hannah taking another selfie with my car, does it all feel so wrong? More wrong than it did yesterday, and the day before. My rationalizing is beginning to waver.

And yet, I stop those thoughts when they come in. Sure, the MLM has its flaws, but everything has flaws, right? Every job has its ups and downs, and I have been pretty good at learning how to ignore the downs. I bat away the complaints from my family that I'm always gone. I ignore the signs and the cries for help from Hannah, and the fact that other team members aren't ranking up. Instead, I listen to the Beckys and Allisons and Kimberlys, and I watch the successes of the Madisons. "I'm a lifer," I tell myself. "I believe in this!" I ignore the drinking and the wild nights and the backstabbing and the fake friendships. I ignore the fact that despite how "successful" everyone says they are at the top, no one ever seems content.

That unsettling feeling that maybe I'm ignoring something really important is stronger than it's ever been, but I've become adept at hiding my reservations and smiling for the camera and my adoring fans. I raise my glass and toast all the women in the room: "To ladybosses!"

They reply back, "To ladybosses!"

I chug the rest of my glass, and as much as I wish I could tell you about the rest of the night, I can't. I remember writing the check to the owner of the donut truck and him asking me how I will be getting home. I think I might have pointed to the car with the big red bow. I remember saying goodbye to Hannah, who was also swaying in the wind. And I remember ripping that massive bow off and tossing it to the ground of the restaurant parking lot, before getting in my new Mercedes and driving home.

But what I really remember is seeing blue and red lights flashing behind me. It takes me a second to realize what's happening. Probably too long for the cops who saw me swerving across the road. By the time they make it to my window, I know what they're going to say, and I know how to respond. I remember being told by one of my MLM friends that you never, ever agree to a Breathalyzer.

I smile when the cop raps on my window and asks, "You mind stepping out of the car?"

I agree to a field test, ignorantly confident that I'm capable of passing it. I don't even bother taking off my five-inch heels as I stagger around along the side of the road.

"Do you want to take those off, ma'am?" the officer asks.

"No, I'm good," I reply with a thumbs-up, but then I realize that I'm far from good. I take off the heels, squatting down to unbuckle them, fingers shaking and short of breath. Unfortunately, it doesn't help.

The officer interrupts the test. "Ma'am, I think you've had too much to drink. I'm placing you under arrest for driving under the influence."

He snaps the handcuffs on my wrist just as the tow truck arrives for my car. I'm placed in the back of the squad car and made to wait while they load my new FREE car onto the bed. I watch the license plate get smaller in front of me as it drives away. Tears fill my eyes as I realize that I am fucked.

When the police officer returns to the car, he asks, "Do you have someone to call when we get to the station?"

I know immediately that I can't call my husband. I wonder whether Hannah might still be up.

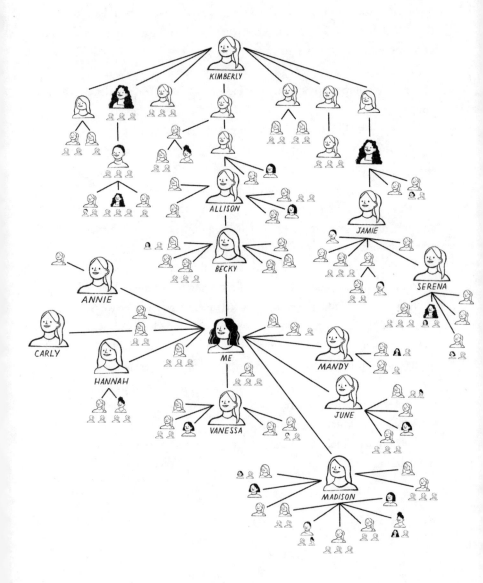

Elbow, Elbow, Wrist, Wrist

+ +
+

Now, I really liked my team, and the trips. What I hated? The vulnerability porn. Needing to tell my deepest darkest secrets as a way to connect, and hearing other people's deep, dark secrets. It made me think: Is this collateral? Why do I need to do this to be in this club?

—WINNIE, former MLM rep

Six months after my car party, I find myself at a coffee shop with a new addition: an AA sponsor. It wasn't a straight line that took me to my first AA meeting in a church basement, and it wasn't the DUI either, because I didn't get sober right away. In fact, it took the DUI arrest, a Breathalyzer in my FREE car, several attempts to cut back on drinking, followed by more failures and numerous hospital stints, including an overdose of sleeping pills, for me to begin to accept that I needed a change. It was waking up in bed hungover for the thousandth time, listening to my kids downstairs, realizing I was eliminating myself and that the only rock bottom lower than a failed suicide attempt was a successful one. All of that was finally enough for me to seek help.

What shocks me is how much everyone in my MLM has embraced my newfound sobriety. Though for a long time they encouraged my drinking, even celebrating it (I was always praised for how "fun" I was when I was drunk), they congratulate me and support my new alcohol-free path. Even Madison, who isn't exactly someone I'd consider a dear friend, sends me a card with kind words. I begin to feel "with it" for the first time in my life. In fact, I am so "with it" that I start feeling gross about some of my behavior: the cold messaging, the high-pressure sales tactics, the long-winded biz ops while I was hammered. I can't bring myself to prospect strangers anymore. It makes me realize how much of this I had been doing drunk. Being inebriated with lower inhibitions helped me do the things that I likely wouldn't have felt comfortable doing without it—what I used to consider liquid courage, I suppose. And yet, Madison is growing, and my downline is making me money.

I still feel, for the most part, that money means I am successful. In fact, it has seemed to balance out the other parts of my life that had fallen into abject failure. Before I quit drinking, my alcohol issues and the antics that accompanied them had led my husband and me close to the brink of divorce. Thankfully, we're repairing those parts of our relationship, too. And the friendships I'd destroyed are slowly but surely being healed.

Over the next few months, despite me not recruiting or reaching out to people, my team continues to grow. Of course, Madison is recruiting almost all of her clients and many hairstylists in the Seattle area, so the numbers are huge. My paychecks have doubled since she joined. Because of that, I hit the very top rank of the company just a few months after getting sober: Excellence Circle. Sure, I "helped" a few team members get to their ranks again by placing a few orders (getting them to the top 3 percent in order to get me to the top 0.05 percent). However, this time, I feel a bit weirder about the decision; the alcohol isn't there to numb my behavior or make me forget about it altogether.

Before I stopped drinking, I was worried my sales would fall off if I quit, but since getting sober, they are only improving. Word started to get around that I quit drinking and corporate became interested in my story: cautionary tale meets inspiring reversal meets cold, hard cash. It's the stuff of MLM lore, and since I am now a top leader in the company, they want me to tell the tale.

My regional manager, Seth, reaches out, encouraging me to share my "inspiring journey" with others. Not long after, I am asked to speak at Convention. This is only six months after I got my DUI in my brand-new FREE car; now, here I am, being asked to go on stage in front of thousands and spill the tea.

MLMs tend to be value-agnostic in this way, using any opportunity to spin someone's sob story to their advantage, even if the MLMs' culture is directly related to dopamine hits and addictive behavior. I've heard keynote speeches from women who had lost children or spouses, dealt with cancer, gone through painful divorces, become paralyzed, or survived domestic-abuse situations, all spun in a way that would lead you to believe the MLM unlocked their ability to process this trauma. Indoctrination through other women's pain. And now, I am the new inspirational tale. I actually feel honored.

Looking back, this is the part that might be the hardest. Because getting sober was an incredibly painful, intimate affair. After I got the car, even after the arrest, the pressure to stay on top increased. And at first, I couldn't imagine doing any of it sober. But I was faced with a choice: Rejuvinat or my family? I realized that if I didn't get sober, I'd lose a lot more than my #bossbabe job; I'd lose my husband, my children, my life.

I was on top at Rejuvinat, and apparently, my greatest heartbreak was its greatest success story.

Sobriety isn't just a catchphrase for me; I am desperately trying to salvage my marriage and my relationships with my children and friends, which were severely compromised by my behavior. I have to rebuild a lot of trust. But Rejuvinat is still my family. At this point, I have been with the company for over four years. Becky, Serena, Allison, and even Madison have become like sisters to me. We have walked with one another through so much, and so even though Rejuvinat is directly connected to some of my bad choices, I can't help but be honored by their invitation, seeing it not just as exploitation, which it clearly is, but also as congratulations.

I am riding the emotional roller coaster that MLMs count on: the dopamine hits, the promise of what's possible—a higher title, more money, more accolades. At this point, I'm deeply overwhelmed, and without alcohol in my system, I have become an adrenaline/serotonin/dopamine/cortisol machine. I have to actually process feelings I've been numbing out for years. I'm seeing a therapist, working with a sponsor, exercising, meditating, journaling; with the absence of alcohol, I'm clinging to any life raft I can find, including the love bombs from Rejuvinat. Make rank? Get asked to speak at Convention? You're the star. Someone outranks you and leaves you in their dust? You get ghosted. It makes you want to keep the praise coming.

There's a reason why the first rank in any MLM is easy to hit—so you start feeling the benefits, emotions, and love bombing right away. Because then, as with any addiction, you continue to crave and romanticize the drug. And in the case of MLMs, the drug is attention. It certainly is for me.

For SAHMs, who often feel ignored, this attention is addictive. The rise of "momfluencers" and the fake authenticity of social media only increase our tendency to criticize and compare. Jo Piazza, host of the podcast *Under the Influence*, dove deep into the multibillion-dollar industry of momstagrammers, which allows women to monetize motherhood with unrealistic, curated, and idyllic expectations. She says that what we see on social media "feels real, just real enough, but never real real . . . it's anxiety-inducing for mothers—this highly stylized perfect content is a very American aesthetic." It's very in line with MLM culture to ask, "What can I monetize here? How can I turn this into a sale?"

INSTEAD OF SCROLLING my drunk texts, trying to remember what I did and who I need to apologize to, sitting at a coffee shop with my sponsor every Sunday has become my new normal. After our step work, I tell her about speaking at Convention, bragging about my opportunity at the ultimate bossbabe summit. My sponsor finally cautions me about MLM life.

"Just be careful," she says. "You're still so fresh in sobriety, so make sure it's the story you want to tell."

I am taken aback. This is the person I've been more honest with than anyone—she knows all my grievances, my amends, everything. She is my confessional.

"Why wouldn't it be my story?" I ask, defensive. "You know how transparent I've been!"

"Well . . ." She hesitates. "Have you noticed a theme with your amends?"

She references the list on my fourth step, the things I still hold shame or anger around, the things I need to "find my part in," and then make amends where appropriate.

"So many of them are around people you brought into Rejuvinat, or things you did while you were in Rejuvinat. Do you see a theme here?"

I suck in my breath. Yes. Maybe I am just realizing it for the first time, but I can see it all in black and white, literally because I had written it all down—my guilt for selling people a business kit when I knew they didn't have enough money, shame for bugging the crap out of people for the sake of the numbers game, cringe about getting drunk on "business trips" and not remembering what I said or did.

The wine trip, the blackout in Vegas, the car party . . . I know what she's getting at.

"Yes, I do see a theme. But isn't it like a chicken/egg thing? I don't think I would have behaved that way if I hadn't been drinking. Like, now I'm not doing those things." I fail to pick up what she is putting down, that the "opportunity" was the toxic part of these interactions, and the alcohol was just the catalyst.

"I'm just saying, make sure when you share your story, it isn't being used to sell something else. Don't let other people use your pain to sell things."

I nod in agreement, but it isn't registering. I have been conditioned to smell a hater from a mile away, and even though my sponsor has helped me see so much about my life in a short period of time, I know she's wrong on this one. My Rejuvinat defense system is fully employed as I think, *This is for people already in the company; it's not like this is for prospects. It's just to inspire! And sharing my sobriety story is a positive thing for everyone!*

I can't see the level of exploitation I am willing to put up with just yet, despite the warning signals that have been bouncing off my Rejuvinat armor from all sides for months now. I can't see that this isn't about me being a great leader or sharing an inspiring story; it's just another way to indoctrinate more people and keep them stuck in Rejuvinat.

I think we would all agree it's not ethical to share your personal trauma or tragedy in order to attract customers, but where would the wellness industry be without that marketing gimmick? In MLMs, the strategy becomes weaponized because you already know people, meaning you know their vulnerabilities, which makes them feel closer to you but also makes them more susceptible to indoctrination.

Even as I sit across from my sponsor acting like she doesn't know what she's talking about, I remember an icebreaker activity at a reward trip from the previous year: the "I am" activity. It was essentially a trauma-dumping exercise, where we had to write "I am" on a piece of paper, be as open and vulnerable as possible, and then walk around the room sharing them with each other.

I read things like:

"I am an incest survivor."

"I am in an abusive marriage."

"I am severely depressed."

I read deep, heartfelt things, brimming with personal pain, about perfect strangers. You know what my list started with? "I'm hungover."

This ritualistic public confession of sins is a common practice in MLMs but also in most cults—to get you to reveal all your tucked-away vulnerabilities so that they're able to tie their cart to your sad, pathetic horse. *It was this business that brought out my greatness, and it can bring out yours, too!*

As if selling face creams is going to heal your trauma.

After I pack up and head home from our Sunday meeting, I think about what my sponsor said. I think about how I used my cancer journey to sell skincare. I think about how the pain points of motherhood, womanhood, and all of our insecurities are placed under a microscope and exploited to sell an opportunity. And praise be, Kimberly, I even begin to think that wine-mom culture, diet culture, and MLMs may be shilling the same narrative: "Don't fix the problem—fix yourself! Don't worry about the fact that your size doesn't matter—buy this cleanse! Don't accept yourself for who you are—just drink your way through it! Don't stay poor—be a bossbabe!"

I think about the first day I met Becky for wine, desperate for human companionship and an escape from my real life. And though it's just a crack, I begin to see how exploitative this might be, even as part of me still believes I'm helping people.

But quickly, my Rejuvinat senses overpower my conscience. I remind myself that my intentions have always been good. Sure, some people are exploitative, reaching out to women who've just had babies to lose baby weight, DM-ing people with acne to suggest something to fix their skin, even cold-messaging widows to suggest they need a new source of income—but I *genuinely* mean well. Don't I? Maybe I've reached out to new moms in the past. And I've suggested skincare to someone with visible acne, as well. But before I can dwell on the internal tug-of-war much longer, I get a phone call.

"Hi, Andrea!" I cheerfully welcome the interruption.

Andrea is a good friend from high school, and she's also a bossbabe for a different company; we are both about the same rank in our respective companies. In fact, she reached out to me quite a while before I joined Rejuvinat, back when I thought direct sales was kind of weird, but I just didn't understand it then. Plus, Andrea works with an exercise/fitness company, and I was pregnant at the time, so fitness wasn't a fit. But since I've been in an MLM, I've watched her cruise up the ranks in AdvoCare, just as I have in Rejuvinat. It's cool that we can talk about our experiences because there are so many similarities—leading leaders, trying to motivate people (sometimes, wake the dead), and dealing with everything that comes along with being a bossbabe. There's a weird dynamic among MLM people— that is, we are stern about defending our company in the sales pitch: "Join me, not her! Join this company, not that one!" But once people are entrenched in their own commercial cult, we're in a similar sisterhood. We're defending against the same objections from people who (rightfully) don't believe in or understand the MLM business model, or who (rightfully) think it's predatory, so we stick up for and support each other.

Andrea and I buy each other's stuff, have events together, and share our products with each other's customers, because it's a win-win! It gets a little sticky when one of her customers wants to join my company, and vice versa, but for the most part, we've stayed connected and it's worked out. I'm excited she's calling, since my personal reach outs have been tempered by my sobriety. I can't cold-message anymore. I can't do the "just checking in!" messages to people who have told me no over and over and over. It feels icky.

I'm hoping she might be able to offer some advice to get over this new hump in my business, but immediately, my hopes are dashed.

"You will never believe this," she says in tears over the phone. "Advo-Care is leaving MLM. My paycheck is gone." She chokes back a sob before telling me, "I'm losing my whole downline."

What. The. Hell.

Apparently, the Federal Trade Commission ruled that AdvoCare has been operating as an illegal pyramid scheme. According to the FTC, AdvoCare rewarded distributors handily for recruiting other distributors, convincing them to spend large sums of money to pursue the business opportunity. But like most MLMs, the majority of distributors either made no money or lost money. AdvoCare and the CEO agreed to pay $150 million for consumer refunds, and two of the top promoters settled for $4 million (most were suspended because they weren't able to pay) and all were banned from multilevel marketing.

I remember a few years earlier, Andrea freaked out about some exposé that was done in a national magazine talking about how most of the highly paid AdvoCare reps (which was a very small percentage) made their money by signing up distributors rather than through product sales. It discussed the exaggerated claims of financial success, and the strong use of religion as an integral part of the business model. I also knew that Andrea happened to do all of those things. She's definitely posted on Facebook about high earnings and God and how the more devout members hold more power in the company. But I *knew* her. I knew her heart and her intentions. Or did I? This is why white women, just like me, can be so dangerous. "But I know her" is a great excuse for bad behavior. I was willing to overlook these predatory practices because she was a friend. And it's easier to overlook bad behavior when it doesn't impact you personally, and especially when you're mimicking much of the behavior yourself. Regardless of how she built her huge downline, ethically or not, now it was all gone.

"Shit, Andrea. I'm so sorry," I console her over the phone, listening to her tears and anguish. I am stunned. Her organization is now one level, not multiple. So instead of having thousands of people in her downline, all with their own customers, with income flowing to her, she now has no downline, just her own customers. Her $50,000-plus monthly paychecks aren't just being slashed; they are being decimated. She'll be lucky if she makes $500 a month. Because the money is always in the downline, not the sales. All I can think is *Could this happen to Rejuvinat? But Rejuvinat is different, right?*

Very shortly after the call from Andrea, Rejuvinat (and probably every other panicked MLM) goes on the defensive and sends out a damage-control email:

Rejuvinat is a leading brand thanks to YOU, our powerful community of consultants, and top-notch business model! Unlike other companies that have been the target of FTC investigations, we have a robust customer base and a compensation plan that does not depend solely on distributors! We are proud that the majority of our sales are to customers. We also place great importance on education for our consultant community. We do not sell this opportunity with improper income claims, and we have a transparent income disclosure statement. AdvoCare, on the other hand, has been the subject of high-profile press and is a defendant in a class-action lawsuit. They have also been investigated by the FTC for two years. Please know, none of these things apply to us at Rejuvinat. Thanks again for your commitment to our brand!

Immediately, red flags go up. Maybe I am bristling from the conversation with Andrea, but I'm not buying this. First of all, Rejuvinat has *many* challenges; we've had numerous class-action lawsuits brought due to product problems and customer complaints. But beyond that, the vague "majority of sales to customers" is bullshit. I know it, and they know it. Sure, maybe my "pyramid" is more customers than consultants, but only because I recruited consultants who brought in those customers. The acquisition of customers is *dependent* on recruiting all of those people! Also, the compensation absolutely depends on consumption by consultants because we have minimum product purchases per month, and product auto-shipment programs that are difficult to cancel.

And transparent income disclosures? You have to dig to find them. We are always discouraged from sharing them, told only to reference but never link to them, though every post you scroll on social media has income claims, or is selling the opportunity: on the beach, living your best life, work from anywhere, never miss a moment. Graphics the company prepares for us to share. These are *absolutely* income-opportunity claims.

Though I'm sure the corporate letter quenches the fire for most, the crack that has begun to form in my own loyalty begins to widen.

Gray Chapman explains in her Vox.com article, "MLMs Take the Worst Parts of the Gig Economy, Then Make You Pay":

MLMs and the gig economy both capitalize on a deeply American cultural mythos that self-reliance and grit are all it takes to succeed. Yet by neglecting to provide workers with basic protections or clear, predictable understanding of income, they're simultaneously complicit in some of the very same drivers of socioeconomic inequality that force people to seek out a side gig in the first place. It's capitalism with hashtags and a Snapchat filter, but it's still capitalism, propped up by laborers whose efforts reward the fortunate few who sit at the top of the pyramid.

I certainly don't want to lose my downline, but this email doesn't alleviate my concerns. If the FTC could shut down AdvoCare, why not Rejuvinat? But then I begin with the rationalizing game once more. Why don't more MLMs get shut down if they're really all that bad? They *can't* be that bad, right?

The truth? When it comes to the FTC's power, it's all politics. MLMs have deep connections to powerful lobbying groups. Trump was the progenitor of his own MLM, The Trump Network, which sold vitamins, mood-infusion beverages, and other health products. Betsy DeVos made $75 million from her involvement in Amway during the Trump administration alone. Most US senators who publicly state that they don't believe MLMs need more regulation have taken huge donations from MLMs, or the DSA itself. Marsha Blackburn (a Republican senator from Tennessee) has taken contributions from Herbalife and the DSA, Mike Lee (a Republican senator from Utah) from Young Living and dōTERRA, and the list goes on. Beyond that, many politicians who are *not* involved in MLMs, as well as the general population, typically don't understand what MLMs are.

Doug Brooks is a lawyer in Massachusetts who, over the past thirty years, has litigated a variety of civil cases nationwide, including matters involving franchises, dealerships, and product distribution, as well as securities, antitrust, and consumer-protection class action. He has substantial experience representing the victims of fraudulent and deceptive MLM schemes and has represented former MLM reps in class-action lawsuits in state and federal court. According to Brooks, since the 1970s, the way the FTC has tried to rein in the MLM folks is by doing case-by-case prosecutions of organizations such as the now-defunct Vemma, which was shut down in 2015 by the FTC for engaging in deceptive practices and pyramid scheming. Similarly, in 2016, the FTC fined Herbalife $20 million, saying their compensation plan was unfair because it "rewards distributors for recruiting others to join and purchase products in order to advance in the marketing program, rather than in response to actual retail demand for the product." The FTC picks an MLM, analyzes it thoroughly, brings a case, does a great job, shuts it down, and maybe recovers some of the money lost to give to victims.

Others receive huge fines and rebrand with different names (Nerium, now Neora, and Newys, now Modere) or change their structure in order to stay in business, like Herbalife, Nu Skin, and now, AdvoCare. They do this every couple of years, which is great, but unfortunately, there are hundreds more MLMs with which to contend. It's an industry-wide problem. Deceptive and unfair conduct is ubiquitous and not at all rare or unusual; you see at least a few of the same deceptive strategies in every MLM. Although the FTC should be applauded for the prosecutions they have done, it's not enough.

What the FTC has proposed, very recently, is to develop a regulation that will apply not only to MLMs, but to any gig economy, any industry that makes an earnings claim: "Join our biz, take our course, follow our plan, you'll make money." If this regulation does end up passing, it would apply to all MLMs and make it easier for the FTC to prosecute companies that don't follow this rule. But passing a federal regulation is very difficult.

How has the MLM industry avoided regulation so well up to this point? The FTC has a franchise rule that was passed in the 1970s. If you're going to buy a franchise (Dunkin' Donuts, Burger King, Subway), you need to sign a disclosure statement from the company with everything you need to know well before you invest any money. However, this regulation doesn't apply unless the required payments in the first six months are over $500. This is how MLMs avoid being scrutinized under the franchise rule; if you look at MLMs, there is always a buy-in business kit that is less than $500. Sure, there are many that cost more, but as long as they offer a buy-in within their product portfolio that is *less* than $500, they can skirt the regulation. Disclosures should be given and agreed to well before you sign anything or pay any money. After all, you need time to understand what the hell you're getting into, and to do your own research, which doesn't include listening to the parroted script of your potential upline.

A few decades after the franchise rule, the FTC decided it needed a rule about business opportunities. Finalized in 2011, the Business Opportunity Rule's intention is to protect consumers by requiring an MLM to give potential recruits basic income disclosures. When the rule was proposed, the MLM industry collectively lost their shit. According to *The Verge*, in 2014, they increased spending for lobbyists and begged members of Congress to tell the FTC to leave MLMs alone. The DSA got more than seventeen thousand people to send letters to the FTC opposing the rule. They basically overwhelmed the FTC, and they were successful; the FTC exempted MLMs from the rule. Sidenote: The DSA in itself is a joke, as I referenced in the previous chapter, with its bang-up job breaking down the (non)diversity of MLMs. It is a self-regulated nonprofit that pretends to police MLMs, yet every single person on the board is an MLM CEO or has strong financial ties to an MLM. The DSA formerly had no code of ethics, and in response to scrutiny about its lack of checks and balances, it established a self-regulatory entity known as the Direct Selling Self-Regulatory Council (DSSRC) at the beginning of 2019. The DSA fully funds the DSSRC. The council was created to shield the industry from further scrutiny and regulatory oversight, rather than to protect customers from deception.

But to the outside observer, it *seems* legit! It has a logo and official-looking photos on its website, after all. It's enough to set the minds of prospects at ease: "Oh, don't worry, we're endorsed by the DSA and regulated by the DSSRC."

Which is a bit like saying you're a gun-control group endorsed and regulated by the NRA.

Along with the FTC, the SEC can also bring cases against MLMs. The SEC protects investors by enforcing securities laws and ensures that investors are treated fairly and honestly. However, there are shortcomings in enforcement when it comes to MLMs, according to Gary Langan Goodenow, a former trial attorney in the SEC enforcement division. Because by the time the SEC enforcement division comes in to freeze assets, the money is long gone. The empty promises made to the recruit are generally from an independent contractor of the company, not the company itself. And since all contractors sign on the dotted line of a consultant agreement form before they join, even if they don't read it, they technically agree to the risk, and there is very little the SEC can do.

And what about those income disclosure statements I mentioned earlier that bossbabes are always posting references to in tiny fine print under the photos of them posing with their shiny FREE cars in front of an ocean view with one of those wide-brimmed fedoras ("Results not typical, please search for our IDS")? Is that enough of a disclosure? Yes and no. The interesting thing about these statements is that they are not required by law. The reason MLMs encourage their consultants to copy and paste the statement along with any reference to income claims is twofold: (1) It's their way of saying, "See, we provide income disclosures—you don't need to order us to do it. Please don't regulate us more!" and (2) If they ever get sued, they can blame the victim. "See, victim? You got this income disclosure; you *knew* your chances for success were very low and you took them anyway." It's a defensive move, plain and simple.

The good news? As of this writing, the FTC is revisiting the business opportunity rule. The difference in the last fifteen years is that more people are speaking out and sharing their stories about being burned in an MLM.

And at this point in my own journey, I am starting to feel the burn.

I AM BACK IN LAS VEGAS. Stone-cold sober and at another Rejuvi-convention. I know I shouldn't be traveling back to Las Vegas with a carry-on of fragile sobriety, but speaking is a big deal. My husband was initially worried, but his pride in and support of me eventually won out. Only nine months ago, he wasn't sure I was going to live. With my newfound "celebrity," my business has exploded, just as it has for most of the women around me. Feeling that I have done a good deed with respect to my Rejuvinat sisters, I'm momentarily on the upside of my conscience.

Kale and I decide it would be best if he comes with me; plus, it will be a fun getaway for the two of us. Because we'll both be away, we leave the au pair with the kids, missing their first day of school.

Now, many people have to miss kid events because of employment, so I don't want to shame those who do, but Rejuvinat schedules this event every year around the start of the school year. About 70 percent of the women in Rejuvinat have school-age children. But then again, it's our choice, right?

Although this is not a necessary activity for doing our business, had I not gone, I would have been shunned and ostracized for failing to show up as a leader. Instead of watching Convention from the sidelines, I look at photos of my kids' first day. The business I started to have more freedom and spend more time with my family is now making me miss the things that matter most. Earlier this week, I posted a photo with my daughter as a piece of corporate propaganda with the caption "Never miss a moment."

What a crock! I am missing tons of moments.

But my celebrity status has definitely increased this go-around, and a part of me is still here for it. By this point, I have far surpassed Becky in title, and with Madison's massive recruiting efforts, my downline is growing like wildfire. Again, this cognitive dissonance has me believing that my sobriety has unlocked my potential. At the same time, after the AdvoCare news, I am seeing more fissures in the system. I'm noticing where people are struggling. And I can no longer drink away what is happening to them. I watch Hannah bicker with her husband about this company while I tell her to "just believe." I text Vanessa a congratulations on her new "real job" promotion but feel conflicted for being proud of her, because I wish she was here and still invested in Rejuvinat. I continue to watch Andrea's life fall into financial ruin as her company folds. But Rejuvinat is different, I promise myself, and I know my downline will find success just like Madison has, despite not having the money or the network. I just have to *believe*.

Something else happens the day we arrive: the mass shooting at the Mandalay Bay hotel in Vegas. Just a mile down the road, more than fifty people are shot and murdered by a sniper in a hotel room. Despite the largest loss of human life in a mass shooting in the United States, the company moves forward with the Convention. Kale is concerned, and we both wonder if we should turn around and go back home. As usual, I turn to the company to decide what to do. Of course, my field leader insists that life marches on, and since we are staying in a different hotel, I should continue with my plans to speak. We oblige and stay put.

Instead of being gracious and canceling the Convention or just giving their best wishes, sending a donation, and not capitalizing on the tragedy, Rejuvinat doubles down, using the shooting as a way to promote the company. Much like my use-cancer-to-sell-eye-cream scheme a couple years earlier. Overnight, there are signs, propaganda, and shareables, emblazoned with the company logo, made available to us with sayings like "Rejuvinat stands with Vegas." There are donation links, and yes, they are attached to product purchases.

Photos of consultants posing outside the broken windows of the Mandalay Bay hotel and even at the attack site, flanked by inspirational quotes and prayers, start flooding social media. Instead of actually shutting the hell up and mourning the loss of life, the ladies of Rejuvinat go about our fancy Convention pretending we're actually doing something about it. Including me.

Despite the awful circumstances surrounding the terror attack and the performative charity, my personal antics are a far cry from the previous year. Staying in the same hotel, in the same town, but now with Kale, I can't help but reflect on my week of drinking and blacking out, and I have gratitude for where I am now. The complicated part is that my gratitude is directly connected to my belief that this company really *did* help. I promise not to run myself ragged this year. I pare down the number of events I participate in, and I make it a point to hang out more with friends and my husband.

Kale and I do a few slot machines, see a few concerts, and eat great food, yet I am still busier than I want to be. And to top off the annoyance of the busyness, Serena and I are stopped constantly for photo ops since we are both ranked at the top of the company. I'm honored and overwhelmed at the same time, thinking, *This must be what celebrities feel like all the time, and it sucks.* I can't walk to the pool or to a restaurant without getting tackled by someone in the company wanting their picture with me, and I am subsequently tagged on social media. Serena and I exchange glances and grin through our irritation because she hates it even more than I do. Though I admittedly once relished the spotlight, and at this point still do, Serena never loved it. Especially now, since she quit drinking as well, her emotions are raw and it's more difficult to escape the crowd's uncomfortable gaze. Although she didn't have any rock-bottom consequences, she realized that the toxic culture of drinking in Rejuvinat was not serving her, so she set the bottle down a few months after I did. It made our relationship even stronger, yet made the cracks in the Rejuvinat façade even more visible to us both.

In some ways, having her as a friend reduces that cognitive dissonance that "not everyone makes it to the top." Look, we both made it! It helps that we don't live in the same neighborhood, aren't financially linked, and have different networks. We aren't recruiting each other's competition, either. Meanwhile, both our teams are growing in size, increasing our titles and our bottom lines, even if the majority of the individual people on our teams aren't ranking up. Our paychecks might be increasing, but theirs aren't.

I'm making over $30,000 per month at this point, and Serena is close behind. But our downlines? Nope. Only my unicorn top earner, Madison, is making any significant income, at around $5,000 or so per month, and the next runner-up is June, with $1,000, with another handful in the low to mid hundreds. Everyone else? Breaking even or losing money. But our paychecks keep growing. The more people who join, whether they make pennies or not, the more our profits are enhanced.

Kale makes nice with some of the other husbands. He is certainly happy with our getaway because he isn't obligated to attend all the sessions and just wants to see me speak. As the week goes on, he becomes slightly more annoyed by all the fangirling I'm getting, as well as the questions he's being asked by other top leaders and their husbands. "How did she do it? Give us the secrets to her success! How did she climb the ranks so quickly?" At the tail end of a (required) leader luncheon, Serena's husband and Kale are chatting as Kimberly's husband makes the rounds. I'm sure he's a nice dude, but you can tell Kimberly dressed him; he looks so uncomfortable in his ridiculous Gucci gear, and he *never* talks about anything but Rejuvinat. It's his entire personality, and hers. We refer to him as the Rejuvibot. Nobody ever says his name; he's known only as Kimberly's husband.

"Hey, guys, would love to have you check out my new Lambo. Just off the factory floor!" Scratch that, he talks about his cars, too, as an offshoot blessing from Rejuvinat.

Serena's husband smirks as we sit at lunch, passing a bread dish as Serena rolls her eyes. "Hey, cool, yeah, maybe after this is over."

Kale looks down at his phone, fielding work emails; I can tell he's praying Kimberly's husband walks away.

"Still working a day job?" Rejuvibot snickers. "Dude, you have to get Emily to put a little more into this."

Kale grunts but doesn't look up from his phone, just as Kimberly saunters up. I swear she has an earpiece with her husband's conversations piped into it. She joins just in time to offer an addendum to her husband's mind-blowing financial advice.

"It's true, Emily. Now that you're at the top, it just looks bad to have a husband who's still working. I mean, what do people have to strive for when they see that you still have a double-income home?"

Crickets.

I swear to God.

Kale, who generally keeps his cool and can segue out of any situation, bursts into laughter. "You're joking, right?"

He and Serena's husband look at each other, size up their mutual offense, and walk out. Serena and I awkwardly look up at Kimberly and Rejuvibot as they sheepishly walk away. We push our plates to the side and follow our husbands out.

"What the hell was that?" Serena's husband scoffs. "Are they out of their minds? Who says something like that?"

I reflect back to Serena's statement about not being able to bang a guy who quit his job for this, and I have to concur: Watching Kale stand up to Rejuvibot was extremely hot.

Kale laughs as we catch up with them in the lobby. "If you want to be a stay-at-home dad or whatever, that's great. But I like my job. It's so odd that they think *this*"—at which point he gestures around to the entirety of the situation—"is real or remotely stable and has to be your entire world."

Serena's husband nods in agreement. "It's a cult, dude." Serena and I look at each other and know what the other is thinking. *Yep, we know.* But what do we do with that knowledge? Leave? How do you walk away from that kind of money? I used to wonder why people stay in bad situations, but now, I know exactly why. It's easier to stay the course than to change. It's easier to stay in a rocky marriage than it is to either get marriage counseling or get a divorce. It's easier to keep drinking, no matter the consequences, than it is to get real help and dig yourself out of rock bottom. I've trudged through both of those scenarios. And I know for a fact, it's easier to continue to collect money than it is to leave a cult, even when you know it's a cult.

It's no question that this will be the last Convention Kale will attend with me.

FINALLY, IT'S TIME for my moment, my presentation. I'm telling my story in front of the biggest audience I've ever spoken to. Sure, I've shared my story in front of my AA group, and with friends, but this is in front of *thousands* of people! I feel pangs of nervous energy as I get mic'ed up backstage, and I peek through the curtains to see June, Carly, Annie, Mandy, Serena, Becky, and Kale, all sitting in priority seating in the front row. Phew. I reflect on the comments from my sponsor. I still believe I'm doing the right thing, but I'm not sure if I'm doing it for the right reasons. I try to ignore the fact that 80 percent of the women have champagne glasses in their hands—super huge thanks, Rejuvinat, for making trays of champagne more plentiful than water at these events. It's ironic, considering what I'm going to be talking about.

Before I can think much more about it, I'm being introduced. "Please welcome your Excellence Leader, Emily Paulson!" Music blasts and applause roars as I walk to center stage. Wow, there are a lot of people out there. I start with an introduction about how I joined this business, give a shoutout to Becky, and go into my spiel about my topic: "The Highlight Real versus the Highlight Reel." I want to share about how, although my external success looked so great, people didn't know what was going on behind closed doors. Of course, I throw in bits and pieces of corporate speak and leadership tips, since this has all been previewed by the corporate team. I offer my best practices and take-aways: staying motivated, setting goals, evaluating priorities, much like any typical Convention leadership presentation.

But I close with my own story. A collage of photos pops up on my last PowerPoint slide, all photos of "success" that I shared on my social media: a snapshot from Vegas last year, walking the stage; a photo from my car party; and multiple other photos where I was blackout drunk but looked totally fine. I say, my voice quivering slightly:

I told you my Rejuvinat story at the very beginning when I got up here, and you see all of these impressive photos of my highlight-reel moments. Maybe these are photos that make you envious or compare your journey to mine. But these highlights have a very real component that is neither happy nor celebratory. One thing you should know about me is that I'm recovering from substance abuse. I've gone through this sobriety journey very openly this past year. You can see up there a photo of me walking across the stage for the first time at Convention in a red dress. What you don't see is the fact that I don't actually remember this moment, because I was a high-functioning blackout drinker. My water cup used to be filled with champagne, and many days, especially really busy, stressful times like Convention, I drank from the moment I woke up until the moment I went to bed. Nobody knew how bad it was. All of those memories are only memories by photo. The photo of me posing in my car, I don't remember, but what isn't pictured is me getting pulled over on the way home from that event and getting arrested for drunk driving. You also don't see a photo of my shiny brand-new car that I earned literally that day, getting towed away and impounded while I sat handcuffed in the back of a police car. You also don't see photos of me when I woke up in the hospital with alcohol poisoning. I could fill this room up with photo highlights, but there are many, many more shadows. The final straw for me, after those rock-bottom moments and many more: I woke up on the morning of New Year's Day 2017. I was hungover as usual, and I couldn't recall the previous forty-eight hours of my life. So I lay there in bed, and I heard the sounds of my kids downstairs with my husband, and something about that moment made me realize I was listening to my kids' future. That I was missing out on my life, my family's life, and I was just training my kids to live without me. Something about that day woke me up, and it was enough for me to march into my first AA meeting. I decided it was better to say for the rest of my life that I'm an alcoholic, rather than pretend for one more day that I wasn't. And I haven't had a drink since. What I want to share most of all today is that you see everyone's highlights, but you don't know how dark the shadows might be. Please do not compare your journey, because you never have the whole story. Thank you for letting me speak today.

The room erupts in applause. There are tears, even from me, and I am not a person who is often moved to tears. After the presentation, I have dozens of women (with alcohol on their breath) letting me know they totally understood. One tells me she just got a DUI, too, and others disclose that they are sober, or struggling to get sober. I hadn't realized there are so many of "us" out there! They thank me for being brave and vulnerable, and it is at that moment I realize I want to share my story—because I want to feel this kind of pride, not only for getting through a presentation without a drop of alcohol, but because it was incredibly cathartic. And I am appreciative to be given the opportunity to do it. I wouldn't have been able to share my story with so many people had it not been for Rejuvinat. Though I am starting to see the harsh light beaming down on Rejuvinat, it's not with 100 percent clarity. As I leave the stage, I know that I want to focus on sharing my story and helping others embrace theirs.

I'm at a crossroads, and again, this is where it gets hard.

Rejuvinat absolutely gave me the platform that I still benefit from today. I got this book deal partially because of my follower count, which was established by the social media love bombing that was Rejuvinat's love language. I made friends but also followers, people who trusted and respected me, and who later, when I began to build a sober community for moms, followed me there out of the MLM world. I was standing on the platform that Rejuvinat built, and some of that platform was offering me heartfelt transformative experiences.

At the same time, this is precisely why people stay in disastrous situations. Just because something is negative overall—the bad job, the crappy boyfriend, the addiction—doesn't mean it's *all bad*. We get drawn in by the momentary good things, and we assume that because there *are* good times, it's still okay to hang on. When I was drinking, it wasn't all bad. Most of the time it was good, but if I still continued to hold out for those good times, I would be dead right now.

I can look back and feel happy that I had some good times, but I also know that I'm better off without Rejuvinat.

I consider that Convention presentation to be one of the defining moments of my life, one of the best things I've ever done, and also, the moment that marks my journey out of Rejuvinat. It led me to what I would end up doing eventually, which was recovery coaching, writing, and speaking about addiction. As grateful as I was to Rejuvinat, a deeper desire within me was catalyzed that day. I began thinking that maybe this business wasn't everything; maybe there was something else for me, something more. I didn't want to keep sharing my story to sell skincare and supplements.

I ride the wave that evening, talking to so many people and feeling on top of the world, and yet, I know something isn't right. That night, I walk the stage (again) and see the same people sitting in the same chairs as last year. Nobody else has grown, ranked, or leveled up; I've just gained more of them at the bottom, always feeding upward. And here I am, being praised and congratulated. What is this doing for me? What is this doing *to* me?

Instead of feeling proud about being at the top of the pyramid, I feel weird about the people still sitting in those chairs, about the money I am making despite not sending cold messages and despite my downline not making any more money. It's hard to sit with the fact that so many people are working as hard as or harder than I am, and they aren't growing.

Thinking of the lights flashing in my eyes, the roaring audience before me, and my celeb status growing even more, I feel dizzy. I want to believe I wasn't full of shit all those years. I want to believe in the person I am telling people I am. But by the time Convention is over, that person isn't sure she aligns anymore with Rejuvinat.

On the plane ride home after Convention, instead of sitting at the computer sending cut-and-paste messages, I write. I start working backward and write more of my story. I start writing what I've learned this past year, and the things I've begun to uncover about childhood trauma and wanting to belong, and how alcohol played a huge part in that. And while I am writing, I continue to realize how wanting to belong and feel less alone is what led me to Rejuvinat. I keep writing what will eventually be my first book, even though I don't know that's what it will be at the time.

I start untethering myself from the belief that I need Rejuvinat.

But before I can think too long about where my business is going, the plane lands and I receive a call from my doctor. I'm faced with another obstacle—my cancer is back.

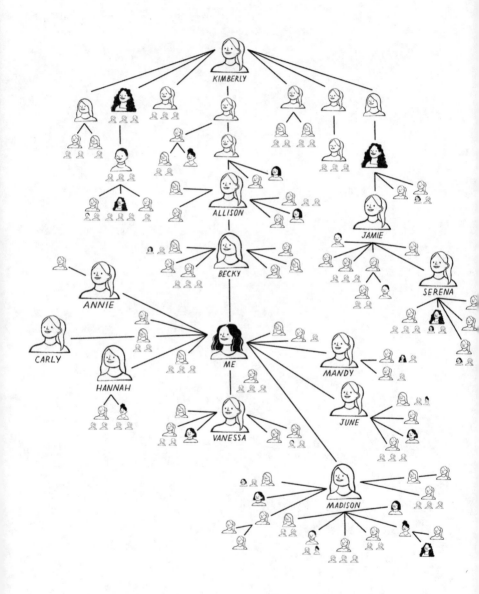

Pray to the Gurus
and Goddesses

I joined multiple MLMs over many years, unfortunately. I thought it
would be different; it never was. Every year at Convention (I kick myself
for paying so much for these now), there were gurus and speakers selling
the same personal-improvement bullshit. From MLM to MLM, it was the
same circuit of speakers, yet I looked around and saw that these women
were hanging on every word, as if they were endorsing the company. I
could never get that invested. I never understood how you could worship
people like that.

—TIFFANY, former MLM rep

On my one-year sober birthday, I am in the hospital for a
relapse—but this one isn't about alcohol. During a routine
follow-up, my doctor discovered that my cancer had returned.
It was a punch to the gut that I'm sure all cancer survivors can attest
to; there is nothing to prepare you for it.

Once again, my people gather around me, both my Rejuvinat network and my non-MLM network. I am able to put Rejuvinat on the
back burner for a bit as Serena helps by hosting my events for me and
taking on the role of "Seattle Leader" while I am busy with doctors'
appointments and surgery. My local friend network makes a meal train

and orchestrates rides for my kids to and from school. The mode of treatment is a radical hysterectomy, lymph-node removal, and thankfully, no additional treatment. Though it is more invasive, I am much more at peace with this surgery than the last, probably because I am in such a better place with my mental health and sobriety. I don't have issues with pain medicine, and I don't feel any particular obligation to return to the hustle.

After my recovery, I have found myself even more conflicted with Rejuvinat. Taking time off, partly because I am distracted by the stress of my diagnosis and impending surgery, partly to recover, I begin to become more disenchanted with the business altogether.

But just as I am continuing to feel less attached to Rejuvinat, the cancer diagnosis leads to another barrage of love bombing by my upline and corporate. They are so sweet after my surgery, sending me money for housecleaning, care packages, flowers during my recovery. I know the friendship isn't fake, yet I wonder at the same time if they would be doing this if they didn't *need* me to continue. It's almost as though they feel me slipping away and want to keep me invested. I don't doubt for a minute that these women care about me, but if I wasn't such a key player, would they be doting on me like this? Would they even be friends with me? As I begin to pull away from Rejuvinat, I also begin to fear their rejection.

I don't use my cancer to sell shit this time, so I feel good about that. And I also don't spend my time in the hospital or recovering at home sending messages or posting glorified ads for Rejuvinat, which lets reps "work from anywhere." Instead, I heal, I rest, and I spend more time writing. I also start online coursework in Certified Recovery Coaching and Addiction Awareness. I am really passionate about learning and sharing my alcohol recovery journey. I always thought I was helping people with Rejuvinat, but what I find as I begin sharing more of my story out loud is that I can help people in a way that doesn't prey on them, that doesn't require their financial buy-in. All of these conflicting thoughts are a moot point, though. Because the checks are still coming in from my downline, making me believe there is no way I can walk away from the amount of money I am making. I keep having the same conversation with myself, going back and forth on the pros and cons of leaving. How do you walk away from money that you use for your family? It is during this time that I earn my highest paycheck: a whopping $40,000. And like any pair of golden handcuffs, the more you have, the more you spend, making it even harder to automatically reduce our household income by five figures every month.

As they say, money talks. And it's why so many women stay stuck, why people like Serena and me don't leave, because we seemingly can't afford to—the pain of leaving seems worse than the pain of staying.

The reviews from my talk at Convention have only made my celebrity status skyrocket. In fact, I am now one of Rejuvinat's biggest circuit speakers. I am traveling more than ever, which, as you can imagine, has caused more strain at home and only added to the guilt I already had about not being there for my kids. But like many women in MLMs who were jobless or part-time workers before the MLM, I feel like I still have a right to this version of freedom. I spent a decade chasing children while my husband worked fourteen-hour days and traversed the country for work. Isn't it my turn?

And with the cancer diagnoses and treatments, I feel like I deserve to be free, which includes being fangirled and spoiled. Even though I am sober, I still need a break from my life.

I am whisked off to France, Mexico, and New York within a few months' span, on the company's tab, but on my taxes at the end of the year. And again, we always spend more than the allotted amount from the company. More money in, more money out. It is a whirlwind. And yes, it's incredible. But every time, I am just sharing my story to sell whatever needs to be sold at that particular moment. Consultants losing faith in the company? Throw in some stuff about belief with your tale of redemption! Volume tanking? Toss in some inspirational BS about reading more personal development! I am getting burned out, not on sharing my recovery story, but on allowing it to be co-opted to indoctrinate women into Rejuvinat—something I swore I would never do. I know that every time I stand on a stage and talk about the pain of my experience, someone is connecting to it and assuming that the MLM is the remedy for their own trauma, which I know isn't true. And I can no longer ignore what I am seeing: how the sales are benefiting me, and not everyone I brought into the company. After all, I've taken months and months off for my recovery, and my paychecks keep coming.

I can't deny it any longer: The most successful reps (like me) keep earning money because new recruits and products are continually recycled; it's basically a continuous collapse, with the people at the bottom of the pyramid consistently being crushed. Because, assuming the MLM lasts long enough, a whole new generation awaits a newly repackaged opportunity, and the MLM can continue exploiting. I stay at the top despite how little I work, and the people at the bottom fail to rank up despite how hard they work. And it becomes harder for me to sell the dream that I know no longer exists.

The Seattle Rejuvinat bubble is beginning to burst, people are quitting, and I just don't have it in me to convince them to stay.

I am flown out to New York, on a trip that will include a "surprise guest speaker" on day one, a "business meeting" for the tippy-top leaders on day two, and a final closing session on day three, for which I'll be the keynote. As most top consultants know but would never admit, these "business meetings" are all smoke and mirrors; top leaders are invited to a "secret" meeting with corporate where you sign NDAs and talk about programs that are already decided, pretending you have a say in them. It's all for optics, so you can share a selfie of yourself signing an NDA on Instagram ("Ooohhh, look at me with the secrets!") to further indoctrinate the downline into being excited about the possibility of "achieving" these trips. It also instills a sense of agency in the higher-ups, to keep us believing that the corporation gives a shit about what we think and what we say (they don't). But while I hate things like this, it's still a trip, and Serena will be there. We're going to spend the weekend seeing *Hamilton* and eating amazing food. If we have to tolerate a fake business meeting or another self-help guru, and she has to hear my alcohol sob story again, so be it.

As you can probably already see, the process of waking up to the great ruse that is multilevel marketing is not necessarily a rapid or linear one. If you speak with anyone who has ever left a cult, they will tell you they had their moment of realization months, if not years, before leaving. There was a crack where the truth slipped in, and then, slowly, began to flood. Even if the indoctrination to remain loyal to the cult (or, little difference, the MLM in my case) runs strong, the cracks only get bigger and bigger every day.

As I sit in another conference room, listening to another big-name speaker, a massive influencer whose blog and books are consumed by every white middle-class woman in America, I feel the crack widen. I'll give Rejuvinat credit—they've got their speakers pegged, because they're always the perfect combination of righteousness and faux self-deprecation. "I know I'm right, but look, y'all, I'm also crazyyyy!" They become false idols, even if they are self-described "experts" with no actual training or credentials.

Real self-help would entail using critical thinking to understand where your information is coming from. If a self-help motivational speaker isn't qualified and is trying to sell you something, they won't want you to analyze where they're getting their information. Better to remind you to "believe" and "have faith" and follow their unproven system of operation than to dig any deeper about why the hell you should listen to them.

We kick off day one with our "guru," a self-help speaker named Caroline. She is bubbly and cute in her super-relatable pair of jeans and a floppy sweatshirt that falls perfectly over one shoulder, with blondish beach waves. Just the right amount of authenticity to make us believe that she wasn't up at four in the morning getting a blowout. She gushes about bravery, a very common talking point among these motivational speakers.

It's so funny to me that these gurus validate the "bravery" it takes to be in an MLM. "Oh, look at you, being unfollowed, unfriended, outcasted! Look at you, still making it!" Pay no attention to the fact that the people who unfollowed you probably just didn't want to get sold to, or that if you've been outcasted, it's likely your own doing because you're told to block the haters. You're not a revolutionary; you're simply perpetrating the financial exploitation of women seeking community and being drained of their finances by the process.

And here you are, with all these other women in the room who feel the same way and have "suffered" the same injustices! Because nothing will bond a group of people together like mutually perceived slights. Divide and conquer is real, but so is insult and band together.

Caroline knows what's she's doing even if she's not in an MLM. The bravery argument strengthens the resolve to stay in the business even longer, even if it goes against both intuition and common sense. I have my foot out the door, but as Caroline flicks a stray piece of hair out of her face, even I have to admit that what she's saying is pretty damn compelling.

When you join an MLM, you are a contractor, not a superhero. You're not brave. But you *are* a victim—a victim of financial exploitation, a victim of toxic positivity, and for many of us, victims of our own white supremacy. Because this constant push for personal development is actually just a symptom of a world that requires perfection to be in community—and perfection in this context is defined by white, Christian, upper-middle-class women.

Caroline hits all the talking points, but the real defining moment comes on day two: our fake business meeting. All the top leaders are freaking out because the bubble is starting to burst everywhere, not just Seattle. One woman cries about having to sell her (second) house because her paycheck has decreased so much. Another complains that she has to fly coach instead of first class. As I listen to the protests from these women, I wonder if any of them have any financial sense, or perspective. Did they all put *every* egg in this basket? I bet they aren't so pleased that they retired their husbands anymore. My lack of empathy for their complaints only adds to my mounting cynicism.

It has become clear that the "growth plan" that everyone had been so thrilled about the past few years—opening in Australia and Japan—was only carried out because we'd become saturated in the United States and Canada. Rejuvinat (any MLM, really) will assure you that's not why, but none of us can make sense of it. Corporate has continued to raise the bar on titles and rewards, making it more difficult to reach the things that keep people engaged in the first place. The monthly car reward amount was lowered, but the title needed to earn the lowered car payment was increased. So, you have to do more hustling and Tetris to get less money. It makes no sense. My car allotment was reduced from \$1,000 to \$750 per month. Never mind that the payment is \$1,950—so much for that all-caps FREE car, eh? I start thinking about my downline, how discouraged they will be, and how guilty I feel for being here, on another "free" trip (not really) while they are going to have to work *harder* to strive for anything, stacking my gold while they count their pennies.

"I don't get it. They tout these sales figures, and they're pulling back money and rewards and making qualifications more difficult if more people are achieving? It makes no sense!" I whisper to Serena as we sit in the very back of the room (on purpose) and listen to the new CEO announce all these program changes.

"I'm shaking my head," Serena responds, literally shaking her head. "I mean, look at this," she gestures. "This hotel is not cheap, our rooms aren't cheap, and they flew us all out here to tell us something that could have been put in an email. And on top of this, they're pulling back rewards?"

Serena feels the same way I do. We are skeptical, and our husbands are *very* skeptical. But our husbands also like the income. It's easy for them to detach from the emotional and mental labor that Rejuvinat requires, because all they see is money in a bank account. For Serena's husband, and even Kale, putting up with some culty shit isn't that big of a deal.

Serena scoffs and picks up a Kate Spade bag, one of our swag rewards (again, to post on social media). She's right, once again: This trip is unnecessarily lavish, ridiculously over the top. Yet the women in our downline haven't been able to experience anything like this, aside from reward trips and retreats they've had to buy into, or the gifts we give them out of guilt. Now, even the small reward trips they've been able to earn, the prizes they've been keeping in their sights, are even further out of reach?

When you look at the numbers, it ends up making much more sense. In a report published by Robert L. FitzPatrick, the longest-standing MLMs (Amway, Avon, Herbalife, Primerica, and Nu Skin, among many others) now face a no-growth future. Saturation has finally caught up with the scheme. The possibility of enrolling more people than the millions that quit each year will eventually run out. While saturation for recruits should be obvious now (no possibility of the requisite number of recruits to join your downline so it can become sufficiently profitable), we are now seeing that the dinosaur MLMs that have seemingly stood the test of time are shrinking, even as they falsely claim to offer an unlimited income opportunity. Even if companies move from country to country to try to keep up with saturation, eventually, you run out of countries. And though the MLMs continue to expand to other countries, they don't seem to thrive as much as they do here. In places like Europe, there are tighter laws around ingredients and marketing, and many other countries have stricter regulations around MLMs. Combined with the rags-to-riches storyline that is woven into our culture, the American circuit of motivational speakers, and devotion to hard work in exchange for wealth, MLMs are seemingly as American as apple pie.

The corporate team continues to talk about changes in our programs, and also changes in what we can/should share on social media. Many things are happening around this time in the social media landscape. Instagram and Facebook have become more of a marketplace to sell things, so the "free" sales of MLM don't go far, since the platforms don't promote posts that aren't sponsored or paid ads. A few years ago, Serena actually brought this up with corporate as a potential problem, but they brushed her off. We now exchange glances as they spout off the exact scenario she'd previously described. It wasn't long ago that you could post about a Rejuvinat sale, and it was like blood in a shark tank—so many people would purchase the promo, ask for the sample, and inquire about the new product. In the early and mid-2010s, Facebook didn't have the complex algorithms and filters that weeded out MLM posts, so sales spread like wildfire on the platform. But now? A post might get two likes and zero comments, and the likes are from other Rejuvinat reps. Facebook even discontinued their "live sale" feature to discourage MLM reps from conducting sales over their platform. The social media algorithms don't like MLMs, and I kind of have to give them props for that. After all, why would they want their platform to be a sales page for a product they aren't getting a cut of?

Not only that, but at this point, you can buy *everything* online. Great supplements, good skincare, even prescriptions, can be mailed with nothing more than a virtual appointment. Why would someone buy from a chick in an MLM when they can get actual prescription-strength ingredients and anything under the sun from actual doctors delivered to their door? The reality is, we're way too expensive for what we offer. Because so many layers of payments are built into the product (every level in the pyramid gets a cut!), the prices aren't remotely competitive.

The last factor (and probably the biggest at this point) is the ascendancy of influencer culture: the personal brand. I'm going to admit that I still don't understand it, and though I get called a "sober influencer," I cringe at the term. It's 2018, and Instagram is now flooded with social media influencers, mostly celebrities or public figures with huge followings, who are recommending stuff from companies like Sephora, Amazon, and Nordstrom. Between 2014 and 2016, statistics show that consumers were beginning to be more influenced by social media marketing and influencers. Influencers are the new advertising campaign. Nothing wrong with that, except it makes it impossible for MLMs to compete. The products are easily available online, for anyone to order— and who *doesn't* trust Kim Kardashian more than your neighbor down the street when it comes to eye-cream recommendations? Plus, Kim won't be in your DMs bugging you to join her team. Influencer culture perfected what MLM bossbabes have been trying to do for years.

Rejuvinat is realizing it has to change its social media strategy *fast*— which means, no more silly graphics with platitudinous buzzwords and products nobody cares about. Now, we are being asked to sell *ourselves*. Sure, we've been posting this way daily on Facebook, having Facebook sales parties, and texting and messaging our prospects. But Instagram influencing is different. Posting once per day is not enough; now we have Instagram stories (and later, TikTok), which requires staying relevant 24/7. Rejuvinat is trying to emulate influencer culture; we're now supposed to post filtered photos, the prettiest product layouts and curated content, multiple stories per day, and targeted hashtags—with the goal of gaining as many followers as possible. As someone who is working hard to be more authentic, I want to barf. And yet, I am still gaining followers. I understand the need for this, as the platform has served me well. Social media has been such a necessary evil.

Serena and I eye-roll at each other for the next hour while we're coached on how to build our "personal brand." In a way, this is a genius move for MLM, because they can reduce their liability; instead of selling products, we can sell *ourselves* and people will (allegedly) buy our products as a side effect! If you do something that is against policy, as an independent contractor, the company can just axe you, instead of assuming liability for anything you were saying. We are encouraged to make personal-lifestyle videos, selling the opportunity without *saying* the opportunity. "Join my team, but I can't tell you what that is until you DM me." Not only that, but our life has to become a part of our brand; we need to become 24/7 personal reality shows in order to be successful. Going to the store with your kids? Share a video! Make sure you show up in Insta stories every day and post every day, so you can stay relevant and at the top of people's minds! Hashtag that shit! Oh, and by the way, lip-sync and dance, too! It's an amplified version of what we're already doing, but now we have to do it every hour of every day. I hate everything they are saying. Serena and I duck out of the session early.

"Why would we try to become influencers? What happened to fitting this into the nooks and crannies of our lives? Now we need to be on blast 24/7?" I fume to Serena, probably a little too loudly. Serena has worked in (actual) marketing and advertising before, so she has some understanding about the industry and how it's changing,

"To be honest, it's an insult to actual influencers to associate with us," she says. "They get paid to promote a product; we don't. We only get paid if people buy it. What they're doing is straight-up paid advertising. We're asking people, actually, *begging* people to join us lately. Not the same."

She's right. Despite every bossbabe regurgitating the line "Get paid to post on social media!" you absolutely do not get paid to post on social media as an MLM recruit; you only get paid when someone purchases. In contrast, an influencer gets paid for a *paid* endorsement. They have control over the brands and products they endorse and a choice in who they partner with; they negotiate their own deals, are transparent about promotional posts (though some have been called out for not being transparent), and have comparative control over the process. They don't recruit human beings or post and pray for a sale. It's a huge distinction. Though MLM bossbabes will refer to themselves as paid influencers, or compare themselves to paid influencers, they are not. Say what you want about celebrities; maybe they use the products, maybe they don't, but at least they're receiving a check for attaching their name and face to a product or service—end of story.

Serena continues, clearly burned that they brought up the algorithm and MLM post suppression, "Isn't it funny that they didn't even blame Facebook or Instagram? They blame us. We just need to work harder, believe more, change our marketing strategy. What a crock of shit." She's right. Given her expertise, I understand how frustrating this must be. She is disgusted by so much of what they are saying, but the reality is, she needs the money Rejuvinat provides; she's paying for her mom's assisted living. And she has a family just like I do, all of whom have grown accustomed to her paycheck. But the veil has been lifted, especially since she also quit drinking. In some ways, we check each other's consciences, and yet, probably also keep each other stuck in Rejuvinat.

At no point during this meeting (or any meeting, come to think of it) does Rejuvinat ever admit to culpability for anything. When we ask why our Facebook posts aren't getting as many likes, we get rote responses: "You just need to market differently, sell yourselves! Social media is changing, so get with the program!" If we ask why numbers are dropping: "Lack of belief and work ethic! Your team must not want it badly enough!" If we ask why so few new consultants are joining and questioning market saturation: "You're enrolling too many customers, not enough new recruits! You've gotten lazy with your recruiting!"

Throughout my time with Rejuvinat, it was a constant assault of victim blaming, which we then turned around so we could "duplicate" their rhetoric down to our teams, telling them the same thing. And how could we possibly prove it wrong? It's a sacred science nobody could crack; we were constantly told that *we* were the reason things weren't working out, so we only had ourselves to doubt. And if we were at the top of the hierarchy and our paychecks were starting to dip and our teams were shrinking, who else did we have to blame but our downline and ourselves?

In the age of the personal brand, people are expected to act like corporations but aren't held accountable, as corporations are. Influencer culture monetizes the human desire for belonging and intimacy, but it's false intimacy. You feel like you know influencers because you're invited into their homes and their lives, but they don't know you. In a 2021 article for the *New York Times*, "When Grown-Ups Have Imaginary Friends," Jessica Grose explains this para-social relationship, which happens when there is an illusion of friendship between a spectator and a performer. Social media has only added another dimension, because sometimes the performer (influencer) will interact with you! Or rather, her social media assistant will interact with you. Regardless, the feelings we have for these influencers are virtually the same as the feelings we have for people in our real life, even though the influencer has no idea we exist.

With influencer culture began the rise in gurus, self-help speakers, and personal coaches, all there to help you "get unstuck." It's the reason our Conventions always had people like Mel Robbins, Jen Sincero, Gary

John Bishop, Russell Brunson, Brendon Burchard, Rachel Hollis, Amy Porterfield, Jenna Kutcher, Marie Forleo, Tony Robbins, and Jay Shetty, among dozens of others—people who had supposedly pulled themselves up by their bootstraps and made it big because they "just believed." But they didn't just believe; they all had influence, power, and money. And they made (and still make) tons of money speaking for the MLM circuit because their messages are so similar. They are all intertwined in a web of click funnels (web pages that lead you to other web pages and sales pages) and affiliate links (sales links that are embedded in everything from news articles to Instagram pages), spouting the same message to whoever will pay them for their motivational speak. MLMs co-opted this bullshit: "Look at Jeff Bezos in his tiny apartment office; he was so poor and now he owns Amazon!" Okay, sure, maybe he had a tiny office, but his parents gave him $300,000 to invest in Amazon. And in 1995.

This isn't to discount any of the aforementioned influencers' achievements, but we bought their books and paid money for their conferences and held on to every word, precisely because they told us we didn't need money. "All you need to do is believe!" Who doesn't want to eat that shit up? Who doesn't want to believe that you're in charge of your own destiny? It sounds great, but it doesn't pay the bills. And it doesn't even begin to dig into the truth of how systemic flaws trump this doctrine of personal self-determinism. The dream that's being sold is not available to most.

And it definitely doesn't pay the bills if you're on food stamps and come from generational poverty. Rachael Kay Albers, a disruptive voice in marketing, stated in an article for *The Week*, "Fake it till you make it is no longer just the stuff of scammers; it's increasingly the cost of doing business with an internet culture that privileges perception over true innovation. Who has time to painstakingly build a reputation when the girlboss next door can invent hers, seemingly overnight, with a little help from Facetune and Rent the Runway?"

These people stand up on stage and sell the dream, all telling us that we need to level up to become extraordinary—but why is an average life not good enough? Why, in order to have a happy life, is it assumed that you need to constantly hustle and earn the top rewards and titles and biggest paychecks no matter the circumstances?

These gurus sell white supremacy, nothing more. It has nothing to do with greatness or improving society; it's all about getting caught up in the hamster wheel that is late-stage capitalism.

SERENA AND I go out on the town in New York City, heading to dinner and Broadway. It's a beautiful night in a beautiful, vibrant place. As galling as the trip has proven to be, I still feel grateful that we are able to experience this. But before dinner, we make a pit stop: I meet with a publisher to whom I'd sent my manuscript several weeks earlier. We were introduced through a mutual friend, and we've been corresponding via email and phone. I consider it kismet that she emailed me back last week and that I would be in town, so I asked if she'd be willing to meet. I'm not totally sure what I'm doing, and though I pretty much trust the process, I bring Serena with me just in case I'm being catfished by an axe murderer. You never know.

Lucky for us, she is not an axe murderer. She's a gorgeous brunette named Anna, and she's fantastically dressed and right on time.

After a few introductions and small talk, she leans over the table and grabs my arm. "Your work is really good. I think you can add more. I think we can go even deeper with your story, but this is something that needs to be out there."

Serena gives me a side-eye "I told you!" and all three of us laugh.

"The one thing that might make this difficult," she says as she pulls her hand back, "is the MLM girlboss stuff."

Shit.

For the record, I now hate the term *girlboss*. I used it during my time in Rejuvinat, along with *bossbabe*, *She-EO*, and other infantilizing monikers for women in business, but I now know that there is nothing less empowering than these titles. The term comes from a 2014 book called *#girlboss*, by Sophia Amoruso, which was a phenomenon (spoiler, the Netflix show tanked) and was celebrated by MLM women everywhere. Fast-forward to 2015—Amoruso stepped down from her company, and in 2016, she filed for bankruptcy. Ironically, the same year she was named one of *Forbes*'s richest women. She was accused of poor communication and a toxic work culture (sound familiar?) yet still went on to found Girlboss Media in 2017. They put together girlboss rallies and instructional events (which cost $500 to $1,400 a pop), supposedly "creating a platform for women to be entrepreneurial," with no actual business training of any kind. Then, in October 2020, she stepped down once again from Girlboss Media, citing the pandemic and declining revenue as her reasons for leaving.

So, maybe she's a girl and isn't the best boss? But she's not the only girlboss to be worshipped like an idol, only to be pulled off her pedestal. Sheryl Sandberg, the former COO of Facebook, wrote *Lean In* in 2013, a treatise all about the lack of women in government and upper leadership roles. It was an instant bestseller, and Sandberg was praised for being a lone female in a male-driven tech world. She has since been slammed for her elitist attitude and accused of being tone-deaf to the struggles of women in the workplace, and of mothers—especially single mothers. Her critics say that she tells women to "lean in" and then avoids doing the same herself; she's perceived as a COO who avoids engaging in the actual crises of women in the workplace by offering anything other than inconsiderate advice.

Then, of course, there is Rachel Hollis.

How much do I need to say about her? She received a ton of flack for wanting to be relatable, but then not relatable, and then back to relatable once more—and for selling expensive conferences promising to disclose her personal secrets to success, when her actual secret was marrying a rich Disney exec—and then selling expensive marriage conference tickets, even though she would later admit that her marriage to that exec was actually falling apart, while simultaneously patting herself on the back for being the reason she's able to have a "sweet woman clean her toilets" twice a week because she gets up at four in the morning every day. The meritocracy queen fell from her throne in a major way.

So, there you go. The takeaway? Female CEOs can be just as shitty as male CEOs because all of them have been indoctrinated into hustle culture, which is just a symptom of white supremacy. *Maybe* women are influenced by power and greed, like anyone of any gender, which can lead down a path of exploitation.

These days, *girlboss* is just an internet meme and joke: "Gaslight, Gatekeep, Girlboss!" Even if it started from a positive intention, to empower women into leadership, it's completely materialistic, commodified hashtag. It's performative feminism, where participation in change is only as meaningful as a slogan on a T-shirt or social media. It doesn't liberate us; it keeps women right where we are. So basically, it's the perfect name for women in MLM.

Because there's no empowerment in MLM. You're making money off the backs of people in the name of female empowerment. You're not leaving a legacy or making an impact. You're recruiting people into a failed system so you can rank up and make more money. You're expected to work more, be less authentic, and talk to anyone with a heartbeat and a credit card number. Recruit everywhere you go. There are plenty of white women out here emulating Amoruso, Hollis, and Sandberg, and co-opting feminism for profit, with zero intention of ever lifting anyone up. So I understand why the publisher is concerned about the girlboss MLM stuff. Who would take me seriously when I've aligned myself with a joke?

After our *Hamilton* performance, Serena and I both walk out of Rodgers Theatre on a high. Until we check our phones. We have both been blown up by multiple other top leaders and some of the corporate team, asking why we ducked out of the seminar early. It wouldn't be a leadership event if our behavior wasn't being monitored and controlled, after all. I have an out in that I still have to speak at the consultant training session tomorrow. "Tell them I had to practice my speech and didn't want to walk back to our hotel alone!" I whisper to Serena. I'll do a fourth step for my little white lie tomorrow.

By now, Serena and I have bared our hearts and souls to each other about how we're really beginning to feel.

"I'm so done with this. I feel completely exploited," I lament. "They're having me talk about 'not caring what others think about you.' I shit you not. And it's ironic because I *do* care. That's why I don't think I can keep doing this. I want to write my book and finish my course-work and completely put Rejuvinat to the side."

I figure I have another few good years left, so I can continue to collect a check and let it ride until it dries up. And the way the business is going, the changes the company is making, and the fact that I don't have it in me to bring anyone else into this scheme, I know it will eventually dry up. Over the last year, my monthly check has significantly decreased to around $25,000 a month, but it's still a lot to walk away from.

Serena nods. "I know how you feel, but can't we just do *this*?" She gestures around at the breathtaking skyline. "What if we just stayed in and just did this stuff? I mean, how fun was today? Minus the Rejuvinat junk."

I start to respond, "But why can't we just do this stuff anyway—" and before I finish the sentence, I know why. Because we wouldn't make something like this happen. Because life, kids, spouses, and responsibilities get in the way when it's just "for fun," but since it's "for work," we set it in stone on the calendar. Isn't that why so many of us join MLMs in the first place? Because we want an excuse for an escape or a village? Maybe the only way to gain a village and a break is to buy them. The real question is: Is it worth it?

What am I willing to overlook for $25,000 a month? Apparently, still a lot.

"Oh God, another text, from Kimberly this time." She freezes, then bursts into laughter. "She asked if we could meet before the session tomorrow so she can pray over us."

"Over my dead body, Kimberly!" I groan.

I generally tolerate the shoutouts to God at our Conventions, even though I find them inappropriate. Multiple times in biz ops and presentations, from both corporate and top leaders, I have heard the message in one version or another: "You would be more successful in this business if you found Jesus. This business is a gift from God, so treat it as such." The worst was when I once heard a top leader at a retreat saying that Jewish people needed to convert to Christianity because the rapture was coming. I thought my ears were going to bleed.

Christianity and MLMs are not compatible, and I don't mean that you can't be a Christian and be in an MLM, but bringing other people into your business opportunity doesn't align with what I see as Christian principles. I think it has something to do with trading in the temple. So many of the top leaders in Rejuvinat are white and Christian, and brag about being raised in a church, and about how much they love Jesus, even singing hymns on their social media channels. They preach unwavering faith with a clear absence of critical thinking, which only bleeds over into the MLM. "If you can't accept this, you need more personal development, or the Bible, sweetie! You have a negative mindset—that's the devil talking!" Not to mention, the pervasive purity culture around Christianity infiltrates everything, from the judgment around what people are wearing and saying, and how they act, to the expectation that MLM reps walk around with a shit-eating grin and a good-girl disposition—always obeying, never questioning.

Christians are supposed to be good stewards of resources by giving to the needy, loving thy neighbor as thyself, etc., which means in theory, they should want nothing to do with exploitative, unethical ventures like MLMs. Now, I personally believed I was helping people for a long time, so I can completely understand why anyone, Christian or not, becomes convinced that their MLM is actually helping thy neighbor. However, when you recruit someone, you are putting *your* financial gain first, no question. If it didn't benefit you, you would never recruit them.

Greed is considered a sin, so monetizing relationships is the least Christian thing you can do. Also, MLMs go against Christianity's focus on family and community because it strains family relationships when a business depends on talking about a product or biz op nonstop to anyone who will listen. Alienating loved ones will bring your credibility into question, and people will lose trust. But the object of capitalism is profit, and it can allow some to become wealthy while others can't afford to eat, for the sake of "getting mine." And if Christianity is seen as "truth," people who stand outside the dominant cultural normal of being white and Christian will ultimately be demonized, "deserving what they get." This ties into the idyllic vision of a majority-white, Christian nation over which God is lovingly smiling while castigating all outsiders.

Hard pass on being prayed over, Kim.

I have one more day left in this conference, and today it's my keynote that will instruct and inspire. It's also an open attendance day, which is another retention event; any consultant who can pay (a lot) to join can be there—and clearly, many are, as the conference room is packed! They have FOMO from our last two days of secret meetings and the sneak peeks we've posted online (ahh, if they only knew). They can't wait to get training from the top. I remember back to when I was in the same seat, fawning over Kimberly before she became so intent on praying over me.

It's nice being outside the bubble of Seattle, since for the most part, these women are from the East Coast, and we have no financial ties with any of them. There will be some photo ops (oh, look, a balloon arch) and small talk, but it will be fairly low-key. I have given this same talk different ways a dozen times, so it's no biggie, but this time all the top earners are here to listen. Who knows? Maybe I can inspire a few of them to slow down the ten o'clock mimosa train. Not likely, but we'll see.

Serena gives me a thumbs-up, and I return a wink and start my talk. The consultants in the back of the room are gazing directly at me, hanging on my every word, but the top leaders in the front row are chatting among themselves, phones in hands, not paying attention to anything I'm saying. And many of them are already tipsy. Seriously, ladies? I find it rude that they're talking during my presentation, but more than that, what kind of example are they setting for their teams and the consultants who are here? It's hypocritical.

But then, I remember—it doesn't matter. They get paid regardless, and so do I. They don't need to listen. In fact, *nobody* needs to listen. As I continue to speak, gazing out into the conference room, starring as today's guru, it's like I am seeing it all for the first time—the fake friends, the toxic positivity, the cult of personal development, the curated perfection, and the FOMO. As I scan the nearly all-white room filled with modern-day Stepford Wives, I am torn between compassion and contempt: compassion for the women who paid to be here, and contempt for myself, for continuing to sell this impossible dream.

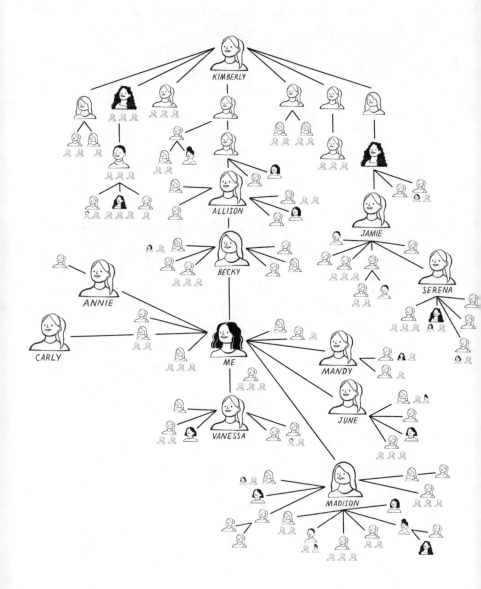

KIMBERLY

ALLISON

JAMIE

ANNIE

BECKY

SERENA

CARLY

ME

MANDY

VANESSA

JUNE

MADISON

Cult Defectors Pay the Price

I spent a few years selling nutritional supplements and coaching for an MLM, but I felt gross calling myself a coach when I'd never actually been trained in anything. I loved the workouts and posted videos of myself doing them, but when I inevitably had the conversation getting people to join me, I just felt like a fraud. When I sent in my termination form, none of my MLM "friends" ever talked to me again.

—ARIANA, former MLM rep

The problem with knowledge is, now you know. I feel like Eve in the Garden of Eden. I've eaten the apple and can never go back.

I'm in Nashville at what will turn out to be my last Rejuvinat Convention, filled with equal parts dread and excitement. I have agreed to speak again, ignoring my own desire not to participate in this one. I'm also being inducted into the million-dollar earner club. Yes, I'm one of them now. Although as I've learned, the term *million-dollar earner* is deceptive, falling in line with much of the MLM vocabulary. It means that a consultant has earned a million dollars total, over the course of their entire tenure, before taxes. Now, I've been in Rejuvinat almost six years, and $1 million divided over that time is an average of $166,000 per year. Still nothing to sneeze at! But after taxes and expenses, cut that in half, and you have around an $80,000 take-home. Still great income, but it certainly doesn't match the "millionaire" lifestyle of the rich and famous that is portrayed on social media, or what you would expect to accompany a title like million-dollar earner. And of course, it comes with stage recognition, to rub it in the faces of all the women losing money. Not excited for that.

What I *am* excited for is my Nashville book-launch event.

My book came out last week, and I've gone on a promo tour from Seattle to Los Angeles to New York, and now Nashville. The response has been awesome. It's amazing to me how many women can identify with at least one part of my story, whether it's a traumatic childhood experience, sexual assault, or substance abuse. I can't say I was surprised, but it was validating that I felt my words helped people, and writing the book was cathartic for me. I've finished up my addiction awareness coursework and recovery coaching certification, and I've been working with an organization doing recovery coaching on the side, which is incredibly fulfilling. In fact, pursuing something that has real meaning has only made my work at Rejuvinat feel that much shallower and more predatory, and yet, the reason I could afford to do the training and coursework at all was because of my Rejuvinat money. The cognitive dissonance still remains—that I'm able to do "this other thing" that's meaningful because of something I've swiftly come to view as harmful.

Although my paycheck is drying up bit by bit each month (there's been a mass exodus from Rejuvinat lately, thanks to all the policy and payment structure changes, brought on by saturation and declining revenue), it's still a lot, around $20,000 per month, especially since I don't have to do much for it, leaving me time to focus on recovery coaching, write a book, and go on a book tour. Again, all of these things require a financial investment up front, so I relied on the Rejuvinat income. But I suppose if I really looked at the numbers, I would have also seen how much money was still going out: product purchases, gifts for my team every time I earned a trip, upgrades to hotels and airline tickets, and outfits for trips and Convention. This year alone, I've gone to Mexico (again), Spain, San Francisco, and New Orleans. Every time, I spend *well* over the allotted amount from the company, and again, everything is added to my taxes as income at the end of the year. I've been showered with a Louis Vuitton suitcase, diamond jewelry, a computer, and so much more. Meanwhile, my downline has continued to see nothing. My guilt has me purchasing things for them, which only detracts from my bottom line.

I am actually stunned at my profit and loss statement from my accountant for this past year, though my annual 1099 was sky high. After taxes and expenses, it is much lower than I'd expected—over 75 percent lower.

As I look at the filing from my accountant, I am excited to see I had $370,000 in gross earnings, but then, of that, a whopping $100,000 of it was in "free" trips, "free" products, promotional items, car allotments, reward gifts (like that diamond necklace and the Louis Vuitton suitcase) listed as income. I spent another $15,000 on overages for trips that were out of pocket, $10,000 on products (for myself as well as to "help" team members or fill quotas or titles), $10,000 on gifts and incentives for my team, and $5,000 on promotional materials, biz ops, and other "business expenses" like postage, etc. But as I continue reading, I see I also spent $22,000 on childcare, $8,000 on clothes and shoes, and $36,000 on my personal assistant. After taxes, my income was $85,000. Now, $85,000 is a great income, but I was living a $400,000 salary lifestyle on less than $90,000 in take-home pay.

I realize that if my profit is so low compared to my "paycheck," those of my downline must be even lower. As a business-building exercise (that ends up backfiring because my team realizes how little they are taking home), I have my team members fill out a profit and loss statement of their own and calculate the money they are making hourly. The results are astounding.

Megan Williams, a mental-health counselor who has been working in the mental-health field since 2005, spent three years as a rep for an MLM. During that time, she experienced many psychological affronts and decided to use her expertise as a therapist to help others who chose to leave an MLM. She wrote a workbook called *Cutting Ties* that offers a process to help those who are leaving an MLM and has an amazing example of how to make a profit and loss statement, which is what we used. It includes a list of all possible expenses including professional photos, childcare, travel costs, increases to internet or phone plans, new clothing, samples, website fees, and so many more, as well as instructions for calculating your actual hourly rate.

My team and I are totally blindsided by the results. I realize that most of my key players—June, Annie, Mandy, even Vanessa—are basically dumping money into the machine just to stay active, and most are barely breaking even. Despite their "sales" being in the tens of thousands on my corporate-provided sales software, and despite being on my top-ten leader lists every month, they are most certainly not killing it like their social media profiles would make you believe. The truth is, those sky-high numbers for the leaderboards include the sales of the people underneath them, and while the sales volume looks high, the amount they make off each sale is minuscule. Their monthly paychecks are in the high hundreds or low thousands, but thanks to taxes, expenses, required purchases, nonpaid trips and overages, products purchased under family members, and other things they aren't taking into account, these women are making *maybe* a few hundred dollars a month. And with the hours they are putting in and the wage per hour they calculated? They could make more working at Starbucks. *Much* more. The ones not on my top-ten list? They're losing money, no question.

This adds more conflict: First, how can I stay in this when I explicitly know how much people are losing? And two, how can I have brought them in and not continue to stick it out myself? I figure as long as I am here and still showering them with love and gifts and get-togethers at our conventions and conferences, it will be worth it to them, and it will also ease my guilt. At this point, I should have told them to leave, but I didn't.

Unknowingly, I am love bombing them to perpetuate their own sunk cost fallacy.

Plus, how can I quit *now*? The village of consultants has been so supportive of my book. Becky, Allison, and so many others in the greater consultant community, even some of the other top leaders, were part of my advance reader team and loved the book, posted about it, and left great reviews. It makes me feel guilty for pulling away from Rejuvinat, so I stay mildly engaged; when corporate once again asks me to speak, I can't say no. At this point, I still believe that while maybe this won't be my "only thing," I will keep Rejuvinat going because I love the community. And I truly do; many are still my good friends.

Becky is the ultimate sunny-side-up optimist, whom I also consider a friend. Not only is she my upline, but we've vacationed together. Our kids are friends. Our friendship goes beyond proximity. So, by this point, I have finally talked to her about how I feel about the company. She had already felt me pulling away and knew I wasn't happy with all the corporate changes. When I turned down the last keynote speech I was offered, before this Nashville outing, she asked me why, and I told her that I felt like the company was using my story to sell the opportunity and products. She could see my point, though I'm not sure she was totally on board with the sentiment. She also knows I still harbor guilt about my downline's lack of success.

"Look, Emily, I'm a lifer. I love everything about this company. I'll never leave. *Never*. And you've been the biggest leader on my team. I would be appreciative of you no matter what you decided to do. But you built this. The only way you fail is if you quit! Why quit now? If you decide to step back, do the bare minimum, and take a check, that is totally your right."

In her own way, I feel like she is giving me permission to step back, even though she does have a few key people call and text to try to reengage me. Allison and a few other women in my upline send me texts encouraging me to stay; they share the same sentiment—that I only fail if I quit. I listen to Becky, for better or worse, and I decide to keep pushing my nagging feelings to the back of my mind. Though her words offer me relief because I finally admitted to her how I was feeling, they also keep me stuck even longer, which perhaps was the point, to begin with. After all, she still makes over $40,000 per month, much of which comes from my downline. And if I looked more closely, I should have recognized the platitudes—that she was employing the same cult techniques to make me think I was free to go, but also shaming me for wanting to leave.

I have already detached so much from Rejuvinat. I rarely post on Instagram anymore about the business. In fact, I started a new Instagram account after I decided to publish the book, since most of my forty thousand Instagram followers are the bossbabes already in the company. Plus, a fellow recovery advocate told me that mixing the two would be a deterrent to book buyers, clients, or potential followers. Our conversation reminded me of the caution my sponsor expressed to me a couple years earlier about mixing business with my recovery.

"If you mix an MLM with your sobriety story, clients will think you're going to try to sell them shit when they work with you," Laura, a recovery advocate whom I highly respect and consider a friend, tells me over the phone one day.

"But I'll be sharing my book on there, as well as my recovery coaching—isn't that selling?"

"Apples and oranges. When you're sharing a book and sharing a service, you aren't asking your audience to sell shit for you. You did a ton of work and put in labor and personal effort to make a product— your book—and now you're asking people to buy it. And with coaching, you've put a ton of work in to be trained and certified to perform a legitimate service. You're selling those tangible things. You're not asking people to then turn around and write books or become coaches themselves. It wouldn't be an issue if you were just selling eye cream; that's not what you're doing with Rejuvinat. You're trying to get them to join you in your pyramid. So as long as you're doing both on the same platform, people are going to think in the back of their mind that you're going to eventually attempt to recruit them to join your team. At least, that's what I would be thinking if I didn't know you the way I do."

She's right on both counts; I don't want people to think I have an ulterior motive. My brain is still sorting out how selling to people who want a service or product is not bad but exploiting people financially for something that will likely never benefit them is. It has taken me a long time to reconcile this. But thanks to Laura's advice, I dedicate my new Instagram account to recovery advocacy and education only, sharing my book, the articles I've written, and podcasts I have been interviewed for. Though many of the MLM network "followed me" to the new account, it feels more authentic to talk about topics that are near and dear to my heart, instead of products and a business that I don't believe in. The business that I have to dedicate one more weekend to for Convention. Time to put on a happy bossbabe face. I can do anything for three days, right? Even in Nashville.

"Are you thinking sparkling waters here, or do you want to have your stack of books?" Serena asks for advice on my book event setup. She and I are staying together again; she's my saving grace, as always. We rented a huge suite (again, more money) so it would fit a book-launch party and also include space to spend time with our friends outside the chaos of the convention center. I want to avoid the fangirling as much as possible and try to enjoy myself. First on the docket for this weekend is my book-launch event, then I give my (last) talk, then my (last) stupid stage walk, and then I can go home and put Rejuvinat on autopilot. Before I can answer Serena's decorating questions, there's a knock at the door.

"I got it!" I say, as I open the door to see Kimberly, standing in a bright-pink dress, mile-high blonde hair, and stiletto heels that look downright painful. Before I have a chance to ask, "How in God's name did you get our room number?" she is standing in our suite.

"Hi, ladies! So glad you picked this hotel, too. I opted for the presidential suite, but this is . . . cute." She looks around. God, can she *ever* skip the pissing contest?

"Yes, it's great, such good lighting!" I make jazz hands around the large picture window as I attempt to hold a cordial conversation, wondering why she's here.

"You know, Emily," she says as she saunters to the window and admires the view, "I have people asking me about your book. Wondering if they need to write a book to be successful in this business, too." She pauses, a smug smile on her lips.

I shake my head and look at her, hoping she'll do me the courtesy of offering more context.

"Okay, and?" I ask.

"I mean, you are a tippity-top leader and you've lost focus, and now, people wonder, *Do I need to write a book to be at the top, too?* It just really looks bad that you're so publicly doing something else now."

She cocks her head and looks at me with an arrogant, judgmental expression, as if she's challenging me.

I'm speechless. First, fuck her, and second, she's written a book of her own, too! It was a pretty basic "how to be in a pyramid scheme" personal development hybrid, in the territory of many other network marketers, but on top of that, she ran her own coaching program outside of Rejuvinat, helping other people in MLMs (or anyone willing to pay her) with her "secrets to success." It seems like every top leader has her own backup plan, whether it's coaching or books or something else.

In the last decade, and especially with the growth of online businesses, many high-level distributors at Rejuvinat and other MLMs have developed "business coaching" programs that essentially assert: "If you follow this proven system, you will be successful in your MLM." So the lowly MLM rep at the bottom who doesn't know why they aren't succeeding can buy courses, sales aids, books, and techniques on how to recruit and grow a downline. Some distributors make more money selling sales aids than they do in the MLM, building the case for the sunk cost fallacy that keeps people in the company. The FTC warns against these coaching programs, because like MLMs, they claim that you can make money with no experience and little effort. They often say their "experts" will teach you a "proven method" for building a successful business on the internet and may even claim that they are affiliated with well-known online sellers or companies, which may or may not be true. We've all seen the pitches and paid placements:

"Learn from EXPERTS in the field!"

"Make seven figures by following our system."

"Make money from home, NOW!"

They pitch that it's simple to make money, and for a hefty fee, they'll show you how! Unfortunately, you'll find out, once again, after losing hundreds or thousands of dollars, that these promises were empty. Now, the internet is flooded with people who have never actually *achieved* success selling their proprietary secrets to it, but their only real success is the scam that so many unfortunate people have bought into.

In effect, it is more lucrative to sell sales aids to other current MLM reps than it is to try to get new ones to join their own MLM.

Watching videos of people coaching when they aren't actually business coaches is weird, but listening to the advice of people preaching their version of the prosperity gospel and their own money-making secrets when they have nothing to show for it is even more than weird—it's unethical. Keep in mind, I'm a certified coach. I have nothing against coaches who come out of legitimate programs. Sadly, the industry is notoriously underregulated, much like MLMs, which is why people can call themselves coaches, even if they aren't trained. Generally speaking, coaches should be recognized by a major credentialing body (International Coaching Federation, Board of Certified Coaches, Association of Coaches, European Mentoring and Coaching Council, etc.). It's best to ask a coach for their credentials because personal life experience does not qualify as certification.

Though I am a woman in recovery, I also went through extensive training and certification that was no joke. I am qualified to coach around alcohol issues and recovery, but I would *never* try to act as someone's business coach. Despite being in an MLM (or perhaps because of it), I'm very much not qualified! MLMs do not train you to run a business. At. All. MLM business coaches may be giving you tips or sharing a story from their own experience that gives you a renewed sense of purpose, but they are not partnering with you, holding you accountable, or supporting your growth in any tangible way. And you can find dozens of self-described experts selling themselves as mindset coaches or business coaches, even self-described recovery coaches, with no qualifications other than being involved in an MLM.

How do you pay for expertise that doesn't exist?

I reflect on a conversation I had on a reward trip earlier this year in Cabo with a fellow consultant, Calista. Like me, she had a fast start, so she asked me for some pointers. She'd made it to "car volume," the total sales number required to achieve your monthly car payout, but didn't hold it; her numbers dropped back down a few short months in, leaving her stuck with a car payment she had to pay herself, which is quite common. She had asked for my opinion on what was going on at corporate because she knew I had insider info. I was at the point where I didn't really care anymore, and in a rare moment of letting my guard down, I told her that I felt like Rejuvinat was a sinking ship. She appreciated my candor, and I didn't see much of her after that. I assumed she quit and found a legitimate job or jumped to another MLM. Imagine my surprise a few months later when an Instagram post popped up from her: "I started a new fun project! Do you have a network of people who think MLMs are predatory? I want to change that! I'm launching a coaching program with speakers, secrets to success, language ideas, and all the top tips to recruit your teams BIG and make your paychecks HUGE! All for $50 per month!"

She hopped off the sinking ship, per my advice, but instead, she collected all the other suckers who were hanging on for dear life. Not only could she prey on all the other women failing in Rejuvinat; she'd opened her offering up to any and every MLM bossbabe. If that doesn't drive home how this industry is all about the people, not the products, I don't know what will. Despite the fact that Calista made her post sound like she was offering a great deal, she was purposely targeting easy prey, promising someone they could level up for only $50 per month, when they had already spent $1,000 on a business kit to "level up" their life. It's also incredibly hypocritical. Calista put her own failing MLM side gig on autopilot because she knew it wasn't tenable or sustainable, but she went on to hoodwink people into staying in their MLMs by seducing them into the premise that it's possible to be successful. And she raked in the money doing it.

So I'm having a hard time swallowing Kimberly's "feedback," since I already consider her to be a self-described "expert" whose entire focus is enticing people into Rejuvinat and making money off those in other MLMs. I'm not sure if she's annoyed that I'm doing something outside the MLM world or that the spotlight is off her.

The big difference with my book versus hers or any of the other reps who've written books is that mine has nothing to do with the MLM world. I didn't write it to bring more people into Rejuvinat or any MLM, or to sell a product; it's just my story, nothing more. And I have no doubt that the "people asking" Kimberly about whether writing a book is a way to get to the tippity-top is a flat-out lie. Nobody is asking her anything; she just knows that none of the related success will flow up to her, unlike my Rejuvinat sales and recruiting.

Unsurprisingly, her false concern is purely self-interested.

I respond as kindly but flatly as I can muster, "Kim, I'm not following. I wrote a book, you wrote a book, lots of people have. Corporate is fine with it, so if anyone has questions, just send them to me."

Seriously, get out of my room.

She gazes at me with an intense look in her eyes. "I just wonder, what happens to people like you? How did you get so off track? Honestly, I started your book and I just . . . I couldn't. But I just want you to know, I'll pray for you."

Serena sees the steam coming out of my ears and butts in, sharply defusing what could easily turn into a catfight. Perhaps a divine intervention, my phone rings. "Thanks, Kim, BYEEEEEEE!" I say in as singsongy a voice as I can and walk the other way. Serena makes a little small talk as she walks Kimberly to the door.

What happened to you?

I am fuming as I consider the absurdity of her question. *Life, Kimberly! Life happened, and instead of pretending everything is pretty and pure white and shiplap and filtered, I'm actually talking about it. Sorry if that gets your panties in a wad, you uppity cow.*

I welcome the distraction of the phone call, but had I known what was on the other line, I would have continued the conversation with Kimberly.

"Hi, Emily, it's Sheila, from the Compliance Department at Rejuvinat," a chirpy woman announces on the other line. Compliance, eek. Compliance's job is to send an email if you post a graphic you shouldn't or make a false income claim. It wasn't great to hear from them, but also, nothing ever seemed to come of it.

"Hey, Sheila, what can I help you with?" I assume they need clearance on a photo or a PowerPoint slide for my Convention presentation.

"Well, we've had several consultants over the last few days send in a recording of a podcast interview you did for your book. Congrats, by the way! But in this interview, you talked about some, well, sensitive things. And you used the company name, and we need to ask you to have it taken down."

Sensitive things? Shit, I've done so many podcast interviews in the past few weeks. Did I talk about the company? When did I talk about the company? Did I accidentally share a product ingredient I shouldn't have?

"Oh, thanks for letting me know. Can you tell me what sensitive information I shared? Because I honestly don't recall." At this point, I still assume it's proprietary company information. Boy, am I wrong.

"Well, it's just . . . ," she sheepishly continues, like an awkward health teacher trying to talk about puberty. "There was some, you know, things of a sexual nature that you spoke about, and in the same interview, you said our company name. We just can't be associated with it."

We sit in silence for what felt like minutes, as I process what she is saying. Yes, I remember the interview now. My publisher was asking me about Rejuvinat in the beginning of the interview, very briefly, then she later referenced a section of my book and made a comment about how people need to "deal with their sexual trauma, or it would deal with them down the way," or something like that. That's the only reference to sex, and the only reference to the company, I've made. This is absurd. I've been carted around to dozens of events over the past couple of years sharing my story, albeit a sanitized version of it. And now that I'm sharing some real shit, they don't want to associate with it? It's too . . . *sexual*?

"So, you're saying I need to have them bleep out the company name? Even though I've been asked to talk about my recovery over and over and over at company events? Even though I'm here now, again, ready to sing the company's praises and tie it to my recovery story? So my book is just a little too 'real' and not the pretty, manufactured story you're used to? Do I have that right?" I practically spit out my words, though I want to say so much more.

"If you could just avoid referencing the company from now on in your interviews, that would be great," she replies in that same maddeningly perky voice.

"Got it." I hang up the phone.

Thankfully, Serena has gotten rid of Kimberly. I regurgitate what Sheila just told me, and Serena's jaw drops. "Those assholes."

My thoughts exactly. What bothers me even more are the "several consultants" who sent the interview to corporate. Were they honestly offended by what I said? Was it impossible for them to simply divert their attention? Everything I shared in my book is my personal story and has nothing to do with this company . . . and maybe *that's* the problem. So much for the sisterhood.

From the beginning of joining an MLM, you're taught to look for people's vulnerabilities. You're not told directly that this is what you're doing, but rather, you're taught to find what people need and show them how this business can fill that need—the "hunger"—that Becky told me about the first day I joined. "Lonely? Join a group of bossbabes. Fat? Take part in our workouts! Have gas and bloating? Do a gut cleanse with our supplements! Depressed? Spray some essential oils on it! And best of all, join our community!" MLMs are the Band-Aid for all that ails you. They supposedly comprise women supporting women, all while using the sales tactics that marketers know will make us vulnerable and self-critical. And all of these are tied to mental health, because you are not remedying the depression or the low self-esteem or the shaky sense of self—you're offering a distraction.

When you relate to others through vulnerabilities, the intent may not necessarily be shady, but targeting people who are at their lowest is predatory: "We have a job and a lifestyle and a network and personal development for you! Join us!" After all, how many MLM bossbabe stories start with "the low point" that got them into the business? "Woe is me! I was so sad and lonely, then this legging company fixed everything!" When every success story starts as a sob story, doesn't that speak to the kind of manipulation that is being employed? Sure, targeting pain points is not exclusive to MLMs, but unlike TV commercials you can turn off or magazine pages you can flip, a bossbabe comes directly to you in a Facebook message, or sits next to you in the PTA meeting, or carpools your kids to soccer. It's more personal and more difficult to evade.

The most sinister, in my opinion, is the health and wellness advice. Since I became sober, I have been stunned by the number of "wellness" coaches who promote gluten- and dairy-free anti-inflammatory diets yet post about guzzling wine. No shade to people who drink alcohol, but as a "wellness expert," you should know that alcohol is the worst thing you can ingest for your physical, mental, or emotional health; no diet or exercise or cleanse can cancel out a literal poison. And don't get me started on the "clean wine" MLMs, since the dirty part of wine is alcohol!

But these women aren't scientists. Most MLM reps are completely unqualified to be promoting diet and health, especially with respect to an already vulnerable population. Of course, there are exceptions, such as actual nutritionists or dietitians who buy into the system, but the majority have zero training in anything related to nutrition, dietetics, exercise science, or another related field of study beyond what the MLM provides in their "consultant welcome kit," which amounts to a brochure on how to sell. They are not licensed or certified, and definitely not qualified to work with someone's medical history or physical limitations. And if they are licensed or certified nutritionists, one has to wonder about their credibility if they join a community of completely untrained self-described "wellness reps" who did nothing but buy a business kit.

Unfortunately, diet culture—the pervasive belief that appearance and body shape are more important than physical, psychological, and general well-being—is rampant. Americans spend over $30 billion on diet products a year, and 45 million Americans diet every year. This is a huge vulnerable population that MLMs target. By telling new moms the "secret to losing the baby weight" or messaging a plus-size friend about the "secret to keto weight loss," MLM reps are reinforcing, not remedying, disordered beliefs. They are contributing to the problem, not solving it.

As described in *The Fuck It Diet*, by Caroline Dooner, most diets are designed to fail; otherwise there wouldn't be a diet industry. Diets seem like they work at first, but since weight-loss studies don't last long enough to take note of the weight that's gained back, people continue to jump on claims that certain diets work. This is very convenient for MLMs, and their reps can sell people the supposed antidote to living a life consumed by food fixation and exercise: a different program that makes them consumed with clean eating and exercise. The motive is *not* others' well-being; it's financial gain.

I'm not saying that people can't and don't love the products they use and share about them because they genuinely worked for them. Sure, many reps love their company; sure, they love their products. Call it brainwashing or not, but that "love" will prevent reps from clearly seeing what other people's needs really are. When I was fully on board with Rejuvinat and singing its praises, regardless of how much I loved a product or not, I saw a new acquaintance as a dollar sign. They were someone to sell to or recruit. If they had a genuine need for connection, money, fewer wrinkles, or literally anything else, I would find a way to make Rejuvinat fill their need. When you're deep in an MLM, you're exempt from being an accurate judge of what is actually good for someone.

If there was zero compensation for sharing, would MLM reps still be sharing in the way they do? Would they still get all their friends together and have parties? If their behavior is changed in any way by the possibility of compensation, that's predatory. Selling things is fine. But if you tell people you just share the products because you like them, you're full of shit. You are sharing because you have an underlying hope that you will earn commissions. Moreover, you are encouraged to lie about your intent. I would never have shared the way I did on social media, inserted awkward conversations about the company and products into small talk with friends, or harassed acquaintances through DMs about my "business opportunity" if I simply liked the products. I shared the way I did because of the potential financial benefit.

This extends beyond MLMs, of course, to the white women wellness space. Take a gander at Goop, Gwyneth Paltrow's wellness brand. Celebrities have a knack for convincing women that they can afford the designer lifestyle and all the products that go with it, and it will make their lives better. Goop has made headlines for selling vagina crystals and co-opting controversial doctors (ones who argue that HIV doesn't cause AIDS, for example). Many find that the health benefits of their products don't quite match up to what they sell, and why would they? Goop's goal isn't health—the goal is to make Gwyneth Paltrow richer.

Similar to MLMs, wellness companies are largely unregulated, and prey on desperation and women's mistrust of conventional medicine. After all, women's health care is a huge problem in America, especially within marginalized communities; this disproportionately harms people of color and those in poverty, or who live in areas without medical resources—many of whom cannot afford the detox bath soaks that claim to improve health.

As Amanda Mull writes in her article for *The Atlantic*, "I Gooped Myself": "The company's products embrace one of America's oldest health myths: that physical beauty is proof not only of a person's health, but of her essential righteousness. If the outside is perfect, the inside must be too. It's a retrograde vision of womanhood for a company that so frequently deploys the word *empowerment*."

Just like many wellness brands selling empowerment, they'll lead you to believe that they can solve any problem as long as you have money to spend. They even have their own themed cruises, which are surely lucrative for Goop, driving home the wealth disparity in wellness and centering white-girl power that isn't remotely accessible or even marketed to lower-income women or women of color. Despite the criticism, Goop marches on in the spirit of white women's self-improvement. And surprise, surprise, the Goop website doesn't allow people to review their purchases. Even Goop doesn't want haters.

This desire for any type of self-improvement can lead people to view MLMs as the answer. I saw this often in my recovery communities. People in recovery are often focused on improving their lives and their health. MLMs (falsely) promise a better life with low barriers (just a small investment, no step work, and no amends!), more health, more money, and a supportive community. I understood the draw, as someone in an MLM and as someone in recovery. When you get a DUI, it's expensive, and some extra money sure sounds good! When your friends shun you for the antics you pulled when you were drunk, an ostensibly accepting community meets a key need! I saw many women in recovery fall prey to MLMs when I was in the rooms of AA. And I understood it. I myself had exploited people's vulnerabilities for so long: their desire to stay home with their kids, to have better skin, to feel more vibrant and alive.

Vulnerability has always been a key part of my success, but it's also what made me susceptible to Rejuvinat in the first place, because I was understandably lonely and looking for a community. But now? My vulnerability is just a little *too* much. They wanted me to share enough to make myself relatable but not enough to make the company look bad.

SERENA AND I SKIP most of the sessions at Convention. And honestly, it's the most fun I've had at a Convention because I don't actually go to any of the MLM-curated lectures or parties. We spend time with June, Carly, Annie, Mandy, and a few other consultants whom we actually consider friends. Luckily, Madison has grown such a big team that she leads her own parties and events, and I don't feel obligated to include her. It actually helps our relationship quite a bit, realizing that we don't work well together. She does her thing, with huge over-the-top events replete with photographers and posed filtered photos, and I do mine, with none of those things. Becky entertains her, so I don't need to—it's a win-win! All the while, Madison has continued to skyrocket, and to relish the praise and fangirling I now loathe. She also continues to support my bottom line, which is enough for me to keep putting on a happy face and faking it.

Serena and I go out in Nashville, dance, listen to music, and eat *so* much greasy food, retreating to our suite at the end of the night. *This is what I will miss*, I think to myself. This is the part I enjoy about these Rejuvinat trips. But I remind myself that I don't need to be involved in an MLM to take girls' trips disguised as business ones. I just need to make sure that I continue making time for friends once I can no longer use "work" as an excuse, even if the work is fake AF. After all, moms like us aren't afforded as much leisure time as our spouses.

According to research, fathers with children under eighteen spend about three more hours per week on leisure time than mothers. And while leisure activities for men generally include playing sports, exercising, or watching TV or other media, mothers' activities are often expected to be normal day-to-day activities chalked up to self-care. "Go take a bath! Go take a nap! Go to bed early!" Gee, thanks, society. When we aren't momming, we are expected to be working; and when we aren't working, we are expected to be momming! Maybe this is why mothers feel more exhausted and stressed during their leisure time than fathers do, and why co-opting a business trip for some R&R is the best excuse there is to do business.

It's unfortunate that MLMs make these trips so busy and stressful, devoid of any actual relaxation. And it's funny that even our leisure time we are supposed to use as a marketing opportunity. It's the reason the company gives us branded towels and water bottles, and why you see bossbabes posting about working "on vacation." This is a nod to the "flexible work" option, but not the flex they think it is. Nobody—I mean, nobody—wants to have their face in their phone or their laptop on vacation, or be tied to a Zoom call when they are supposed to be vacationing.

After our fun night out, we all connect at our suite, ordering room-service pizza and kicking off our heels. Carly pipes up, "Where are Vanessa and Hannah, anyway? I'm sad they aren't here!"

I am, too. Vanessa is easy to explain: She's still my very best friend, and I see her all the time, but her career has exploded—in a good way! She's worked her way up and is traveling a lot. She's still involved in Rejuvinat but just sells a little on the side and doesn't take it too seriously. I often wonder, *If I hadn't risen to the top, could I continue to be blissfully unaware and just sell products whenever?* Maybe I'm not that low-key of a person. Maybe it's my personality that makes me feel like I have to strive for the top, or maybe it was just the luck of the draw, since I found Rejuvinat first and Vanessa found it second, and I had a second income and she no longer did. Either way, she's happy, and that makes me happy for her.

"Vanessa is doing so well. These trips just are too much time away from her family," I explain.

Hannah is a different story. Things finally came to a head with her husband. He questioned the credit-card bills, and even found some that he didn't know about. When he confronted her, he told her that she could no longer spend any money on Rejuvinat. Since she was no longer able to fill her monthly quota, the small team she had rolled over to me. Yes, that's right, I absorbed her team because she couldn't afford to keep them.

It's sinister, actually. MLMs require not only a minimum title to keep the team you recruited, but also a minimum title to earn money on any team you have. Maybe you've heard the term *leaving money on the table*? If you recruit an absolute rockstar networker who makes it big, you don't necessarily make money on their sales, unless you're hitting and maintaining a certain title. It's the reason women can feel so desperate and end up buying multiple "legs" with family accounts, just to make themselves eligible for a certain level of pay.

Didn't make the minimum title? Shoot, you must not be working hard enough. Instead, that team is going to roll to your upline. Hannah's team did just that. Ironically, Carly herself was a "roll-up" from someone I recruited years ago who eventually gave up. Many consultants will leverage this by "buying out" their downlines. After all, if you offer a few thousand bucks for someone to terminate their business but gain a downline of thousands per month, it's worth it. I'm ashamed to admit that I once offered to buy out Hannah, since her downline would help me with my title more than it would help her. But I ended up not needing to, as she finally gave up herself.

"Hannah's not with us anymore," I respond flatly, as if I'm announcing a death. And that's how it feels. Even though it's good news for Hannah, I know she went into debt. She would have been better off never joining.

"Didn't want to work hard enough, huh?" Carly shoots back.

I know that's what we've been told to believe, but I don't buy it anymore. All of these women in this room work harder at Rejuvinat than I do. But with constant changes in the social media landscape, saturation in the field, the fact that I got to most of their networks before they did, and so many other factors, the odds are stacked against them. I saw how hard Hannah worked. She busted her ass for a really long time, but she didn't have the disposable income or the huge network, and to top it off, working this "opportunity" destroyed her friendships and self-esteem. And I know it was my fault.

When she finally sent in her termination form, I was relieved, and not because her downline rolled up, but because she was finally free. And selfishly, I was free from the guilt of knowing I put her there. I decide to admit to these ladies what's really going on.

"You know, she did work hard. You all do. And meanwhile, I'm not, and I'm still making a ton of money." I put down my slice and make a cringe face.

They all know I've been busy with the book and my certification programs. They know that I refer them to Becky most of the time, that I am barely plugged in, don't post much on social media, etc. But I've never fully admitted to them how I've been feeling and why—and they deserve to know.

"Ladies, I haven't been happy with Rejuvinat for a long time. When I was doing my twelve steps, many of my amends were about things I'd done in this company. And I keep trying to convince myself that I can ignore the red flags, but it's not aligning for me anymore. I know you all have felt me pull back. But today was really the last straw."

I tell them about the call from corporate, and the complaints from consultants in the company who once praised my "pretty" recovery story but sent the dogs after my real one. I tell them about Kimberly's talk, and the pressure I'd been under to "retire" Kale, and the ridiculous amounts of money that we are expected to spend at the top. I pull back the curtain on what it looks like, and I apologize for selling them a dream that never existed.

"Emily, I've had so much fun the past few years. Honestly, since you've toned down a bit—well, a lot," Mandy laughs, "I've felt so much less pressure to hit any numbers or achieve trips or whatever. I think you're doing it right."

"And we're all big girls," June adds. "We made our own choices when we signed up. Maybe we didn't know what we were getting into, but knowing what I know now, I would still make the same choice. It's been an awesome ride, and a little bit of side money."

The ladies all give their feedback, and selfishly, I feel better, like another weight has been lifted off me. I have made my amends, and I decide that I'm no longer going to participate in any of the pomp and circumstance: no more speaking at retreats, no more Conventions, no more posturing or recruiting or keeping a happy face for my team. I wouldn't have met Serena if it wasn't for Rejuvinat. I wouldn't have had these fun experiences in Hawaii and London and France and Spain and all over the world. I wouldn't be publishing a book and moving into a new field of recovery advocacy if it wasn't for everything I've learned (good and bad) over the past few years. Yes, it came at a price sometimes, but this weekend and the conversations with these women are the closure I need. I know that these friendships will remain intact, no matter what happens. And it certainly helps that my stepping back doesn't impact their bottom line, like it does Becky's and those of the other women in my upline.

"Awesome. Well, I have surprises for all of you!" Now, I feel even more elated that the gag gifts will land the way I want them to. The only downside is my friends may need to pay for extra baggage on the way home.

I pass out bags full of all the swag I've ever earned. Even the bags are swag bags from Rejuvinat, all with different reward trips or Conventions written on them. Inside the bags? Bracelets, necklaces, products, and personal development books. Everything here, I'm regifting. I've literally unloaded my warehouse of MLM recruiting shit. Giggles fill the room as we dig through some of the ridiculous items. Who thought glittery slippers were a good idea? Then there are all the gaudy trinkets that literally nobody would ever wear, like charm necklaces that would embarrass a seven-year-old and T-shirts with the most heinous empowerment slogans on them ("Rejuvinat 4 ever," "Good things come to those who hustle," "I have the POWER to EMPOWER," and "Hustle until your haters ask if you're hiring," to name a few). There's even a masquerade-ball mask with glitter, sequins, and tiny little *ichangedmylife!* hashtags on it. I share stories about when and where I got all these gifts. Some I have trouble remembering, but Serena is there to fill in the details from my heavy drinking days. It's a walk down memory lane, a stroll through a tacky museum, and a cathartic release of everything I have been through in the last six years, since that first meeting with Becky.

I tell them, "You can keep this, use it, sell it, send it to your teams, or burn it. I don't care. It is a gift to me to get rid of all of it. Thank you for letting me do this."

It's probably one of the most fun evenings I've ever had during my time at Rejuvinat, and a springboard to move on to the next chapter. I will go on to close my team Facebook page and tell my uplines not to include me in emails anymore, or put me on top-ten lists, or invite me to Zoom calls. I stop posting anything about Rejuvinat. I let everyone know where I stand. I am going to reap the rewards of what I built (according to Becky), collect a check until it dries up, fill my monthly product purchase obligation, and that's it. I feel that the pain of this burden is finally over, and I can move on.

How wrong I am.

KIMBERLY

ALLISON

JAMIE

BECKY

SERENA

ANNIE

ME

MANDY

CARLY

JUNE

VANESSA

You Can Check Out, but You Can Never Leave

+ +
  +

I lost my job when the pandemic hit, and I was in a really low place. My "friend" who had been bugging me for years to join her team finally wore me down. I was desperate, and I didn't know where to turn. I spent my stimulus money on a stupid kit, and I would give anything to go back in time and reverse that decision. By the time I realized that I didn't want to prey on other people who'd lost their jobs in the middle of a pandemic, it was too late to get my money back. And my "friend" and I are no longer friends.

—MELISSA, former MLM rep

The first nine weeks of 2020 are great. My book sales are still coming in strong, and I'm making TV and podcast appearances and writing articles. My coaching business is going well. I haven't replaced my MLM income by any means yet, but I am keeping up with attrition. My Rejuvinat paycheck has been declining, but it's still around $15,000 per month, and I am able to make up the difference by doing something I feel good about while spending less money. Plus, I can see how at some point, I'll be able to walk away from Rejuvinat entirely. But for the moment, I feel fine about leaving it on autopilot.

And then, March 2020 comes. Need I say more?

In some ways, I'm glad that my conscience has gotten too loud to continue publicly selling Rejuvinat, because the desperation that comes in the next few months is no joke. Suddenly, the internet is flooded with messages from MLM reps.

"See, this is why I'm building my own dream!"

"Put that stimulus check to good use!"

"Have time for a plan B now?"

"The world may be shut down, but network marketing is not."

During the pandemic, you didn't see any other company attempting to profit from the crisis quite like the MLM world. And it's not like other companies weren't making bank. Zoom stock went through the roof. Netflix was a daily staple. But do you recall seeing any advertisements from Zoom or Netflix bragging about how popular they were, or about how their numbers skyrocketed while people were in lockdown? Imagine if you saw a hand-sanitizer company saying, "Yay, we hit record numbers! You're in the wrong business, you lazy fucks!" The pandemic and the resulting death toll were tragic, not something to be used as a recruitment strategy.

There was also an uptick in the number of buy-now-pay-later services during the pandemic. MLMs frequently used companies such as Afterpay, Affirm, Klarna, and Fingerhut. Now, credit is nothing new, but the difference with these services is that they are unregulated, with no affordability checks. If you need a buy-now-pay-later service to buy a $50 eye cream, chances are your money situation is not great. They do not check your income or your credit, or your ability to pay the debt back. It's a way to target people who cannot afford products. In fact, over 34 percent of people who use these services are unable to pay them back.

Every day, more and more MLM reps were flooding the internet with rhetoric touting the benefits of a nontraditional job. In fact, most of the language was anti–traditional job. It peddled the idea that when you work for someone else, you aren't in control. After all, you don't pick your own hours or decide when you get a raise. And when the economy tanks, people lose jobs. "But guess what? A side hustle will protect you!" The lack of job security, the fear that your livelihood is up in the air, is a critical fear tactic to push MLMs. In fact, they are not secure. They can (and do) shut down and change their structure, and there are no protections like unemployment, Family and Medical Leave (FMLA), severance, or Paycheck Protection (which I will talk about in more detail later).

Beyond trying to recruit, MLM reps now had a new sales pitch: "We can cure/help COVID." The faux wellness experts were out in full force, ready to exploit a pandemic.

"Everyone is out here buying toilet paper and paper towels, and here I am ordering my immunity booster! Send me a PM!"

"Our essential oils attack on several fronts: lemongrass in your diffuser, tea tree and oregano internally! Don't be afraid of COVID!"

Don't worry about the fact that you are never, ever, *ever* supposed to use oils internally. The misinformation machine was in full effect.

"Facts: Essential oils prevent and kill bacteria. We can make the difference—prevention is always better than a cure!" Hey, genius, COVID is a virus, not a bacterium. And facts actually have data behind them. Where's your source and study? Reps were posting data that you shouldn't be posting unless you're an immunologist, but we've already covered the ethics issues among MLM reps.

My favorite is a video from an MLM rep stating, "I believe I don't exist in the same realm as COVID. I don't energetically hold space for it. Our beliefs create our reality. No matter what, I've always chosen to be optimistic and positive. My energy is too positive. Join my team to feel the same way."

Oh, honey, *please* talk to someone with a microbiology degree. Scientifically baseless or not, none of these screeds were meant to help people or kill a virus; they were meant to make a buck.

The FTC took note of all this misinformation and sent letters to sixteen companies (dōTERRA, Pruvit, Total Life Changes, Tranont, Modere, Arbonne, IDLife, It Works, Rodan + Fields, Zurvita, Isagenix, Juice Plus, Melaleuca, Youngevity, Vivri, and Plexus) whose reps were claiming they could cure or prevent COVID or offer an option to make money from the confines of your quarantine. The FTC was rightfully concerned that people might delay or fail to use accurate treatment, considering the wave of COVID misinformation that surged over the next two years (and continues to). Now, I don't knock anecdotes or "natural" remedies, but I'm also a trained chemist and have significant experience in research, studying sources, and vetting where data comes from. I'm not against alternative or adjunct therapies by any means. I know the limitations of vitamin C and zinc when I have a cold, but I still give them a shot, while continuing to rely on proven scientific facts and modern medicine.

Saying something like "This may boost your immune system" is vague enough so that it could be helpful with no real harm done, but saying this product will prevent COVID and filling your post with exaggerated anecdotal information is something entirely different. MLMs also have very limited liability around reps making claims, because reps aren't official company spokespeople! They are independent contractors, so if they say something that isn't the official company line, the company can say, "Aw, shucks, sorry, we didn't tell them to say that!" Then, they can either give the rep a slap on the wrist or terminate them. The company doesn't have to take on the liability themselves.

Unfortunately, the FTC letters had very little impact, according to Truth in Advertising. TINA is a nonprofit organization that uses investigative journalism, education, and advocacy to empower consumers to protect themselves against false advertising and deceptive marketing. They conducted a follow-up investigation after the FTC letters were sent and found that reps from all sixteen companies continued to make unsubstantiated health or earnings claims.

According to Bonnie Patten, TINA's executive director, the FTC simply doesn't do enough and isn't effective in its enforcement. She states, "TINA is urging the FTC to stop playing a game of whack-a-mole and instead implement an enforcement program that will finally deter the systemic harm caused by the constant and continual use of deceptive marketing within the industry. The FTC needs to put the MLM industry on notice that it's time for using deceptive marketing without facing substantial penalties is up."

This pseudoscience runs thick in the so-called "clean" movement: clean beauty, clean living, clean eating, and the greenwashing of science that's thick with fearmongering and pseudoscientific claims that have zero science behind them. Not a week would go by without my seeing MLM reps share facts from the Environmental Working Group (EWG), like the "Dirty Dozen." These are twelve conventional product items that supposedly have the highest rates of cancer-causing chemicals in them.

If you're not familiar with the EWG, it's an activist group funded by organic farms. Not exactly an unbiased source, since it's funded by the producers of the products it's promoting. The EWG has faced a ton of criticism for its exaggerations of toxicological risk and lack of scientific method. It uses buzzwords like *cancer-causing chemicals* in an effort to get people to purchase—surprise, surprise—organic products. As a chemist, the demonization of "chemicals" has always been laughable to me, since literally everything is a chemical. Water (a chemical!), which is necessary for life, can kill you in multiple ways, just to use one example. Human blood contains over four thousand chemicals, many that you cannot pronounce, *all* that you cannot live without, but most could kill you in large doses. Because as any actual scientist knows, it's the dose that makes the poison.

Every year, scientists from the USDA, as part of the Pesticide Data Program, sample, test, and report on pesticide residue on a wide variety of foods. The data shows year after year that 99 percent of samples have residues well below the EPA limits. Still, the EWG manipulates this data to make their Dirty Dozen list. They count the number of pesticide residues, without regard for what the chemical is or in what concentration it occurs. The EWG even states on its website, "This guide does not incorporate risk assessment into the calculations. All pesticides are weighted equally." In actuality, none of the twelve dirty fruits or veggies actually contain any significant level of pesticides. It's all marketing. What's even more interesting, which, of course, they do not mention, is that the organic versions of these same twelve foods also have pesticides but are *not* monitored for safety or residue levels!

Their goal isn't to educate you; their goal is to instill fear and make money. And it doesn't stop at the EWG or any other people making "clean beauty" claims. You'll see false claims all over the MLM marketplace. Sorry, not sorry: Shampoo can't regrow your hair. Water additives don't penetrate your skin because you aren't a freaking sponge. Eye cream can't change your molecular structure. Your liver and kidneys detox your body, meaning you don't need those teas or shakes that make you shit your pants. Essential oils can't cure disease. And for the love of God, alkaline water doesn't change the pH of your body, and if it did, you would drop dead immediately.

Beyond false claims, even as the pandemic marched on, MLM reps posted photos next to stacks of their products, despite company policies against inventory loading and despite bossbabes parroting that "there are no minimums" to shill their benefits, blasting the FOMO far and wide. This was nothing new, but it was a markedly gross display of privilege that people were so obsessed with wealth and their company that they needed to demonstrate how much product they purchased as a pandemic raged on and people were out of work—or worse, dying.

That kind of greed and desperation is hard to accept. At this point, the fact that MLMs were not, in fact, communities, but rather, product-based cults preying on human desperation had become as clear as day to me.

The FTC knows that recessions and other disasters, like a pandemic, have a "positive" impact on MLM revenue. MLM reps use these times to boldly push and target the most vulnerable people they can find— and this time around, it only escalated. The claims were wilder and more widespread, especially the financial claims. I remember an upline telling me that when the real estate market crashed in 2008, it was the best time for her business in Rejuvinat, because MLMs thrive in economic downturns.

According to a DSA report (which we should probably take with a grain of salt in general, since the DSA is the lobbying group for MLMs), the number of MLM reps went from 15.1 million in 2008 to 18.2 million in 2014 (which is, ironically, when I joined). Rejuvinat became a billion-dollar company during that recession. It says a lot about who you are and what you are doing if your "business opportunity" is doing its best when people are at their worst, giving those who are struggling a seemingly seaworthy life raft as they are being told to sink or swim.

So, make no mistake, MLMs were *excited* about the pandemic.

There was also an increase in people using the pandemic to solicit "donations." Again, this was nothing new. As I mentioned previously, Rejuvinat consistently did promotions like "Buy this kit and we'll send sunscreen to the troops!" and "Purchase this supplement and we'll send donations to hurricane disaster relief!"

It was no different from my "charitable" cervical-cancer event, which earned money for charity only while I was simultaneously lining my own pockets.

The DSA has stated that direct-selling companies and their salespeople are often involved in charitable activities that support their communities: "Direct sellers will be an important part of recovering from this [pandemic] crisis, and DSA is confident that our member companies and their salespeople will make charitable contributions with the same level of responsibility, concern, sensitivity, and ethics with which they should always conduct their business."

How sweet. But really? Because reps have to continue to maintain purchase volumes, and this "loophole" only allows people to piggyback on a tragedy to increase their bottom line. Robert L. FitzPatrick, president of Pyramid Scheme Alert, agrees:

They've been doing this before, but the pandemic provides a nice rationale for this arrangement. MLMs are in deep trouble now in their own peculiar way from the pandemic. They can't hold meetings which are highly orchestrated for emotional response and for dominating and influencing the recruits with visions of money, etc. So, they are now claiming MLM is the perfect business for the pandemic—work from home and work online.... It is a myth, a come-on.

During this time, I'm just happy I'm not participating anymore, at least not in the same way I did in the past—but every time I scroll Facebook, I cringe. Here I am, home with my entire family, trying to build a new coaching business that requires me to work one-on-one on a computer, while sharing an office with a loud talker who's in meetings all day (love ya, Kale), all while splitting an internet connection with six other people, five of whom I now have to also *teach*. With my diminished hours at Rejuvinat and the kids getting older, we decided to say goodbye to our au pair, so we are back on our own for childcare again. I am stressed, worried about how I can make it work, and of course, worried about the virus, which is still so unknown. And yet, I am so glad I no longer have to hustle with the MLM. I know that no matter what happens, I will make it work.

And, in retrospect, I understand the privilege I have to be able to say that.

Like many people who started organizing their homes during the pandemic, I spend time purging my inventory of bossbabe paraphernalia. I sell my Louis Vuitton luggage, Convention gowns, and diamond jewelry on Poshmark. I donate many other items and throw away the old desktop awards and plaques that I used to display so proudly. They are meaningless to me now. I go through my social media and delete old braggy posts and spammy sales graphics.

Beyond the cringe, it's an interesting dichotomy when I scroll Facebook, because I notice a huge divide in the MLM community. There are those shouting to support your small businesses (again, MLM reps are not small businesses, but they try to include themselves at every turn). "Support your grocery stores, restaurants, small businesses—stimulate the economy! That is our duty!" But then there is another demographic of people who are pissed at the FTC for "shaming them" for working right now, completely missing the point. It isn't a problem that they want to sell some shit. The problem is the attempt to maximize their own profit at the expense of others. Your "being able to work from home" is getting people to buy shit from you that they *do not need*. This is not groceries and restaurants. It's essential oils (I hate that the word *essential* is tied to that) and overpriced skincare and supplements.

And yet, I completely understand it. At one point, I felt like a savior, too: "I want this for you, not me!"

Bullshit. That's what I was brainwashed to believe. Women are given very few options, and for the most part, they bear the brunt of the mental and physical burdens of childcare and household duties. More power to modern couples who have it all figured out and divided up equally, but that's not true for the majority, and it certainly wasn't for my family. MLMs' largest demographic is moms, so it's no wonder that more moms were targeted during the pandemic.

According to US Census Bureau data, women in the workforce were hit much harder than men during the pandemic. The reasons listed were the higher likelihood they worked in service jobs that were heavily impacted by closures, and the fact that mothers carried a heavier burden of unpaid domestic chores or childcare, which, during a pandemic that keeps everyone home, interrupts the ability to work. This is not new for moms, who have to take off work for summer months, school breaks, or children's illnesses. This is simply a symptom of gender inequality in the workplace, and the pandemic made it more pronounced.

Even a year after the first wave of the pandemic, an additional 210,000 mothers were on paid or unpaid leave compared to the previous year. Unemployment spikes continued increasing during each shutdown. With continued school shutdowns and widespread remote learning, more than 700,000 American moms simply gave up and left the workforce if they had a partner who could handle the financial burden. Of course, this wasn't possible for single moms, who had to continue to work, and if remote work wasn't available, had to leave children at home. Overall, mothers across all racial and ethnic groups faced challenges in the labor market, but Black and Brown single mothers were hit hardest.

Even as the pandemic began to slow down, mothers who left jobs willingly or whose positions were terminated had a difficult time returning to the workforce. The negative impact on their earnings will only continue to exacerbate gender inequalities in the workforce. Is it any wonder "work from anywhere" preys on desperation and empty wallets? Who doesn't want to hold on to the hope that they may be the 1 percent in a 99 percent failure-rate industry?

At this time, I am thankful that I've admitted to my downline that I am stepping away from Rejuvinat, so they don't feel any bullshit pressure from me to perform. I also suggest that they find other opportunities, and some of them do. June starts taking virtual classes, and Annie begins online tutoring for the school district. Some actually end up joining other MLMs alongside Rejuvinat. While you couldn't get me to join another MLM to save my life, I can understand why they would want to stick with what they know, and I happily encourage it at the time. Madison takes the bull by the horns and begins selling leggings alongside Rejuvinat, since her hair business has slowed to a standstill because of shelter-in-place orders. Leggings, sweats, and comfy clothes are becoming a growing industry, thanks to people working from home. I can't blame her at all. When you're prepped and trained to see everyone as a walking financial opportunity, why wouldn't you be looking at other ways to make money? Honestly, it seems like a good choice for her. When she calls me to get my advice, I welcome the conversation. Her texts and phone calls to me have slowed down a ton over the past year, since I basically told everyone not to contact me about Rejuvinat, so it's actually refreshing to hear her voice.

Mandy begins selling for a pet-food MLM—again, a growing industry, since so many people during the pandemic are adopting dogs! I am also happy to encourage both of them, even though a few years earlier, I might have staunchly forbidden it.

I actually had a rule at one point on my team Facebook page that if you were involved in more than one MLM, you could not be on my team page. The reasoning was that I wanted to protect all the women on the team from being sold to by someone else. The reality? If they were selling for more than one business, they weren't "all in." They weren't fully devoted to Rejuvinat. It was a way to compartmentalize information, because as their "leader," I knew best. I can't believe I ever operated that way, and yet, I did. I might not have been Kimberly, and I might have felt guilty along the way, but the reality was, I still did it. I learned going through AA that "the best apology is changed behavior." I'd changed the way I treated people, but by remaining in Rejuvinat, how much had I really changed?

Leaving MLMs for other MLMs isn't something that was spurred solely by the pandemic. However, I know several women who were fed up with Rejuvinat, so they jumped ship to a new MLM and now post ad nauseum about how their new company is so much better, how the women are "just like family." In reality, I can see it's the same shit.

There are MLMs that will even pay leaders to leave their companies and join theirs. I know this firsthand. At one point, I was personally offered more than $100,000 by an MLM to leave Rejuvinat and bring my team with me. Forget the financial exploitation—I was simply too disenchanted by then. Also, I knew there was no way I could have convinced my entire team, and the money still wasn't as much as what I took home that year from Rejuvinat. No surprise, of course, that they asked me to sign an NDA, which I refused. This happens quite often in MLMs, but despite all the NDAs, the secrets are out. Because MLM reps cannot keep their mouths shut when it comes to money. They will post about their new "ground floor" opportunity as if it's any different from what they just left. The new company gets an instant boost by "purchasing" an entire "leg" from another MLM, so they don't have to wait for someone to build a new team. Robert L. FitzPatrick talks about this in his report *Piracy Fuels the Illusion of MLM Start-Up Growth*:

There's an explosion of "growth" by startup MLMs that is the result of "downline piracy," the practice of paying large bonuses to lure away "top gun" recruiters who bring large downlines from one MLM to another, creating the illusion of "growth." This illusion is then spread online as the "next big thing," causing many others to leave their MLMs and flock to what they hope and believe is a better one. This process is repeated continuously, as the new schemes are just like the old ones. The decline of the larger and older MLMs spawns more and more MLM startups and increases the level of "piracy," hastening and increasing the impact of saturation on the larger MLMs. Newer MLMs rise and fall even more quickly.

So, despite my behavior to the contrary years earlier, I wish Mandy and Madison well, but I caution them not to be overly optimistic. The pandemic has to end at some point. Doesn't it?

"MOM, MY INTERNET DROPPED AGAIN!" my youngest shouts, as I realize that my middle-schooler missed one of her Zoom classes.

"Be right there!" Ugh.

As the months march on, I pivot my recovery coaching. I have five kids at home, and I can't do as many one-on-one virtual sessions anymore. Instead, I begin hosting free sobriety meetings online, seeing a huge need in the community and a rise in alcohol addiction rates among moms. I continue writing articles and doing recovery coaching in the hours I can squeeze in between managing all the kids' online schedules. We are still making it work financially, and we still have fun doing puzzles and enjoying each other's company, and frankly, enjoying a reprieve from the busy schedules. We don't know at this time that it will be months and months before my kids will return to school; we simply make it through as best we can.

In some ways, having five kids (and one who is driving, hallelujah!) is amazing. The kids are never lonely or bored. My youngest is in second grade and always has a sibling to watch him if I have to be on a call. This is extremely helpful when my husband has to move his home base to California (thanks, COVID), which means he can only fly home every two or three weeks for one weekend to be with us. So, yet again, it's me, Supermom, holding down everything at home.

Today, I can recognize the immense privilege I have to be able to do that. But at the time, it only exacerbates my ambivalence around wanting to leave Rejuvinat. I'm still receiving checks at this point, even if they are getting smaller, but I'm still part of the system . . . and yet, how can I throw off the financial balance right now?

I continue working on my new company, Sober Mom Squad, which is becoming a success. I still haven't replaced my income by any means. In fact, at this point, more money is going out than in, but I am thrilled that I have the opportunity. I am almost completely out the door, with Rejuvinat in my rearview mirror, collecting a check and doing nothing else. And every time Sober Mom Squad is featured in the media, my uplines, who were seemingly understanding at the beginning, pester me about when I am going to quit or start working again. Becky reminds me of this on a phone call one afternoon.

"Have you had any more thoughts about letting me buy your business?" she asks.

Buying out my place in the pyramid (just like I'd offered to buy out Hannah at one point) means that my entire downline would roll up to her, and she would finally be at the tippity-top like I am. She'd get all the accolades, trips, and perks. Her paycheck would also go up a bit, so it's financially worth it to her. She isn't offering a ton of money, but it's enough to make me bite. I know that my paycheck keeps going down, and it's going to fizzle out eventually. But is it smart to walk away right now?

"I'll think about it. I don't know. I just feel stuck, Becky. I feel like it would be stupid to walk away from a check, but I also don't feel like I want to take your money during a pandemic when things aren't going so well. And yet, I want to be done with this so badly. So. Badly."

I feel that's all I need to say. I want to be done. How much am I holding myself back while continuing to be tied to this black cloud?

Finally, I concede. "Sure, just let me know what I need to do."

"I'll send over the paperwork—it'll be easy. Don't feel bad—it's worth it to me! I know how much you want to be done with this," she says, as if she's doing this favor to relieve me of my guilt and not to improve her own situation. But I don't even care anymore.

She continues, "I'll send over the offer, as well as an NDA."

Shit.

She wants me to sign an NDA that she created agreeing I would not speak negatively about the company or disclose the terms of her "purchase." But there is no way I am going to sign an NDA. If there's one thing I've learned since getting sober, it's that if you see something, say something. I know I don't want to be muted if someone asks me why I left. I know it would only continue this cycle of people leaving and not speaking out, and I don't want my silence to be the reason more people get roped into an MLM. Absolutely no way.

I decide at that point I will have to terminate my consultant agreement myself, or the company will do it. And it won't be much longer. I am being turned in to Compliance left and right for keeping an "outside business." And Kimberly has made it her personal goal to get me out at any expense. Unlike Becky, she's angry that I'm making money without doing any work. Because I am not an active consultant, and I'm not following any of the "rules," I'm supposed to be left off leaderboards and prizes as punishment. The company does this as a way to keep you loyal: Break a compliance rule, sell for another MLM, or otherwise break the system of operation, no leaderboard for you! And that's fine by me. I don't want to be tagged or mentioned in anything Rejuvinat. Frankly, it embarrasses me.

However, Allison decides to start tagging me in everything. She is essentially reverse social media shaming me. Funny how they bend the rules to serve their needs. And yes, my numbers are still high because my team is so big, though I am doing nothing. I think part of me subconsciously stays out of spite.

Madison is under fire, too. The only thing keeping me from getting terminated is that my new business is not a competing MLM, while Madison's is. But who can blame *anyone* for looking for other financial options during the pandemic? I certainly don't. Still, Rejuvinat doesn't like it, and neither do any of the other consultants. And on a random Tuesday, I receive a phone call from Madison. I am surprised to see her number pop up, but I know immediately what has happened.

"Emily, they terminated me. Sent me an email. I cannot believe this," she cries through the phone, stunned.

For nearly three years I have watched her rise quickly at Rejuvinat. Frankly, we never saw eye to eye. Rarely could we ever get through a conversation without being annoyed with each other. But I am filled with nothing but empathy at this moment.

"Madison, I'm so sorry. What are they basing it on? The fact that you're selling for another MLM? That isn't against the rules!" Which is true. There is red tape around where you can share two different businesses and checks and balances to make sure you aren't taking your team with you to the other company. You're left off recognition and leaderboards, but there is no shame in earning a check from another company, and it's not against policies and procedures.

"It was Jenna. And Sienna. And about five other Rejuvinat consultants. They sent in screenshots of me speaking negatively about the company, and they terminated me. So much for sisterhood."

According to Madison, she had private conversations via text with other consultants who were curious about what she was doing with her athleisure business. They trapped her into saying things that were negative but true—that she felt like they were limiting her options, acting like a cult, and putting their nose where it didn't belong. These were personal feelings she had an absolute right to express with people whom she considered friends.

The truth? She got terminated because she's always had a target on her back. She is young and gorgeous and escalated quickly, and the consultants are jealous and think she has it too easy. They were looking for any way to take her down, and they found one—by reporting her "deviant" behavior to their superiors.

I am continuing to see how the business aims to trap and control you. Sometimes, all it takes is the first domino to fall. And I know I will be the next one they will take out. I resign myself to the fact that one of these days, I will be receiving the call because now, the target is on my back. And I can't help but think what a relief it would be. Like all of those years I was waiting to hit rock bottom, the consequences getting worse and worse. What disaster am I waiting for? In many ways, it's easier to do nothing than to do what I know is the right thing.

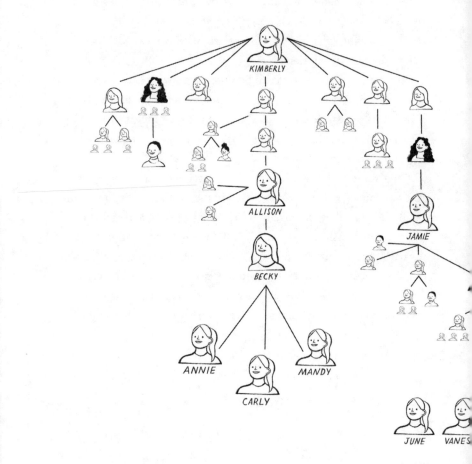

KIMBERLY

ALLISON

BECKY

ANNIE

CARLY

MANDY

JAMIE

JUNE   VANES

Escaping the Pyramid

+ +
+

I was horrified by the fact that my entire upline had started posting QAnon garbage on Instagram. I started to distance myself and joined a different (non-MLM) business that I shared on social media. I was turned in to Compliance and terminated because I violated a rule (of which I still don't understand) yet several of my upline leaders were at the January 6, 2021, insurrection on the Capitol, and they are still around. Apparently, you can break the rules if you are a million-dollar earner.

—TELISA, former MLM rep

I had naively believed the summer and fall would calm down. But then, late May 2020 brings with it the extrajudicial police killing of George Floyd, and in the fall, a heightened political campaign for the upcoming presidential election. And then, there are the QAnon conspiracy theories, as the world becomes politically divided around extreme alternative beliefs about the virus. I see a microcosm of this widespread division and panic among the MLM reps I know. I witness so many of the former top leaders, women I'd rubbed elbows with and sat in trainings with and traveled to Europe with, turn into people I can't even recognize. One woman compares wearing masks to the Holocaust. Many continue to host in-person events and host beach retreats with no regard to what's going on with the pandemic.

One goes online to "warn" her followers that Biden is the leader of Antifa.

Rejuvinat looks the other way.

Before I launch into the final months and death of my MLM career, I want to start by saying that I have always considered myself politically moderate—though not politically neutral. I believe in equal rights, but I also believe in certain personal freedoms, and I think the government spends way too much fucking money. I hate the two-party system. I've voted for a Clinton and a Bush. I'm horrified by the overturn of Roe v. Wade. My beliefs have evolved over the years, and though I'd say I lean further to the left, I've never fully claimed a side. I believe in nuance, and maybe I'm just stubborn enough to refuse to be told what I should or shouldn't believe. However, I strongly advocate people's rights to be who they want to be, marry who they want to marry, love who they want to love. I believe that what's between your legs or what shade your skin is shouldn't dictate the human rights you deserve. I care more that kids can safely go to school than if someone can legally smoke pot. I care more that people can access health care than I do about . . . lots of other things. I was born and raised in a very red state and have spent my adult life in very blue ones. I'm not a political commentator or expert by any stretch of the imagination, and in fact, I try to avoid political bloviating. But what I started seeing was women in my MLM co-opting the beliefs of their upline with no critical thinking of their own. Suddenly, they started parroting certain political and scientific beliefs, only because their MLM leaders spouted those things. Again, having different beliefs is your right, but if your reasoning is to simply cut and paste the thoughts and feelings of your upline, are they really your beliefs?

Also, there is a difference between political beliefs and hatred. The year 2020 ended up teaching me (and many of us) so many things that I didn't know. I don't care about anyone's politics, but I do care about your bigoted, racist rhetoric, and your cherry-picking of science. Especially from people who post about the so-called science of their products. Or women who use culturally appropriated music and voices in their TikTok and throw around terms like *tribe* and *sis*, yet "just can't believe racism exists." Women who will post a picture of their little one and caption it, "I will teach my child to love yours," while simultaneously supporting racist leaders who spew anti-vax and QAnon rhetoric. Women who repeat scripts from their upline but spout about personal freedom.

These are the people I used to claim as part of my MLM sisterhood— and my jaw is left on the floor. And yet, these are women who, just a couple years ago, I happily posted pictures with from an international trip, boasting about "sisterhood" and "friends for life." I fit right in with them, with my hair extensions and designer clothes and studded heels. The truth is, they were always this way, but they looked enough like me for me to believe they weren't. My own privilege has allowed me to be shocked by their current behavior, but perhaps I have been enabling and encouraging it all along.

I'm in my kitchen with my kids putting away our grocery delivery order, miffed that the hand sanitizer is still sold out, when I get a text from Serena: "Email, now!" I open my computer to see an email that has landed in my junk from Rejuvinat. Despite going on autopilot and trying to unsubscribe, there is no way to turn off these goddamn emails. The first image is of a woman wearing the newest product—a black "detox" skincare mask made from charcoal. In the same month that George Floyd was murdered. There is no question that this was planned months before, and obviously, the company didn't know what was going to happen in the world with human rights and Black Lives

Matter. But the optics are unbelievably bad, and it's a monumental fail to continue with this product launch in such a crisis moment.

I text Serena back: "This is gonna be bad."

And it is. All of a sudden, there are women posting photos in full blackface saying things like "We stand in solidarity with the Black community." Why anyone would think this is a good idea is beyond me, but how much more can I say about the opportunistic nature of some MLM reps? More than the opportunistic nature, it's a complete lack of empathy or understanding of what it means to be Black in America.

My God. If that weren't bad enough, this is followed up just hours later with a reminder on the proper way to use the face masks, specifically instructing us *not* to post in full blackface, despite the fact that the first email contains a photo of a woman in full blackface, and the product usage requires that it be placed all over the face. Plus, we've been trained the entire time as MLM indoctrinates to take pictures of *everything* we use. Of course, people posted photos of themselves wearing the face mask, with no concern for the cultural context. Not that I need to make excuses for clueless white ladies, but the reason they've been careless or clueless is that they are insulated from the cultural context, since most of their social circles are also white. Perhaps they don't know better, so they can't do better, but it's not that difficult to venture out of their bubble to learn.

Of course, with the renewed conversation about racism and cultural appropriation proliferating across social media, there's backlash from some of the top leaders, who feel "bullied" that they can't post how they want to.

Give me a break. Blackface during BLM protests? These women are angry about their freedom being taken away, when an innocent Black man was murdered and there is justifiable outrage and pain in the Black community? I am beginning to see the complete lack of awareness and privilege that exists when you believe you are entitled to take up space rather than sitting down and actually listening. Many of the incensed reps end up posting "All Lives Matter" on their profile pictures in retribution. It's more than just insulting—it's violent.

Rejuvinat has never felt more toxic or dangerous. But then again, it has always been toxic and dangerous.

At this point, I have experienced firsthand how racism and MLMs go hand-in-hand, but what I didn't know was that even the Ku Klux Klan was structured as a pyramid scheme for a period of time. Before researching this book, I had no idea, and yet, in 2011, Roland G. Fryer and Steven D. Levitt found that "the 1920s Klan was best described as a social organization with a wildly successful multilevel marketing structure."

The KKK has had many iterations since the early 1870s and operates within small splinter groups around the United States. However, during the 1920s, it experienced a resurgence, incorporated as a Georgia fraternal organization in which the leaders exploited preexisting racism to make money.

A new member had to buy a KKK robe from an approved KKK factory, and there was further pressure to buy other racist swag. They paid a membership fee, and the fee went up the chain, just like in an MLM. But because pyramids only survive as long as they can expand, the KKK (as it was known then) collapsed under this MLM model. Their desire for profit was nearly as integral in the foundation of the organization as their hateful ideology. This is surprising, since the KKK is mostly known as a brutal terrorist group. Hate crimes and systemic bigotry were rampant in the 1920s, but research suggests that at the time, the KKK as an organization didn't have as much of an impact on this; they simply capitalized on it. The IRS noted that the organization was not tax-exempt and slapped them with a nearly $700,000 tax bill. The KKK, as it existed at that point, was taxed out of business. Though splinter groups using the same name continued to grow and inflict terror, the KKK as a financially incorporated organization has never returned.

Though I had never heard of a Rejuvinat rep claiming ties to the KKK, their hate flags are now flying high on social media because they can't post in blackface. In response, Rejuvinat decides to do a pop-up virtual panel on, you guessed it, diversity. It is titled generically: "Respecting All Cultures." What it actually should be titled is "Let's Whitewash This Shit." It's led by nine people: one Black woman, one Black man, one Brown woman, one Asian woman, and five white women. It's so clear that this is all about ticking boxes, not actually trying to make a change. The opening line is "We honor diversity—let's focus on what unites us!" According to this panel, rich white women are the unifying factor. Nobody says anything about antiracism, social justice, or how to prevent harming people of color. At this point in the pandemic, there are also many anti-Asian slurs and hate speech regarding the "Asian flu," which nobody talks about, either. The entire twenty-minute image-control panel (that's right, no need to spend time on such a minor thing as racism) is a sugarcoated "this is fine, everything is fine, we're all fine" plug in a leaky dam. And it is painful to watch.

But here's where it starts going even further south: Instead of telling the consultants to remove the offensive posts about blackface, the company does nothing. *Nothing.* Now, remember, this is the same company that asked me to remove a podcast interview because I talked about, gasp, sex in the same half hour that I mentioned the company name. But now they are responding with "We don't get involved in politics." Yet, as I've covered before, MLMs are *very* political. The lobbying that keeps MLMs in business is political. Even so, the problem isn't that MLMs are too political, or that Christians or right-wing Republicans or any race or gender or particular group are too political; it's that their political agendas benefit them, and only them, at the expense of their neighbors.

Essentially, the company is bowing down to the top leaders, who are acting like entitled brats. And it only gets worse from there.

Not a week later, Kimberly posts the infamous *Plandemic* video to her 150,000 followers.

If you didn't have the pleasure of watching that absolute disaster of nothingness (I'll never get those twenty-six minutes of my life back), it was a video that claimed a dark underground group of elites were using this fake virus and potential vaccine to gain power. It included the commentary of discredited scientists and anti-vaccine activists, and the whole thing was quickly denounced and removed. Unfortunately, not before it received almost 2.5 million interactions, including many other top leaders in Rejuvinat. Allison hopped on the bandwagon and shared it in an email to all of us on her team, and in a post on Facebook. I commented on several of the posts by women I knew, urging them to think critically and fact-check further, but every time I did, I had swarms of other women who believed this rhetoric attacking me and using anti-science logic to fight me in the comments section in all caps. None of these women were particularly versed in science or research. However, fearmongering—spreading frightening and exaggerated rumors to arouse fear and manipulate others—is a common tactic in MLMs. I would go so far as to say it's the official love language of MLMs.

Because fear sells! It makes people emotional rather than reasonable, and with critical thinking out the window, they are likely to fall for anything. In an MLM, it's pretty easy to boost yourself even higher in the ranks by instilling fear in others. I knew this worked, because I'd done it in the past—threatening to remove people from my team page if they didn't follow certain rules or sending shaming text messages asking my team why they weren't at a biz op. A few years earlier, I'd told a team member that she was "lame" for not showing up to a Zoom call, and I told another that her boyfriend was becoming a distraction from Rejuvinat. When customers quit, instead of being gracious and saying, "Thank you for your business," I hounded them for the reasons why, and did everything in my power to make them feel like they needed to continue purchasing products, without listening to their real concerns. I participated in this fearmongering, just in a different way. I was a part of the problem.

And during what will likely be one of the strangest, most tragic, and most dramatic moments of our collective lifetime, who doesn't want to cling to an easy (albeit totally bizarre and unlikely) explanation for why we are in the middle of a dumpster fire? But orchestrated violence, a planned pandemic, a government conspiracy, and a dark underground cabal of celebrities and politicians who eat babies from the basement of a pizza restaurant? *What the actual hell?* However, when you trust your upline, put your livelihood in their hands, and duplicate what you're told and what you hear, why wouldn't you fall for anything and everything they are doing and saying? And this is the difficulty with misinformation—if it's said and shared widely enough, no matter how illogical, it starts to seem plausible.

The fact that so many women in MLMs could so easily be suckered into these posts and conspiracies begins to make sense to me. It makes sense that people who are suckered into a pyramid scheme; who get indoctrinated into every part of the cult, down to the studded heels and those stupid fedora hats; who repeat everything they are told by their upline; and who use all the same products, believing in the benefits and vision of the company, even if there is nothing behind it, would be more susceptible to other bad ideas and false information. Many of them start posting QAnon conspiracy theories, describing themselves as independent thinkers and freedom fighters. Some of them even surmise that the earth really is flat.

Concordia University researcher Marc-André Argentino has a name for people like this: "Pastel QAnon." As he described in *The Atlantic*:

> These women—they are almost universally women—are doing the work of sanitizing QAnon, often pairing its least objectionable elements (save the children!) with equally inoffensive imagery: millennial-pink-and-gold color schemes, a winning smile. And many of them are members of multilevel-marketing organizations—a massive, under-examined sector of the American retail economy that is uniquely fertile ground for conspiracism. These are organizations built on foundational myths (that the establishment is keeping secrets from you, that you are on a hero's journey to enlightenment and wealth), charismatic leadership, and shameless, constant posting. The people at the top of them are enviable, rich, and gifted at wrapping everything that happens—in their personal lives, or in the world around them—into a grand narrative about how to become as happy as they are. In 2020, what's happening to them is dark and dangerous, but it looks gorgeous.

It fits really well into the idea that MLMers have some sort of "sacred secret" to business, so why wouldn't they also have social and political secrets? Why wouldn't they know what's *really* going on? They truly believe that the government doesn't want you to know things. They say that you are living in fear of a virus, but in actuality, they are living in fear of everything.

There is pushback from reps who feel the same way I do—that a general mistrust in the government isn't the issue, but searching for bizarre explanations for a continuing pandemic is dangerous. Many send emails to corporate, comment on posts, and try to talk to their team members, but the pushback is even stronger, and the divide in the

MLM community, seemingly just like the rest of the country on social media, only widens.

It should be no surprise that while MLMers fell victim to the undue influence of QAnon, QAnon promoters then turned to promoting MLMs as a way to monetize their followings. Birds of a feather, as political commentator Will Sommer documented in his article "QAnon Leaders Push Followers into Multi-Level Marketing": "QAnon booster Richard Potcner, who goes by the name 'Richard Citizen Journalist' online, pushed his followers to buy silver. But not just any silver, a very specific MLM silver company. His tagline, 'Patriots are unstoppable together,' falls right in line with the word salad of most MLM marketing-company taglines."

I finally unfriend Allison after a post one random afternoon where she urges her Facebook following to refuse to mask or get vaccinated: "The people who push this fake virus delusion and want us to wear face diapers are the same people who think abortion is health care, there are unlimited genders, Critical Race Theory isn't racist, and BLM cares about Black lives." I can't believe she's the same woman who snuck out with a random dude at that shady Colorado bar just a few years earlier. Or maybe she's been this way all along, and I was too brainwashed to see it.

There's an all-or-nothing, us-against-them mentality with MLMs that seems to be part of the culture wars in general. Again, I can respect Allison having different views on vaccination, but the evidence behind her opinions is shady YouTube videos and other Rejuvinat reps, not personal experience or the opinions of trusted scientists and medical experts. I am beginning to see so many cracks in the system that I ignored for so long—sometimes unknowingly, sometimes on purpose.

Finally, after much back-and-forth, I send an email to Compliance about the rampant spread of misinformation. I feel like I'm tattling, and my desire to enact change in a company I don't love anymore is low, but I've been turned in to Compliance so many times for my book, I figure, why not pay it forward? I forward the inflammatory posts that spread hate and misinformation. I receive a form email back.

Thanks so much for reaching out. Rejuvinat is a company that welcomes and values a diverse and inclusive community of people, which means we will inevitably have situations where differing beliefs and opinions exist on various matters. With so much uncertainty in today's world, let's continue to focus on what unites us, rather than what divides us. By coming together and rising above our differences, we are stronger and greater than we could ever be apart.

Thank you for your support.

Sincerely,
Rejuvinat Compliance

Jesus, what? We are "diverse and inclusive"? As diverse as a box of sugar cubes. Differing beliefs and opinions are great, but hateful ones prohibit inclusion. And now you're gaslighting me for complaining during a pandemic? "Thank you for your support"? I am not supportive, hence the email. Wow. A few other consultants who express concern receive the exact same form email, including Serena, who is also embarrassed by her involvement with Rejuvinat. So, despite having so much "power" in the company as a top earner, I realize it was meaningless. I was a showpiece. My power was in bringing more women into the system and shilling more products for them, not to enact actual change.

Or maybe I wasn't quite powerful enough. I recall a few years earlier when the company changed their logo to a rainbow for Pride month. Kimberly urged the company to remove it, stating that they should refrain from posting about "polarizing" topics. They changed the logo back because of that. So perhaps Kimberly was high enough at the top of the structure with her $500,000- to $750,000-per-month income. After all, if she left Rejuvinat, the pyramid would crumble. If I left? It wouldn't impact the company much at this point. Also, Kimberly was likely speaking to a larger conservative contingent within the organization that believed the face of Rejuvinat was white, cis, and heteronormative. No wonder the rainbow was polarizing. Another sign that using the platform to support equal rights and social equity is not their priority—it's to appease their moneymakers, even if they are bigots.

My words have fallen on deaf ears, so I stop trying. Instead, I continue to ignore the disgusting behavior I see among other reps and curate my own social media feed to serve me and my mental health better. I unfollow people who share things I want to argue with, because like the company, my words don't matter to them. Whose opinion is changed on social media, after all? The idea of seeking accountability from people who have shared problematic articles or opinions on social media seems, I don't know, pointless.

Besides, even among those who seem to be saying all the "right" things, it is impossible to know who is performative and who is actually putting their money where their mouth is, or who is simply sharing what a friend told them. It's not that I don't think people or companies should be called out, but I know better than anyone at this point that social media isn't real. Who knows whether what is shared on an Instagram feed reflects the real actions, behaviors, and intentions of the person posting it? Do your friends really care about BLM, or did they just post a black square because they felt shamed into doing it? Do the people who didn't share a black square actually *not* care, or were they taking time off social media to actually enact change in real life?

I take time to check my ego, which Rejuvinat has inflated for so many years. For so long, I believed that what I was doing and saying was of the utmost importance, and that everyone needed to hear and see me. How is shouting at people online helping anything, though? I also think that, while it's important to combat misinformation, we also need to reconsider the idea of "safe spaces." The internet is not safe if you're worried about being trolled. But when I'm sitting in my warm house with my Wi-Fi and my smartphone, how unsafe am I? And to protect myself from the "harm" that I considered was being inflicted, all I needed to do was delete Instagram. What happened to "Sticks and stones can break my bones, but words can never hurt me"? The internet is all words, and behind them, intentions that we can't begin to place. Maybe that is why so many people like me—comfortable, safe, and white, often insulated from racial-justice uprisings and pandemic misinformation—find we have more to lose than to gain by becoming loud.

I feel called to step back, remove the pressure on myself to comment on every social issue, do my best to educate myself, and enact change in real life. I remind myself that not everyone needs my hot take. In fact, nobody does. I begin to remind myself of how I once used social media for fun, for entertainment, and for joy. That was, until the election of 2020.

When Biden wins, many of the alt-right MLMers effectively lose their minds. Now, as I've said, I don't pick sides, and I'm not going to say that Biden is the best candidate I've ever seen in my life. Great, another old white dude. But getting Trump out of office has been an emergency for many of us, m'kay? The corruption, vitriolic personality, and disastrous tweeting were just a start—please don't get me started on the immigration policies and his inaction at the beginning of the pandemic. I believe in nuance and different perspectives and having the agency to choose your own candidate. But what I don't understand are the women I once called sisters insisting that the election was stolen. Posting "The South will rise" on social media. Making jokes about

Biden hopefully dying soon. All interspersed with posts about their "life-changing" products and business opportunity. Spouting about personal freedom, as though that covers both their desire not to wear a mask and their desire to recruit you into Rejuvinat.

Really? Freedom? You mean, when other people were living their lives and you were glued to your phone sending cold messages on New Year's Eve? Freedom when you were told what you could and couldn't say on social media or in your convention speech? Freedom when you couldn't decide your product lineup, your own discounts, your own pricing structure? That kind of freedom? And now you want freedom to . . . what? Say whatever the hell you want without consequences?

Again, crickets from Rejuvinat. More and more, I am feeling like my allegiance (however distant) to the company is making me complicit in these disastrous messages, even though they are so far from what I believe.

I HAVE A FEW Zoom calls with friends—our new "coffee dates," since we can no longer meet in person. Serena is one of my weekly Zoom friends, and I look forward to our conversations about life as much as I do our bitch sessions about Rejuvinat. She's in the same boat as me but feels even more trapped. Her Rejuvinat money supports her mom's assisted-living facility. She's doing everything she can to try to replace her income. She was interviewing for jobs when the pandemic hit, and now she's frustrated. I know she had a virtual interview with one of the companies this past week. I realize immediately that it didn't go well.

"They said it was between me and one other person, and the fact that I'd been in an MLM didn't look good." Even through the screen,

I can see her holding back tears. "They said it wasn't the type of sales experience they were interested in."

"Oh, Serena, I'm so sorry. There will be other opportunities!" I try to avoid toxic positivity, but I *know* Serena. She was in marketing before kids and before Rejuvinat, and she is brilliant, charismatic, and the kindest person I know, so I know she'll find something. She wants so badly to get away from the MLM, especially now, but she can't walk away from the income.

"You know what really sucks? I knew that it would take me a while to find a job, but I had no idea that being in an MLM would look bad to employers. It's one thing to have a gap in experience, being a stay-at-home mom, but I used to think that being in Rejuvinat would help bridge that gap. Now, I realize it's hurting my prospects."

Like many people who are wary of MLMs, many industries look down on them, as well. As Serena was quickly realizing, it's probably a bad idea to put it on your resume or even mention it, according to some experts. Participation in an MLM may reflect negatively on you. As one HR executive on Reddit shared:

> As an employer, if I see someone put MLM on their resume (and they usually add their ridiculous rank as their title), it's an automatic "no" pile. I feel that putting MLM "experience" shows that the candidate makes poor decisions and also, they obviously haven't learned how poor of a decision they made if they put it on their resume. In addition, MLMs provide no valuable training and I don't want to risk hiring someone who may still be enticed by an MLM and try to bring that crap in my company.

And that comment is one of many echoing similar sentiments. According to Ask a Manager, Pink Truth, and many other sources, almost all employers state that the downside risk of listing your MLM "job" on your resume is greater than any potential upside. Even a gap in employment is favorable to time spent in an MLM.

I feel empathy for both Serena and the company she interviewed with! Knowing what I know now, who *wouldn't* view MLM experience as negative? What company would want someone who considers cold messaging "sales"? It's not a good look. Similar to people in cults who are wholly indoctrinated, while outsiders can see how bizarre certain behavior it is, insiders think it's completely normal. And then, as more MLMers have become synonymous with conspiracy theories and right-wing nut-crackery, employers likely began to get concerned over who they were hiring, and how they might behave in the workplace. As I think of ways for Serena to reframe the experience, she drops a juicy tidbit of gossip.

"OMG, I can't believe I forgot to tell you this. Jamie took out a PPP loan. Totally illegal. She's training the whole team on how to take out loans. And you wouldn't believe how many of these chicks are dumb enough to do it."

What. The. Hell.

Now we come to something that is shocking yet somehow unsurprising: PPP loan fraud. The Paycheck Protection Program was established to provide small businesses with resources they needed to maintain their payroll, hire back employees who may have been laid off, and cover applicable overhead. Now, MLM corporations (the parent company, not reps, which we'll get to in a second) could technically apply, even though they're not actually small businesses. Though they have hundreds of thousands of 1099 reps, as long as they have fewer than five hundred paid (W-2) employees, they still qualify. Since they are getting revenue from so many sources, it's shitty, but technically, it's not fraud. Sadly, those loans took away funds from small businesses that needed them more. You can search the database and see that

MLMs took advantage in a big way. I found about ninety MLMs with loan amounts totaling over $100 *million*. But that's not the worst part of this, and that's where we get to the fraud.

MLM reps were themselves *exempt* from PPP loan dollars. In fact, this exemption was quite literally first on the list:

What type of business does not qualify for the Paycheck Protection Program?

- Multilevel marketers (MLM)
- Banks, lending institutions, and investment companies
- Political and policy lobbyists
- Landlords or businesses who do not manage their own operations
- Religion-promoting businesses
- Businesses that restrict gender patronage (e.g., men- or women-only health clubs)
- Casinos or other gambling businesses
- Marijuana businesses
- Household businesses that contract or employ housekeepers and nannies
- Businesses dealing with sexual material
- Business owners convicted of a felony in the past five years or currently indicted on federal charges
- Any business owner or partner with more than 20 percent stakeholder that is not a US citizen or Lawful Permanent Resident

MLM reps were excluded from taking loans, plain as day. Now, many MLM reps at the top have an LLC or S corporation for their tax structure. Some of them have their own assistants, whom they potentially could pay via W-2, which would technically make them qualify. But if they did have an LLC, or an S corporation, they would also have a business name of their own and the loan amount would be pretty small. You probably wouldn't be able to track down "Shiny Skin LLC" in the database, or whatever LLC or S corporation name the rep had registered. But what you could do was search any MLM name in the database. Go ahead! Put in "Monat," "Beachbody," "Rodan + Fields," or any other MLM you can think of.

Let me tell you what you'll find: multiple listings. Why, you might ask, since there is only one parent company, can the company be listed multiple times? It's because these dumbass reps used the company name to take out fraudulent loans for themselves. MLM reps without their own actual established small businesses, without a business name, without employees to pay, scammed a program put together in the pandemic to help small businesses. It seems outrageous, but it's true. Because as you may or may not know, you can't open a business with the same name as an already established business with a registered trademark. There's only one Pampered Chef, yet there are dozens of loans taken out under that company name by reps who didn't qualify. *Fraud*.

I have the immense privilege of knowing the woman who oversaw the Senate committee that created the PPP. We'll call her Annabelle. She told me that for claims under $150,000, as is the case for MLM reps, the fraud is much worse than I could ever imagine. The PPP received copious applications from MLM reps, who not only filed fraudulently but also listed the cost of products (not an eligible expense even for a legitimate company) and the lost cost of conventions and travel (again, not an eligible expense, *and* let's not forget that airlines, conventions, and hotels were fully refunding everyone during the pandemic for the most part—so this is like triple fraud).

Annabelle found that many of the fraudulent loans were taken out through a handful of certain lenders. It seemed like a concerted effort, since some banks that aren't even banks, as well as some credit unions, make up the majority of the lenders for funds given to these fraudulent claims. To fund PPP loans, the government gave money to lenders to do transactions, and there was a built-in fee, so essentially, these lenders were incentivized to do this. Why wouldn't they potentially look the other way if the reps weren't legit? This is pure speculation, but if there is a financial incentive for Lenders 'R' Us to dispense their PPP funds to some bossbabes, why wouldn't they?

The number of PPP loans taken out fraudulently has completely overwhelmed the Small Business Administration, and they are now slowly trying to dig themselves out. Luckily, they are succeeding in recovering some of the fraudulent money, which is being allocated toward the Restaurant Relief Fund to fund women, minorities, and rural communities who were impacted by the pandemic—you know, the people who should have received it in the first place.

Annabelle continued to tell me that the DSA (remember our friends, the Direct Selling Association?) has been "throwing around money in DC" for so long, and that they are extremely influential, and "very slimy"—all of which is no surprise. They are not in service of the hardworking reps; instead, they lobby to keep wealthy MLM owners in power.

At the time of this writing, a congressional hearing is being put together to find out just how deep this PPP fraud goes. Because of the similarities in the claims and the lenders used, it is believed that some of these companies encouraged their sellers to take out the loans. (Sidenote: If you have any tips related to people who took fraudulent PPP money or who were encouraged to do so by their company, you can submit an anonymous complaint via the SBA website.)

The kicker to this whole scenario? These chicks were all posting on their social media timelines how lucrative their "side hustles" were during this time, and the companies were all singing the praises of the reps' revenue and expanding businesses, deliberately distorting information to make it more acceptable. What a joke.

I am not surprised by Serena's information, but I'm still horrified. "Serena, that is awful."

"I know," she says, defeated. "I don't know how to associate with these people anymore. They are not who I thought they were. And yet, I'm trapped. Completely trapped."

I understand. I feel trapped, too. But am I, really? Yes, the money is good, but what is the cost of being stuck in this toxic environment? My paycheck is still hovering around $10,000 per month, but I will learn the true cost in the next few weeks, when I receive my year-end statement, which nails the coffin on my MLM career: I still hit the top rank of the company. Despite not working for an entire year, not talking to a single customer or recruiting even one person, and despite my entire team losing ranks and losing money, including me, I still hit the coveted 0.05 percent, with all the perks, bonuses, and bling that come with it. *And I have done nothing to deserve it.*

It is such a moment of clarity for me. My cognitive dissonance automatically clears. I no longer can lean on the false notion that "I built this" and deserve to collect a check. I can no longer ignore that all the money flowing up is due to everyone else's hard work, not mine. And I wonder to myself, *How did I stay for so long just for money?* I don't have an answer. Instead, I fax the termination form before I can think one more second about it. I know I will never come to a different conclusion: I cannot be aligned in any way with Rejuvinat anymore. I no longer can follow the status quo for a paycheck, since so much of what is coming out of the company goes against what I believe. The cumulative effect of the unethical and ugly things I've seen through the pandemic, leading to this moment, is an unnavigable divide between who I am and who I once was. And I can't continue to sell my soul for another day.

I immediately receive a form email from the company: "Sorry to see you go." The fangirling, the paycheck, the bling, the accolades, are all gone in an instant.

I was always just a number.

ME

Life Takes on a New Shape (and It's Not a Pyramid)

I left my MLM because I wasn't comfortable with how it had taken over my life. It ruined so many friendships because I was constantly pursuing people. And I realized my upline was constantly pursuing me—the next title, the next sale—because it benefited her. I thought these people were my friends, because frankly, between Zoom calls and messages and conventions and biz ops, I spent more time with them than my actual real-life friends! But proximity isn't friendship, which I realized when I quit, and was dropped immediately.

—ELIZA D., former MLM rep.

In an MLM, you're told to "do the hard thing." I've been telling my downline that for years. Always push, strive, persevere, even if "the hard thing" is just sending a cold message on a Sunday afternoon to someone you went to high school with. But as I've realized so many times in my life, the right thing and the hard thing can be the *same* thing. Having children. Fixing a marriage. Getting sober. And now, leaving Rejuvinat.

Whether it's Rejuvinat or the NXIVM cult or Amway, the structure is the same. You are buying your way into a community whose main goal is to profit off you. Any dissent threatens their sense of unity, their livelihood, their belief about their future potential. Though there might be real friendships tucked inside, the structure is there to drive competition, often leaving women worse off than when they started: in credit-card debt, in trouble with the IRS, cut off from their families, bullied and hurt, or unable to secure real employment. Thankfully, I was departing relatively unscathed, but leaving a commercial cult is still a shock to the system.

According to the book *Merchants of Deception* by Eric Scheibeler, a former Amway insider, leaving a cult can feel disorienting and confusing at the best of times, but the experience is often compounded by feeling like an alien in the big, bad world. Most people who leave an MLM describe relationship problems, low self-esteem, post-traumatic stress disorder (PTSD), and even suicidal tendencies after their exodus. And that can lead to cognitive dissonance, possibly causing them to believe that the cult was the remedy to their pain, which can send some defectors right back into the same MLM or other MLMs.

The many women I've talked to who left commercial cults all echo the same thing: Our life became so entwined with the MLM that it was difficult to imagine leaving it behind. You come to feel deeply ashamed for helping spread the MLM's falsehood, so you stay in the lie, or you wait even longer to leave. I stayed in the lie for years after initially realizing it was indeed a lie. And when you finally leave, you realize that the amazing community you were a part of was conditional. They will likely block or belittle you or send Compliance after you. You might get a cease-and-desist letter. You're an outsider and a threat now. When you leave a cult, you can expect to be abandoned by the "best friends" you met there. They can't afford to see you thrive after leaving, because it challenges the lies they have to believe in order to stay. Your existence, your joys, and your success are a threat to all they've been indoctrinated to believe. This is what keeps so many women stuck: "I can't leave—this is all I know! I can't leave because I promoted this and shouted it from the rooftops—I'll look like an idiot! I can't leave because . . . sunk cost—so much time, money, relationships!"

Staying in the system feels safer, because when you even begin to entertain leaving, you are shamed. You see what happens to those who leave, and you are afraid. You know that you'll be shunned, excommunicated, and labeled a traitor. "Block her. Don't read her posts. Don't read her book. She has a negative mindset. You don't want to receive that negativity." I know this because I lived it and recited it on the other side.

But I've now become the person I cautioned others about for so long.

I start speaking on podcasts, writing articles, and sharing my story of leaving the MLM, similar to when I left drinking behind. I start shedding pieces of the "bossbabe" uniform I acquired over the years. I say goodbye to my hair extensions, and even stop covering my grays altogether. Part of it is facilitated by the pandemic and hair salons being closed, but I also feel like I am discovering myself again, the same way I did when the alcohol was stripped away. I quit working so hard to remain a size two because that's what looked good on a stage and in life-size photos at Convention. I start moving my body in ways I enjoy instead of in ways that make me thinner. I even have my breast implants removed, because they feel so, for lack of a better word, fake. I stop worrying so much about the filters and the name brands and all the things I realize I never cared about in the first place—I just thought I needed them to belong in the upper echelons of the MLM.

The mental freedom from releasing all those things is profound. The ability to unplug from my phone, or leave it behind altogether, to not have to document every waking second of my day on social media, to constantly strive to be at the top of a pyramid. I feel free in a way that I haven't for a long time. I hadn't realized how trapped I'd become.

I also start examining my own need for validation—the fact that I'd been so vulnerable and shared my story freely with so many people. The MLM inflated my ego to such a degree that I begin to question how important my story actually is. It is unnerving—the feeling that maybe, just maybe, your words are simply noise in a noisy world. That if everything the MLM led you to believe was a lie, maybe your own importance is, too. Had I not been in an ego-inflating MLM, would I have ever written my first book?

It isn't easy leaving Rejuvinat. I've built a community there—what I felt for so long was a home. Thankfully, many of my friendships remain. I talk to Serena and Vanessa almost every day. Vanessa is happily still working her "real" job, and Serena is still trying to find one and leave Rejuvinat behind.

June quits after I do and goes back to personal finance, where she thrives. My relationships with many remain intact, even with women who stay in Rejuvinat: Mandy, Annie, Carly, other friends I had before joining the MLM, and most of those who weren't financially linked to me. I make my amends to Hannah, who ends up getting a job at a flower shop that she loves. Madison keeps her distance since she's "all in" with her new "life-changing" company, where all the reps are her new best friends. Same shit, different day. Still, there are many others who never call back, and who are coerced to block or unfriend me on social media. Despite having vacationed together and spent so much time in what I thought was a friendship, Becky stops speaking to me as soon as I leave, making me realize that we were only friends because I made her a shit ton of money. (Sidenote: she did finally reach the top rank when I left, a result of my downline and Madison's rolling to her; though according to social media, it was all thanks to her dozen years of "hard work, mindset shifts, and determination.")

It's interesting comparing my first book to the one you are now reading. When I wrote a book that focused mainly on not drinking, people were able to compartmentalize; that is, plenty of drinkers read it and loved it because they didn't consider their drinking to be a problematic part of their personality. But an MLM is different. It's not something you do in your off hours. It becomes your identity. It's all or nothing. So if someone doesn't like it or leaves it altogether, it's considered a personal insult. Writing about leaving drinking wasn't an offense to my former bossbabe friends, but writing about leaving the MLM is.

The same women who praised my first book and the conversations about not drinking now seethe at my conversations about leaving the MLM. Kristy and Shelly, who begged for my secrets to success during my Colorado trip, send me page-long Instagram messages about what a disappointment I am, how I am ruining the industry for everyone else, and how I am stabbing Becky and Allison in the back. The same boss-babes who used photos of me at my book launch to further their own credibility ("Look! I'm aligned with a company that has best-selling authors!") become the same women who send me toxic messages.

I remember a woman named Esther, who spent over an hour talking to me at my Nashville book launch. She was so enamored with my ability to be honest and step into my own truth. Now, she's commenting "traitor" on my Facebook feed, even though I am simply once again sharing my own truth. Alicia, who also attended my book launch, takes it a step further with an ad hominem attack that I've "gotten fat and ugly" since leaving Rejuvinat. Kimberly sends an email to everyone in her downline to block me and tells Serena that she shouldn't be friends with me anymore. Allison, who used to share my sobriety story on social media as an example of the "change that Rejuvinat can bring to people's lives," opens a burner Instagram account (since I've blocked her) and starts reporting my posts on Instagram and leaving comments like "If you hated it so much, why did you stay so long! What a betrayal! I can't believe I ever called you a friend!"

And the same upline leaders who love bombed me while I made them money stop speaking to me altogether, including those who were my friends—or the ones I thought would always be my friends. And to a degree, I understand. It becomes impossible for many women in my upline to compartmentalize the job so that it's separate from their sense of self. I get it, because Rejuvinat was also a part of me for so long.

And yet, many more understand and quietly thank me offline. Overall, the messages I receive in support of my exodus outnumber the hate mail. Jamie sends me a message, first apologizing for leaving me in the back of a taxi in Las Vegas, but also telling me she is proud of me and understands. A common theme among current MLM reps, she also asks me to keep her anonymous and not tell anyone she is supporting this book. These women are in fear of their fading allegiance to Rejuvinat and the MLM channel being "outed." I receive messages from hundreds of women echoing what I witnessed with Hannah: a wounded self-esteem, a lost sense of purpose, and a feeling of paranoia for questioning what they'd been told was "the way" for so long.

These messages have made my desire to speak about my MLM experience even greater.

At first, my life gets very quiet. Without the swirling storm of social media, and with the ever-present weight of the ongoing pandemic, I am reminded of what it was like before Rejuvinat, when my days were consumed with children and alcohol and not much else. But this time, I don't want a distraction. I have my family, with whom I have a stronger relationship now than ever before. I'm no longer obsessed with my phone and my network, or my image. I have a passion and a purpose. I have begun to build a voice in recovery.

Sober Mom Squad is continuing to grow. Not surprisingly, a number of our members have been in an MLM (some of them still are). But we are creating a new community, one where mothers can find fellowship around sobriety and not sales. Though we formed it during the pandemic, we realize all the ways it can create purpose for sober moms who long to find joy in the quiet and the chaos, and away from the pomp and inauthenticity of social media. We want to create a place of action, activism, and unity, and not just for white moms. We want Sober Mom Squad to reflect women from all over the ethnic, racial, and economic spectrum.

Though most of my network is still very white, thanks to my MLM, and Sober Mom Squad still reflects that, I've learned from the lack of diversity in Rejuvinat and have taken part in antiracism training. I have included BIPOC women among the company's leadership, because I want it to feel like home for anyone who wishes to leave alcohol behind. In many ways, Sober Mom Squad came out of the realization that women need the fellowship that MLMs provide, but perhaps without all the predatory behavior.

Thankfully, it resonated with so many women, and they wanted more—more meetings, coaching, offerings. So, with the help of a few other sober friends in the recovery space, whom I contract to help lead meetings and coach and create content, I build an online paid platform. I have some major hesitation about developing a paid platform. Frankly, it's hard to go back to charging people for things. I don't want to be exploitative, but I want to be paid for what I am trained in. There's been some backlash in the recovery community, mostly from AA old-timers who believe AA is the only way, and that recovery should be free (despite the fact that all organizations require money to flow through them to function, even the free ones like AA). I also know what I *don't* want: a community that requires payment and only rewards a few.

I make sure to offer a sliding scale. Those who can afford to pay for the services allow me to be able to pay my coaches and counselors a very

fair rate, and to offer scholarships to those who can't afford it. It's a payment structure I feel good about, because it rewards those who are well
trained to help people sustain change in their lives, allowing people who
value our work to invest, and benefiting everyone who's involved.

The connection I have with my friends in Sober Mom Squad is built
on a desire to see each other improve, but only in the way that makes
sense for us individually. We don't have a checklist of requirements, and
though many pay for the service, nobody is treated differently if they
receive our free services or use other recovery paths or programs. We
establish real connections to combat the loneliness that leads us to
drink or seek out other unhealthy coping mechanisms. We share, and
we talk about the hard shit. We create community in the lonely pockets
of motherhood. We don't shy away from the hard topics, and we nod
our heads in solidarity.

I'm always open to adjustment, to correction, to the fact that I *know*
I'm not always right. I dug my heels in the sand long enough with
Rejuvinat to understand that I don't always know everything. And I'm
now open to the opinions of those whom my words and actions affect,
knowing I was unreceptive for *so* long. I was unreceptive because I was
taught (and believed) that I shouldn't care what other people think. But
this is an avoidance tactic. I started my business as a Rejuvinat rep to
avoid—working on my marriage, looking at my alcohol problem, leaning all in on motherhood, and stress and anxiety, which only brought
on more. Through attempting to avoid my life, I was indoctrinated to
"follow the system and not give a shit what people think." Back in New
York, I gave a keynote speech on this topic (I merely changed *shit* to
ish to be palatable). This is more information control: Believe what the
cult members tell you, not friends or family, and especially don't believe
your own thoughts or feelings.

This snarky, passive-aggressive rhetoric is everywhere: "We don't
care what the haters think." This kind of attitude conveniently skirts

around accountability and the possibility of meaningful dialogue and change. It's inherently defensive, hierarchical, and supremacist. Because to allow no feedback for problematic behavior is, well, problematic.

When I was in Rejuvinat, we posted memes, quotes, reels, and videos all about how much we didn't care what people thought, not realizing they only revealed how much we *did* care, since we needed to post about it so much. And the bottom line is, you *should* care.

You *should* care what your loved ones think. You *should* listen to people who left the structure you're peddling or thinking of joining. Remaining in the echo chamber of the MLM reps who are trying to recruit you, who supposedly don't care what people think, is not the same as doing your due diligence or being presented unbiased, well-researched facts by your "haters," who might actually have a point or two.

I joined Rejuvinat for connection, to combat loneliness, to fix something in myself that I thought was missing, to help contribute to my family, to better myself and others. Yet, by doing so, I was complicit in hurting many people. I was trapped in a culture of my own making. And even when I saw that I wasn't helping everyone, I rationalized by insisting that I was helping myself, and a few others, *just enough* to make it all okay.

Even the most "woke" among the Rejuvinat consultants, who have "Black Lives Matter" signs displayed in front of their homes, clutch their pearls at my discussion of white supremacy, likely scared to acknowledge their own complicity in the system.

And *this* is the reason that MLMs uphold white supremacy. We live in a world where we participate, not because we believe in the system, but because, by virtue of our whiteness, we've inherited the system. To leave it, you have to renounce it, like a citizenship, and that is very hard to do. It's hard to walk away from a paycheck, even when you know it's hurting people.

And it's not to say that a financial buy-in to a connection is a bad thing. Gyms, organizations, and even meetup groups need money flowing through them to work! But look at the way the money flows: Is it going to pay for a lease and exercise equipment, or an online platform to cover the cost of instructors and teachers, as well as other administrative tasks? Completely different from paying members *inside* the organization, as an MLM does. And look at who benefits from the money being paid: Is everyone being paid fairly within the organization? Look at the options for people who don't have money: Are there scholarships or sliding-scale options?

The way to find true connection is to meet in a community where it's available to everyone who wants access to it. Healing loneliness by joining an MLM makes you a perpetrator, and your helplessness to enact real change and the belief that you are creating real connection will keep you stuck in a hierarchy that rewards a few at the expense of many.

Getting out seemed impossible, but for me, it was the responsible thing to do. It wasn't enough for me to go on autopilot, collect a check, and slowly do less work, which I tried for a long time; I was still complicit in the system. I had to fully leave, quit, stop financially benefiting, and speak about my experience. And despite losing thousands of boss-babe acquaintances because of it, I do believe I have an authentic connection in my life now.

The sentiments from my friends echo what I now understand. My friend Amanda, who distanced herself from me when I joined Rejuvinat, sent me a message after I announced that I'd quit. "I had my own opinions about the women who you were joining, but I didn't say anything. And then, it was wild to see you get in SO DEEP. The gowns, the car, the bizarre sameness of the women involved. I felt like you were being brainwashed and sharing it for all of us to see. I'm so happy you're sharing your story. Cheers with fizzy water!"

Another woman who used to be on my team said, "You were intense. You were absolutely all in. Doing the intensive workshops, the push and the drive. It was a wild, traumatic world. And yet, I still wanted to be at the top, despite losing money. I'm so glad I got out, and I'm so glad you are out, too!"

My connection with those who were never in the MLM is more authentic than before. There was always a lingering fear among others that I was going to constantly be selling them something, the products or the business, and that I always had an ulterior motive. My friend Bridget told me, "I feel like I finally have you back," after I quit. My mom expressed her relief as well. My brother gave me an "I told you so," as only a brother can. Smart-ass.

My relationships with my husband and kids are stronger than ever. Without the pressures of Rejuvinat, traveling, or the financial stress, a space was cleared for us to continue to work on our own relationship and family system. The pandemic and the changes in our employment allowed us to prioritize what we really wanted. We moved out of the hustle and bustle of the city to a quieter, less-populated area, with more space to just be together as a family unit. We moved closer to my parents, since the distance of the pandemic made us realize how important our extended relationships were. Today, I spend more time in real life with my loved ones and share much less about it on social media. I didn't realize what an imposition it was to constantly put my kids "on stage" online, and how much I was missing by always being behind my phone camera, staging the perfect shot. Today, we soak up every memory, instead of proving to the world that we are making them.

What I was seeking nearly a decade ago has finally been found. And actually, it was there all along. I didn't need another distraction from loneliness, or a numbing agent, or even a fake sense of purpose beautifully packaged in a Rejuvinat box. I needed to embrace the relationships around me, lean into them, strip away the layers that were wearing me down, and hold the hands of people who accepted me just as I was. I happily shed the title of bossbabe for recovery advocate, trading in She-EO for (pretty) good citizen and renouncing my fempire for the sweet comfort of my family. And I've never felt like more of a boss.

Postscript

I'm often asked if I think MLMs should be illegal. The answer is, I don't know. I do know that in other countries with stronger consumer protections, MLMs don't prosper. In the United States, we need more consumer protection, but as I've already mentioned, there is so much money and power politically tied up in the MLM industry that I don't think MLMs will ever cease to exist. The double-edged sword of social media has helped MLMs prosper, and yet, it's also helped the anti-MLM movement grow. As more women get burned and feel comfortable speaking out, I do believe that more of us will educate ourselves from sources outside the commercial cult, and realize that MLMs, at the very least, can be a terrible financial decision.

I personally believe that the multilevel structure should be changed to single-level only, no recruiting. I would never have been wrapped up in something so deeply, been publicly brainwashed with trips and gifts and Facebook livestreams, if I were simply selling a product and making a profit. Instead, I was selling a dream and collecting people. I was selling an ideology, an image of success that was inherently tied to the myth of American exceptionalism, with fangirling and ego boosting that had me so enveloped, more than any other "day job," personal relationship, or hobby has ever done. And as a stay-at-home parent, I was understandably attracted to a culture that offered a salve to my loneliness. I was so engrossed in the MLM world, for years, that I did nothing to change the MLM culture. I was focused on staying afloat in the sea of FOMO, even when I started realizing that it was destructive in so many ways.

To break free, I had to educate myself on how the MLM's behaviors mimicked cults. By continuing to reference the BITE Model, I was able to slowly understand how I'd been influenced so deeply.

Through behavior control, I started behaving differently, even dressing differently, and surrounded myself with different people. I realized how Convention and month-end madness manipulated my schedule and deprived me of sleep. I recognized how my leisure time and family time were restricted by the considerable amount of time spent on group indoctrination. I was pushed and pulled constantly by rewards and punishments, and subject to rules and regulations that worked to instill my dependence.

Through information control, I was deceived by deliberately withheld information and lies about the business model and shown only cult-generated materials and propaganda. I was kept busy to discourage critical thinking and was placed in a hierarchy to compartmentalize information at different levels in the pyramid. I was encouraged to share information about my personal life and unburden myself of my "sins," which served to dissolve my identity boundaries.

Through thought control, I adopted a very black-and-white way of thinking, organizing people into us-versus-them categories and adopting the MLM's reality as my own. I *became* my company title and used loaded language to stop critical thoughts and constructive criticism, from myself and others. I used denial, rationalization, and justification to stay aligned with the company and the people in it.

And through emotional control, I blocked my intuitive feelings, believing that my success or failure was completely my doing. I had a deep fear of being shunned by the people in the MLM, and the extremes of emotional highs and lows from love bombing and public shaming kept me stuck in believing there was no legitimate reason to leave.

And I placed all of these controlling behaviors and feelings on other people, as well. I was a commercial cult victim, and a perpetrator.

If you are reading this book to help a loved one, I hope it can be of some use to you. I also hope that it will help you educate yourself on why people get so caught up in MLMs. Please try to understand where they are coming from. Please know that they genuinely love their involvement, and that reacting critically about an MLM will likely push them further away. As with any cult indoctrination, confronting someone will be potentially harmful and alienating. They will feel personally insulted. Don't barrage them with reasons why they're wrong. Ask them questions. Ask them if they understand toxic positivity, and how it can keep people bound to something—a doctrine, a business, a way of life—without them necessarily knowing.

Once they understand toxic positivity, they can look back on their own experiences and recognize that the dream they were sold, complete with trite motivational slogans, was an emotional manipulation tactic to keep them silent and complicit. This makes it easier to understand that it isn't their fault when (not if) they fail. Yet ironically, failure might make some people stauncher believers than skeptics. If that is the case, ask them if they've ever done a profit and loss statement. Perhaps ask them if their involvement in the MLM has changed any friendships, even if you already know it has. Ask them if their upline leaders extend their "friendship" at any other time than month-end to keep numbers in check, or if they receive gifts and other love bombs in lieu of profit. Simply ask; don't judge. Be kind, and patient. Know that they might come around, or they might not. I had plenty of people try to talk sense into me. I wouldn't hear it for a long time. Now I hear it, and I speak it. Give grace and have hope.

I want to reiterate that, no matter how I might come across in this book, I don't dislike people who join MLMs. Far from it. I profoundly understand them, even the Kimberlys of the world. If you're a proud bossbabe, I didn't write this book to call you out or to denounce your behavior, but rather, to shine a light on how it could be different. Perhaps you can evaluate your own values, goals, and priorities to understand how you want to be spending your time and what kind of person you want to be. Look at your social media posts, the language you use, the cut-and-pasted scripts from your upline, and see them through a different lens. Do they feel good? Authentic? If not, why? Ask yourself if you're squashing your own intuition in favor of the messages being fed to you by your company or team members. Perhaps you can have empathy and understanding for women who have done their (actual) research. And by research, I mean from someone other than you or the MLM, because you are an inherently biased source.

If you picked up this book because you have a nagging feeling that something isn't right; or you cringe when you send generic, scripted cold messages but send them anyway; or you have quit or your company has terminated or silenced you through threats of lawsuits or vague NDAs and tiny print on policies and procedures; or you were pressured to join despite your better judgment and regret it every day, please know that you're not alone.

I've listed resources at the back of this book, but the list is not exhaustive. They are abundant, and new resources are popping up every day. Typically, anything listed as "anti-MLM" will have stories and cautionary tales of other women in MLMs, or facts and figures about why they are harmful. There are other books, workbooks, YouTube channels, Instagram accounts, Reddit pages, blog posts, and more. Some may resonate more than others, so use personal agency, ingest them at your own pace, and keep an open mind. And be aware of your own potential for black-and-white thoughts, so you don't swing completely to the other side without critical thinking. You can become cultlike with anything, including anti-MLM education, beliefs, or advocacy. Identify the need within yourself to find complete allegiance and alignment with one specific movement, without any nuance—basically, the same thinking that got you roped into the MLM in the first place.

Maybe you're trapped in a terrible system but feel stuck because you rely on the income or the distant dream of someday "retiring your husband." Maybe, like me, you hate the culture of the MLM but feel too guilty to leave because you brought so many people into it. Maybe you never could have afforded the business kit without putting it on a credit card or borrowing money from a friend—and thanks to capitalism and the white-supremacist rhetoric of the prosperity gospel, you sank further into debt because of it. Or maybe you're someone who made it this far and still happily shills your MLM products day in and day out and picked up this book out of morbid curiosity. Maybe you're Kimberly.

I see you.

All of you.

And I thank you for reading my story.

Bonus Chapter
The Aftermath, Q&As, and Helpful Guides

THE AFTERMATH

After my book launched on May 30, 2023, it was almost shocking how quiet it was from the Huns, especially the first week. It was *eerily* silent. I waited to be canceled or publicly called out by my former boss babe cohort with debunking reels or ad hominem attacks. It never happened. And then, a friend sent me a screenshot of an email distributed by Rejuvinat:

Hello Leaders,

We want to share that a former independent consultant is releasing a book on direct selling on May 30th called Hey Hun. While we don't anticipate being mentioned, the book may spark dialogue on the direct selling industry including media attention and social media discussions.

We are focused on the incredible opportunity at our fingertips and supporting our passionate community of Consultants,

Customers, and employees. We have a lot to be proud of as we unlock our next era of growth with new entrepreneurs and Customers and reaching new audiences to make an impact.

We kindly ask that you do not proactively engage in dialogue about the book. Please forward any media inquiries to corporate.

We will share some brief messages for you should you need it upon the release of the book. As always, thank you for your partnership.

Rejuvinat

Reps from other MLMs sent me screenshots of posts or emails from their respective companies. The rhetoric was almost identical. After reading the book, you probably recognize the hallmark: information control (*Listen to us and nobody else! We will give you talking points!*), thought control (*This is no big deal, really, we aren't freaking out, so you shouldn't freak out!*), emotional control (*We are sharing something important with you and only you because you are so special! You are amazing, keep being amazing, and recruit more amazing people!*), and behavior control (*Don't mention this to anyone, don't comment on any posts, and definitely, do NOT read that book!*).

Coercive methods like these are likely a big reason I didn't receive much pushback, but what is there to argue with? The story and experience are mine. Data and research support the facts. I'm not the only person in the trenches doing this work, either. If it hadn't been for activists before me, like Roberta Blevins and Sarah Edmondson who appeared in documentaries about MLMs, I may not have realized that people would find my story so resonant with theirs. *Hey, Hun* is part of a more significant movement to advocate for victims and raise awareness of how predatory these corporations are. I am one of many in this movement—I just happened to write a book about it. Thanks to many people in the anti-MLM and anti-scam community and other brave activists who continue to speak out, more victims are following the lead and publicly sharing their experiences. They all document what they lost, whether money, friends, or self-respect. These stories are beginning to overwhelm the controlling methods that MLMs use to keep them away from their converts.

For those who've wondered if I faced legal issues with my former MLM, the answer is yes. But I was the one filing against them, not the other way around. I had to send *them* a cease-and-desist letter because the company still had me on their stupid website, and all requests to remove it were ignored. The C&D eventually worked. However, several of my former uplines still have me on their websites, and other former field development reps have YouTube videos of me that they cannot access and delete because they are no longer with the company.

People were very interested in which company Rejuvinat represented, which I understand. As of this writing, the first auto-populated response in Google when you type "Which MLM . . ." is "Which MLM was Emily Lynn Paulson in?" It cracks me up. I knew figuring it out wouldn't be difficult, but I don't regret changing the company's name in *Hey, Hun*. The issues I wrote about weren't a company-specific phenomenon but industry-wide. I didn't want a reader's main takeaway to be, "Oh, well, it was just *that* company." The fact that it was easy to figure out also proved that misinformation is easy to spread. My MLM boss babe traces were nearly impossible to scrub entirely from the internet.

Withholding Rejuvinat's real name didn't protect the company from its karma. Revenue continued to decline, sending many of the "top earners" to other MLM companies, like Bravenly, Oliveda, Master Reseller Rights, Shaklee, Amare, and others. They took their downlines, plummeting Rejuvinat's revenue, while the growth and income of the new companies seemingly skyrocketed. The same trajectory: rise, peak, decline, and mass exodus will eventually repeat itself with the new MLM companies.

To stop the bleeding, Rejuvinat canceled its convention. As you read in my book, Convention was a you-have-to-be-there event, no questions asked. You wouldn't be considered a serious businessperson if you didn't spend the money to show up. The corporate talking heads would spout off statistics showing how much Convention increased business-building activities for those who attended. And yet, in 2024, they canceled it. Guess who they blamed? The consultants! The Rejuvenat CEO explained that people "aren't traveling as much" or "desiring large crowds" and how "statistics show that convention doesn't change your business much—it's your business building activity that does." Doublespeak is hard to ignore.

Despite all efforts to keep Rejuvinat afloat, the ship sank. Rejuvinat completely abandoned the MLM business model. On a random Tuesday in July, corporate scheduled a Zoom call with the field of consultants and told them the bad news. They transitioned to an affiliate structure, offering a 30% commission on personal customer sales, with zero team building or recruiting. To illustrate, if this change had occurred when I was enrolled, my monthly payout of 40,000 dollars would have been reduced to a few hundred dollars, at best. The CEO cited decreased sales due to "Millenials and Gen Z disdain for purchasing from MLMs." He also presented it as a positive change, stating that "90 percent of Rejuvinat consultants would have a higher earning potential based on their current sales performance." How is this possible? Well, because 90 percent of the sales force was already losing money. Those reps in the lower 90 percent *may* have a better opportunity to be profitable with the bar set so low. Whether this holds true will depend on the required product purchases and associated website or affiliate fees, which, as in the MLM model, would likely cancel any profits. As for the women with a significant downline high in the hierarchy, like me a decade ago, they are out of luck, particularly if they 'retired their husbands.'

A few people asked me if this book was the final nail in Rejuvinat's coffin, so to speak, but I don't think so. Perhaps reading *Hey, Hun* helped some reps bite the bullet and leave, but Rejuvinat, along with many other MLMs, was declining well before I left, and certainly before I wrote this book.

Rejuvinat is not the only MLM company struggling, of course. Finmore, Elomir, Dot Dot Smile, Tori Belle, Matilda Jane, TranzactCard, and Black Organic Oxygen were shut down. Rodan + Fields, Seint, Beautycounter, Traveling Vineyard, and Plunder discontinued their MLM model. Monat is being sued by its previous president; Rodan + Fields and Beachbody (Bodi) have former consultants suing both. Rodan + Fields, doTerra, and Nu Skin laid off hundreds of workers, to name a few. Charges have also been filed against many reps who made false income and health claims and those who took fraudulent PPP loans during the pandemic. My source in DC assures me that many are still being pursued.

Since my book was published, my beliefs that MLMs are toxic and my compassion for people involved in them have only grown. These two things aren't in opposition. Women in MLMs are all pawns in a capitalist, patriarchal, white supremacist game, just like I was. I want to dismantle the game, not destroy the players. I know from my experience that leaving an MLM is very hard, socially and financially, and that has been reflected in the *thousands* of women who have written me after reading my book, wondering how they can leave. So, at the end of this bonus chapter, I conclude with more Q&As and resources to help you or someone you know spot an MLM so you can exit or steer clear.

I shared some cringeworthy moments throughout this book that I look back on and can't believe I took part in willingly. While I'm happy to share them because they make for a fun read, they are also a considerable part of the healing process and a friendly reflection that it's okay to have regret, but not shame. I hope readers lead with compassion instead of ridicule for those who fall victim to MLMs.

What I found difficult to wrap my brain around, and something I've disliked, was the very personal criticism on a disproportionately enormous scale. Don't get me wrong, I am the villain in many people's stories. I should be, and I'm okay with that. I also understand the criticism from people still in MLMs parroting back company canned responses. I've been there. What I wasn't prepared for were the random one-star reviews destroying me because I voted for George Bush when I was nineteen, or personal judgments about my history of addiction, or the way I raised my children. I suppose being anywhere in the public sphere puts you under a microscope, but I've had to learn the hard way: never read reviews. They can be so personal and so cruel.

If it didn't come through in my writing, and because people ask, YES, there are things I miss about the MLM life. I really do love those ridiculously expensive, studded Valentino shoes, and I probably always will. I had some of the most fun times during those seven years. However, the scamming and manipulative culture will always outweigh whatever perks I enjoyed, and it continues to bite me. My inner girl boss haunts me whenever I have to promote something.

Being an MLM defector made running a for-profit business like Sober Mom Squad an absolute mindfuck. Charging money for anything pains me. Strategizing for sales pains me. Sharing my work and asking for pre-orders was *painful*. Have I mentioned that it's painful?

Still, my experience in an MLM made me realize how strongly I feel about women being paid for their work and content creation. It can be difficult to hold space for both. Why? We live in a world run by a few billionaire oligarchs (you likely bought this book off one of their platforms). Yet people want to split hairs over a mom in Oregon who runs a community that benefits an underserved population. Apparently, if you're doing something "good," you're supposed to do it "from the heart" and not get paid for it. That's odd to me. What exactly do we value in our society? (Don't answer that.)

Some of my most critical reviews have attempted to make parallels between the sober community and the MLM industry, alleging that I left MLM and found a new way to scam people. These criticisms aren't justified or rooted in logic. I'm not asking people to become sober, become sober coaches, coach other sober people, or start their own sober platforms. They pay for a service, they receive it, end of story. I'm not sitting on piles of money because of it. Just because a company has revenue does not mean it's making a profit. Yes, even a for-profit business. Sober Mom Squad is a revenue-generating business because it has immense operating costs. That is what the payment goes toward, not toward my (nonexistent) boat or my (nonexistent) lake house, but rather toward the platform for the people it serves. We also comp membership to literally anyone who tells us they can't afford it, no questions asked.

I can do that because I'm privileged to have a spouse with an income along with my (small) income from my writing. I say this because I want to highlight that there is always more to the story. The alternative would be not doing it at all, which would serve no one. How is that a better choice? Any online platform requires a certain level of privilege, like a smartphone and an internet connection. I don't believe that if you can't serve everyone, you should serve no one, yet I understand how any community can look exclusive when there is a paywall. I'm happy to explain it, but I won't waste my time arguing about it with people in Goodreads or Reddit.

Speaking of money, it was funny (yet not surprising) how the media focused on the MLM-woman-becomes-millionaire-and-quits-her-MLM clickbait angle of the story because, as you read in the book, I was never a millionaire. Yes, I may have made a million in commissions over seven years, but I never, at any point, ever had more than a few thousand in the bank from my MLM money. The "business" expenses and taxes were immense, as was the highly- encouraged discretionary spending. Removing the Rejuvinat stream of income also removed the stream of expenditure, which came out to practically net zero change in our finances. When angry keyboard warriors say, "You should give the money back," I giggle. What money? It was almost always spent before it was received!

And though I don't read reviews anymore, sometimes I will have friends, fellow writers, or my assistant look for funny, negative ones, as in reviews or comments that make NO sense, give no context, or have nothing to do with my book. Some have since been removed for obvious reasons, but some are still out there. Here are my favorite comments from one-star reviews and social media posts:

"The book arrived damaged."

"Shut up."

"Clearly, this author has been damaged by the C vaccine!"

"White women shouldn't talk about anti-racism."

"She should have talked more in-depth about anti-racism."

"If you want to feel bad about being a white woman, read this book."

"If she hated being a mom so much, why did she have so many kids?"

"She's racist against white people."

"Hit Piece."

"Where is my book?"

"Very irresponsible use of birth control."

"Political agenda, gross!"

"I was supposed to get a different book and got this one. Is there a number I can call?"

"GIVE THE MONEY BACK!"

Readers were very interested to hear more about the people I used to work with in my MLM and what happened to our relationships once the book came out. Honestly, not much changed. Many Consultants I met through Rejuvinat had to stop talking to me, if they hadn't already. There are some exceptions, but for the most part, that was pretty much what happened. And I have no ill will toward any of them because I understand it. What I share contradicts what they need to believe to stay committed to the MLM. However, there are many people involved who feel the same as I do, who speak to me anonymously, and who are not yet ready to leave. That number continues to grow as the façade starts to crack and their critical thinking returns.

I was astounded at the lengths people went to figure out who the characters were despite making it clear that they were primarily composites. I'm so sorry to say this again: there is no Kimberly. She is an amalgamation of numerous people in my upline, the company at large, and other companies from stories compiled from different sources. That might be more frightening—that there are multiple people just like her.

Same goes for Becky, an avatar for many people in my upline and otherwise. Of course, I *did* have a direct upline. We went to high school together and had never spoken before she recruited me through a Facebook message. We *did* become close friends (or so I believed) because we talked daily about "business." We went on vacation together and spent time at each other's houses. I have no idea how she reacted to the book because she's never spoken to me again after she learned about it. I would guess that she was pissed, and I'm sure I would have reacted the same way ten years ago.

However, two characters weren't composites: Serena, and Vanessa, and I received many questions about their whereabouts. "You can't bang a guy who's mooching off of you" is a Serena classic. You'll be happy to know she got a "real" job. Vanessa recently laughed out loud at the dick pic chapter as she read it, having completely forgotten about the incident. She's doing fantastic in her job as well. They are two of my favorite people and closest friends.

Some of the frequently asked questions I've received came from readers asking about their own involvement: *Should I stay on? Should I keep buying products I like? Am I a bad person?* First, do whatever you want. This is all about informed consent. If you need validation, then absolutely no, you are not a bad person. There's a reason these schemes are so enticing—remember, I was in one for seven years! I have friends on my former team who are still enrolled. I have friends who are still high up the chain and fully believe in the MLM. I would be a hypocrite if I said you were a bad person. Also, lean into that cognitive dissonance. You don't have to make any decisions right now, but if that inner voice tries to tell you something, *listen.*

Another way to look at it is to determine the level of harm you are inflicting. For me, it was very high. I had thousands of people on my team who were eventually losing money. Maybe it's not that high for you if you have one customer or buy lipstick from your aunt every few months. However, any involvement in MLM inflicts harm, and you must decide: Are you okay with that? If so, then okay! You don't need my permission. If any harm doesn't sit right with you, figure out what you must do to make things right.

We evaluate levels of harm in life all the time. I should probably recycle more, get an electric car to replace my gas guzzler, or stop shopping at big box stores. Also, I know hot dogs are terrible for me, but those fuckers are so tasty. Analyze the level of harm and what you are personally comfortable with. I cannot make that decision for you, but it is essential to know that any involvement, no matter how small, keeps these companies making money hand over fist. The "not much harm" by many people adds up to a whole hell of a lot of harm. And that's not a moral failing on your part more than a failure of a country that doesn't support our basic needs. Again, bad things like MLMs fester in an environment that doesn't support the good stuff, like affordable housing, subsidized childcare, and paid parental leave.

Perfect example: I'm as anti-MLM as they come. My mother-in-law is a Pampered Chef consultant—she has been as long as I can remember. Yes, she knows my story and she's read my book. And yet, I guarantee that a company-branded spatula or something like it will be in my stocking this Christmas, just like every year. Even I cannot escape it. And, yes, I'll put it in my kitchen drawer, and we will use it because even I know where and when to pick my battles.

Need help finding your level of harm? Check out this *Which Level of #Bossbabe Are You?* list. Notice the one common trait among all these bossbabes and know that I was almost every single one of these women at some point.

Can't find yourself? Congratulations! But stay aware. One of the warning signs of being recruited is believing you never will be.

WHICH LEVEL OF #BOSSBABE ARE YOU?

Guilty Greta

Greta is a friend or family member of a bossbabe who buys her friend or family's overpriced subpar product but never uses it. She shares their posts and hosts parties because she feels sorry for them. Greta supports a predatory business model.

Loyal Linda

Linda likes MLM products but doesn't realize similar products are better and less expensive. She wants to support friends and genuinely believes she is. She recommends all her friends' MLM ventures but refuses to join their teams. Linda supports a predatory business model.

Fence Rider Francine

Francine is a current customer who spends so much money that her rep continues to press the "discount on products" to lure her into becoming a Consultant. She has listened to every opportunity call and watched all the videos, but still hasn't joined, though she's found herself considering it. Those social media posts are inspiring, but she can't shake that cringy feeling. Francine supports a predatory business model.

Wholesale Wendy

Wendy signs up "for the discount," doesn't sell, and believes she's getting a deal (she's not). She has no customers, no team, and now has to buy products monthly, whether she wants them or not. Wendy supports a predatory business model.

Vulnerable Victoria

Victoria is a struggling rep trying to sell overpriced products most people don't want and is paying for inventory to remain "commissionable." She lives for being love-bombed by her upline, who she thinks is her best friend, so she doesn't leave. Her husband is pissed that boxes keep showing up on her porch, but she tells him she needs to spend money to make money. Victoria supports a predatory business model.

Skeptical Sarah

Sarah has an extensive, wealthy network, so she sells on the side as a hobby by posting once or twice a year on social media. She thinks all the rah-rah convention stuff is bizarre and cringes at the TikTok videos of forty-five-year-old women dancing about shampoo. She hasn't made any money but has fun at the parties and wine nights. Sarah supports a predatory business model.

Embarrassing Eleanor

Eleanor wears head-to-toe corporate garb and has a sticker of her MLM company on the back of her car. She goes live daily on social media, whether or not anybody shows up. She doesn't understand her compensation plan, but it doesn't matter because she never sells anything. She gets unfriended daily on social media, but it's okay because her bossbabe friends are her "tribe." Eleanor supports a predatory business model.

Harasser Hillary

Hillary has an endless stream of Stories on Instagram, all heavily filtered with product placement and far too many personal stories about her family. She pushes products on everyone, sends cold DMs, and is obsessed with building her team. All her posts have inflated income claims, and she is probably in debt, but who knows? She hasn't done her taxes yet. Hillary supports a predatory business model.

Sell the Dream Danica

Danica has recruited a small team but pretends to make far more money than she does and posts the maximum number of hashtags on Instagram. She posts many poolside selfies "working" and photos of herself next to other people's fancy cars. She shares photos of her upline "leaders" on trips that she hopes to earn but never will. Danica supports a predatory business model.

Brainwashed Believer Betty

True to her name, Betty believes her company is the best. She is part of the elite group of people who have earned more than a dollar, which everyone knows because she posts about it every month #payday. She would follow her upline off a cliff and doesn't understand why everyone isn't joining this life-changing opportunity. Betty supports a predatory business model.

Top Shelf Tiffany

Tiffany joined the MLM business early and had income (and a second income) to invest, but she claims she's made it all possible thanks to hard work, manifesting, and Jesus Christ. All of her posts contain a Bible verse, a heavy filter, and occasionally a MAGA hat. She is sugary-sweet on social media but a massive bitch in real life. Tiffany supports a predatory business model.

Pyramid Pam

Pam sells seminars, affinity marketing, courses, and coaching containers. Her paycheck relies on others believing in the MLM industry, even though it didn't pan out for her or anyone else she knows. She shames anyone who spends money on drive-thru coffee instead of their entrepreneur journey. Victoria, Hillary, and Danica are her target market. Pam supports a predatory business model.

Shiny Penny Sheila

Sheila quits her MLM and joins another because she doesn't believe the problem is the structure; it's just that *one* toxic company (and the last three she joined and quit). She has closets full of wax melts, collagen pudding, shampoo, and happy juice, and she legitimately doesn't remember which one she is selling now. Sheila supports a predatory business model.

Cringe Caroline

Caroline realizes she may be part of a commercial cult but feels stuck. She is embarrassed to be part of the MLM but is in so deep and has been sold a dream that hasn't existed for so long that she doesn't know how to get out. She collects a check and stops talking about the company and instead starts watching anti-MLM YouTube videos. Caroline supports a predatory business model.

Q & A

Q: **Sometimes, it's hard to tell when something is an MLM. How can we, as consumers, be sure we aren't supporting the industry?**

A: You're spot on, and that isn't an accident. As MLMs become more taboo, they rebrand themselves as other things, even when they are still very much MLMs. Try using the handy flowchart at the top of the next page when a friend pitches you a product or service.

Q: **Talk to me about affiliate marketing—is it an MLM?**

A: It depends. I talked about this in the book as well. If an MLM calls itself an affiliate program to skirt around the fact that it is an MLM, it is still an MLM. Amare, Seint, Savvi, and many other companies are moving away from the term "MLM" and using "affiliate." If you cannot purchase directly from the company and must purchase from one of these brand ambassadors, or the site requires you to "find a

IS IT AN MLM?

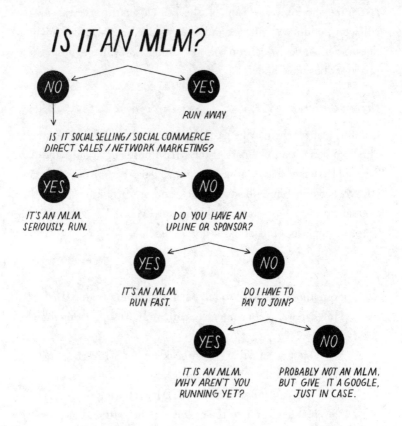

NO → YES

RUN AWAY

IS IT SOCIAL SELLING / SOCIAL COMMERCE DIRECT SALES / NETWORK MARKETING?

YES

NO

IT'S AN MLM. SERIOUSLY, RUN.

DO YOU HAVE AN UPLINE OR SPONSOR?

YES

NO

IT'S AN MLM. RUN FAST.

DO I HAVE TO PAY TO JOIN?

YES

NO

IT IS AN MLM. WHY AREN'T YOU RUNNING YET?

PROBABLY NOT AN MLM, BUT GIVE IT A GOOGLE, JUST IN CASE.

Consultant" or assign one to you, it is NOT an affiliate program, it's an MLM.

Affiliate programs have been around forever. You share a link to the product, and if someone uses your code or link, you get a small kickback. Essentially, it is a referral fee. Companies use this instead of paying for high-cost advertising to connect to networks of current happy customers or people with large networks like influencers and podcasters. This is a one-ended transaction. The company isn't asking affiliates to purchase the products, sell them themselves, get five friends to do the same, and so on, in perpetuity. The payment for the product also isn't going "up the chain" to a series of upline leaders. *Proper affiliate marketing doesn't require you to pay anything.* If it does, it's an MLM.

Something new that has popped up more recently is people selling "courses" that supposedly teach you about affiliate marketing, like Master Resell Rights (MRR), 7-Figure Mastery, and others. This is a straight-up pyramid scheme. The "product" is a course, so they are adamant that they aren't an MLM, but again, it doesn't matter what is being sold—it's the *way* it's sold.

That said, the confusion with affiliate marketing lies in semantics. Don't worry so much about that. Follow the money.

Q: What do you say when someone says, "Well, corporate America is shady, too, why not support the little guy?"

A: That is a false equivalency because MLMs aren't "the little guy." They may seem like it because they hide behind independent contractors, most of whom make zero money, but they are all *massive* corporations. I could write a book about late-stage capitalism and the flaws within it as well, but it isn't a lesser-of-two-evils situation. MLMs are huge capitalist monsters that also throw in the meritocracy to distract from the fact that almost everyone loses money. Multilevel Marketing is a 180-billion-dollar industry. That isn't a "little guy." By supporting the lonely housewife selling products, you are keeping her stuck in the system while elevating the revenue of the MLM corporations. Yes, always shop local and small when you can (I'm talking *real* businesses, not MLMs), but when given a choice between a big box store like Walmart and an MLM, choose Walmart every time.

No is a complete sentence. Please repeat after me: No is a complete sentence.

But if you want to temper it, here are some suggestions (it pains me to make scripts but I know why pages of scripts work; they are easy and take emotion out of it!) Here are some polite but firm scripts to tell people you are not interested in buying:

"Thanks, but I am happy with the skincare/supplements/collagen/etc. that I'm using." When they say, would you like a sample or discount, say, "No, thank you, I won't be changing my current regimen, please don't ask again."

"No, thank you, I don't purchase from MLMs, but I wish you the best." If they ask why, because they will, say, "It's a personal choice I ask that you respect."

"I'd love to support your fundraiser, but I'll donate directly rather than buying a spatula from your party." When they say, give me the $$, and I'll donate it, say, "No, thank you, I'd rather give directly."

As I explained earlier, your MLM friend has been taught not to take no for an answer, so you'll need a secondary, and potentially third or fourth response, which won't feel very polite. To set a hard boundary, here are some ideas:

"I love our friendship, and to continue prioritizing it, I need you to take me off your prospecting/follow-up list. I won't be purchasing from you or joining your team. Thanks for respecting my wishes."

"I already told you I wasn't interested before and won't be interested in the future. I appreciate how excited you are about this, but I don't want it to interfere with our friendship/work relationship, so I'll ask that you not bring it up again."

"Asked and answered."

Any reaction they have to your boundary does not reflect on you, and frankly, it does not reflect on them. It's a reflection of the coercive control they are under from their uplines and their company. Give grace but hold your boundary.

Q: I would love to see Hey, Hun the TV show, how can we make that happen?

A: Stay tuned!

Q: I would LOVE to see some of the MLM scripts you followed so we know what to look out for.

A: First dead giveaway: lots of emojis!

Here's some cut-and-paste directly from an old document I used to share with my downline (that was shared with me and shared with my upline, and so on and so on from the beginning of bossbabe time):

Language Ideas!

If you are a brand-new consultant, send this to your customers:

"<<NAME>>, I just started my Rejuvinat business and need your help. I would like to practice enrolling Customers and get some success stories in my back pocket for when I share this with others. And you will begin your journey to the best skin of your life. Will you help me out and become my first customer?" Then lead them to a three-way call with your upline.

If You Are a Brand-new Consultant,
Send This to Your Dream Teamers

"Hey, Suzy Q, I just started my own business, and when I was challenged with the idea of thinking of the most well-connected, successful people I knew, I immediately thought of you. Can we take a few minutes to chat this week? I think you can help be a connector for me to grow my business. Does Tuesday work for you?" Then schedule three-way call with your upline.

Initial Message to Get a Phone
Number and Set Up a Phone Date

"Hi, Sarah! Hope you're doing well! Wondering if I can steal fifteen minutes of your time this week to pick your brain about my new business? I am looking for referrals and I think you can help me. Does Tuesday work?" Feel free to add this: "I know this might be a little random, but . . ." or "I realize this is totally out of the blue, but . . ."

When People Ask What Is Rejuvinat/Your Business
(or they won't give you their number until you give them a
little bit more info about your request)

"Rejuvinat is a premium skincare company. I am looking for well-connected, savvy ladies to help me get the word out. Does Tuesday work for you?"

Follow Up to People Who Have Never
Responded to the Initial Message

"Hey Sarah, I know we have yet to connect about my business. Let's shoot for a time this week. Would Tuesday afternoon or Wednesday morning work better for you? I only need about ten minutes of your time. Thank you!"

How to Invite to a Three-Way Conference Call

"I'm happy to get you more information. Let's set up a time that works for you and I am going to bring in my business partner Melissa to help me. She has been doing this longer and she will be able to give you another perspective on this business and fill in any gaps I may have missed." You could also say, "I'd love to get you more information about our business. The next step is to jump on the phone with me again and this time I am going to bring my business partner Melissa with me. She has been doing this longer and she will be able to give you another perspective on this business and fill in any gaps I may have missed."

For People You Know

"Hey Megan! How are you? The kids are getting so big ... Keegan still asks about Luke from time to time! I don't know if you have seen what I have been posting on FB, but in my vast spare time (ha ha) I am a rep for Rejuvinat. It's been great, and my business has grown based on word of mouth. Anyway, I know you are very well respected and know a lot of people. If you hear anyone talking about sunspots, wrinkles, acne, or rosacea would you send them my way? It has been so fun to help people love the skin they are in! Thanks in advance, my dear! Hope all is well. Emily."

"Hi, Jane, I hope all is well for you. I realize this is out of the blue but is there any chance I could steal ten minutes of your time this week to get some business help?"

For Male Friends

"Hi Chris! I realize this is completely out of the blue. First off, you have an adorable family! Congrats! Secondly and the point of my message: Since I don't know your wife, I'm hoping that you can connect us? I'm looking to expand my business out of

Washington and I'm hopeful that she might be able to connect me with someone within her network. If you wouldn't mind forwarding me her contact info, so that we could find a time to talk, that would be awesome. Mine is bossbabe2000@hotmail .com, cell 206-555-5555. I appreciate your help and Happy Spring!"

"I'm so excited to have partnered with the doctors who created Rejuvinat and their anti-aging line! I couldn't resist getting involved in this business, and I'd love to tell you more about it! (or something similar)."

"Hi, so-and-so! I love your pics of Easter/vacation/whatever! I wanted to let you know that I'm a consultant with Rejuvinat, and I'm really excited about helping people get the best skin of their lives! If you hear of anyone talking about wrinkles, age spots, rosacea, acne, or other skin concerns, please send them my way! To find the products that would be best for you, please visit my website. Thank you so much!"

Message to Someone You Don't Have a Phone Number for

"Hey, Susie! How are you? I would love to catch up sometime on how you are doing, but in the meantime, I wanted to write to you to see if you could help me out. My direct sales company, which I have been running for three years now, is starting to branch out in the Ohio market, and I am looking for a place to start. I know that this is not something for you personally; you have way too much on your plate as is! I am confident, however, given your background and network, that you would be able to lead me to someone who could help me open up the entire Dayton market and beyond. What does your schedule on Tuesday allow for a quick phone call? Send me your digits!!"

Text for Someone in a Hot Market

"Hey lady! I need help in Cali for work and thought you might be just the person who could help point me in the right direction there! I know you wouldn't be personally interested, but you have a network there who could be. Would love to tell you the type of person I am looking for, what works for your schedule in the next couple of days?"

How to Go Straight to a Call with No Written Intro or Heads-up

"Hey, Laura! How are you lady? Good! So I am running into a meeting here in five minutes and you just came across my mind as I remembered that you live in Florida. FL has made some real promise with my organization, so I am looking to get that market center up and going with some dynamite ppl . . . I know it wouldn't be of personal interest to you, but I bet you could introduce me to some killer people over there. What does tomorrow look like for a quick chat?? I want to respect your time since I called totally out of the blue today!!!" (The next call would be your first intro call.)

Follow Up with a Fence-sitter

"Hey Krissy! I wanted to touch base and see if you closed on your house?! I am touching base with people who have looked seriously at the business in the past, and you were on my list! Some crazy stuff is going on right now with the new launch of our acute care product . . . It gives a whole new meaning to the dermatological experience. I know you expressed interest in the past, so I am running through my list And making sure that I am not leaving anyone out or behind!"

What to Say on an Intro Call

"Thank you so much for taking time out of your busy day to talk to me. I won't keep you long, so I'll get right to why I'm calling. First off, have you heard of Rejuvinat?"

<<Share your why>>

"Has anything that I've said intrigue you?"

If yes, then say, "That's awesome; sounds like you have some great questions. The next step would be to get my friend and business partner on the phone with us. She has been doing this longer and has a totally different background, and between the two of us, we can answer all your questions to see if this might be a good fit for you or someone you know. This was very helpful to me when I decided to hop on board. I'm available tomorrow at two and three, which works for you?"

If they say no, I don't have a personal interest, I will keep trying to engage them with questions. If you want them on your team, describe them! My usual language is, "I look for motivated, driven, and successful women who keep themselves busy! Put yourself in my shoes . . . If you wanted to bring this to your market, who would be the top five people you would ask to help you."

A Product -focused Reach Out with Business Looped in
"Hey XXXX—

"I'm just diligently reaching out to peeps in my network-specifically about Rejuvinat. I would love to talk to you about our regimens or a great exfoliating wash and a moisturizer w SPF. I offer free enrollment and goodies and can work within any budget.

"If you're in the market for skincare, I'd love to be your girl!! If you're curious about the business aspect- we can chat about that, too!

"No pressure. Either way, would love to hear from you again!

"Hope you are doing well!"

Another One for Friends

"Hi, Maria! Sorry you didn't make it for our girls' night, it was a fun time. It was great chatting at football last week. I know this may seem random but had to reach out to you. I'm not sure how much I have told you or what you may have seen on FB but in addition to my full-time nursing job I also have a home-based skincare biz that I am building, and it is really growing huge. I am looking to expand even more and while I think you would be amazing because you are so personable, outgoing, and smart, I have no idea if you would have a personal interest or not. But you have an extensive network, and I would love to pick your brain about who you might know. Can I take five min and tell you a little more because you might know the perfect person. Send me your cell phone and the best time to call. I will drop off a mini facial sample as my thanks! Oh, and we should get the boys together soon!"

That's for moms I've seen around but only recently connected with via kids' events. I had a good rate of at least getting on phone and sharing vs. ignores.

For New Moms You Just Met

"Hey Sally . . . I'm currently in work-my-side-gig mode and you've been on my mind as someone to share the Rejuvinat business with. I originally thought I'd make a little extra per month, but this business has completely surpassed my expectations on every level. I've been wanting to share with you because I know you would KILL IT . . . you are so well-connected and influential in your network. Are you open to hearing more?"

Direct Message on LinkedIn

"Hi Maureen. Nice to connect with you on Linked In. I love that your profile indicates you are an Entrepreneurial Spirit! I know you are very busy, so I will be direct. I have a business opportunity and I am looking for savvy entrepreneurial people . . . especially in the North Country but also in other markets. The opportunity was recently featured on the TODAY Show, our company's founders were recently named to Investopedia's list of the Top 10 Most Successful Women of the Decade, and just a few days ago, they were included on the first-ever Forbes list of the top Self-Made Women in the U.S. This opportunity may or may not be of personal interest to you, but I am certain that you know a handful of people who are just the type I am seeking (including your business students?). Could we chat for 15 minutes so I can describe more about my business and the characteristics of those who I am seeking? If so, let me know two or three good times to catch you and best number to call. Looking forward to connecting with you by phone.

Regards,
Debra"

Random Facebook Friend

"Hey, Sharon! Hope things are well with you! I'm sure you've noticed here on Facebook that I have this little passion:-) and because I just love your spunkiness and outgoing nature, I need to pick your brain! Would Tuesday or Thursday evening work to visit at all? Promise it'll be super painless and a lot of fun! Do any specific times work better than others?"

Someone Who Used to Be in Another MLM

"Hi Robyn! I can't get over how grown up your kids are! Where has the time gone? Wow!

"So, I'm curious if you are still with itWorks? I'm about to offer a big incentive to Rejuvinat new business partners and you came to mind. It's not for you but maybe you know someone. Do you have 15 minutes for me to share with you about it?

"Hope you are well! Hi Rich!—Liz"

Add to Your Script
When Reaching Out to Current Customers

". . . Or you could seriously just join my team, get the insane discounts, make some money, have a blast, get super fun incentive awards along the way and I'll give you a box (Acute Care) as a welcome aboard gift! You would be great and are a walking billboard already—isn't it time?!" 😁

Another for Current Customers

"Luce, I'm racking my brain trying to figure out WHY you and I haven't joined forces and conquered the wrinkled world! Everything is just getting so exciting, and you'd love this! What gives?!"

Good for People You Don't Know Well

"Hey Kathy: So fun to follow your FB to keep up with you and your family.

"I'm sure you see my posts on my Rejuvinat Business on FB.

"So, wondering if you will give me ten minutes on the phone sometime this week to tell you why I think you should try some of my Rejuvinat Products, and/or at home skin care tools, which provide spa and derm-like results for a fraction of the price, in the privacy of your own bathroom. All our products and tools come with a sixty-day, empty-bottle $$$ back guarantee too, so you really have nothing to lose, except fine lines, wrinkles, brown spots, acne, or redness!!!

"I love to share, simply because Rejuvinat offers a phenomenal opportunity to either Change Skin or Change Lives! Let me know when you have a little time this week- I promise it is worth ten minutes!!

"I also know how well connected you are in the Omaha area, and I am trying to build my team there. I would love to share a bit about the business with you to see if you might know anyone looking for a tremendous opportunity, even you. 😊 Let me know a few convenient times to reach you this week and I will give you a call."

Another One That Is Good for People You Don't Know
"Hi Susie-q! Hope all is well! By the looks of things, life is treating you and the family well! So, listen, I wanted to pick your brain about something. Do you have a few minutes in the next couple of days to chat? Either way, would love to catch up!"

Once on the phone and small talk is out the way, the convo either authentically moves to Rejuvinat because people know it's what I do and have been watching . . . or I can say "I don't want to take too much of your time. I'm not sure if you've seen what I've been up to. Regardless, I've got a quick four or so minute history of our company, what it is I actually do, and the kinds of people I'm looking for."

And Another

"Hi xxx, how are you? Love those recent pics of the kiddos you posted! (or pick some other thing from their FB) I'm not sure if you've picked up on this pretty exciting little side gig, I have going with Rejuvinat, but you're actually someone I've been wanting to reach out to! Your energy is so great, and it seems like you have a fantastic network! It would mean the world if I could steal just a quick five minutes of your time. Since Rejuvinat isn't a home parties company, networking can be really influential for business . . .pretty much the more opportunities I have to share, the more I grow! Is there a time tomorrow or Thursday you could chat for a quick five? I'll be in the car around 6 to6:30 both evenings on my way home if that works? Oh, and I'll totally mail you a free product sample for your time."

Old High School or College Friend

"Hey Chica! Glad to hear life is good in Arkansas! Your littles are precious! I know you must be having a blast! You have been on my mind, and I thought today would be a good day to reach out.

"My Rejuvinat business is something I'm committed to sharing with everyone, but you make me smile! You are such a spark plug, with a huge bright smile and warm heart. I think it would be a blast to collaborate with you again!

"I know it may feel crazy to consider something like this - it def was for me too- but would you be up for hearing some more details on what this could look like for you and your sweet family?"

Send Out When You're Traveling for Any Reason

"I'm coming to Austin in September to grow and launch more Rejuvinat businesses. I'd love to focus on Houston too. Could we chat about the profile of career women I work with next week? Maybe someone in your network would love a cool business like you have, but maybe doesn't have time to build it from scratch?? Thank you!!!!"

Another Traveling One to People You Know Pretty Well

"Hey Kim, I'd love to connect with you this week. My skincare business is expanding in Atlanta, and I could use your help. You are so connected and have SO many friends I'd love to be introduced to. Let's brainstorm. I'm available Thursday morning at 11 . . . does that work for you? xo"

To Invite People to an Event in the Area

"Hey Jeff, I'd love to pick your brain about my business. We're growing like crazy in Chicagoland and my corporate team is actually down there this week and I'd like to talk to you about who I'm looking for. You may have an interest, or you may not, no big deal, but I'll bet you'll know some people who are the right fit. When do you have ten minutes for a quick chat? I'm flexible throughout the day, what works best for you, day, or evening? Thanks in advance!"

To Someone Who Has Ghosted You

"Hi! I hope things are well with you, can't believe school is next week! I'm reaching out about Rejuvinat. I know you were excited to have a business of your own, empower other women and utilize your vast network here and overseas. I'd love to share what's been going on lately. Growth has been staggering and new global market launches are about to be announced. Plus . . . I'd love to see you, catch up and I think we would make a killer partnership! Thoughts?"

To Men to Catch Their Wives
"Hi friend! <<Insert random fact or history of your friendship to connect>> I'd love to chat with your lovely wife about my business! Can you connect us?"

Q: I would love to see the objections list and how you were taught to handle people's valid objections.
A: Again, this was *dozens* of pages. Here are a few.

How to Handle Objections
Here is a sampling of effective answers to common objections that you may be having in conversations with your network about the business. Please keep in mind these are suggestions, use them as guidelines and then make them your own. Also, don't forget to relate to people with their objections. Be authentic, as we probably all had some if not all of these when we were looking at the business.

Make sure to get people talking. If they express an objection about money/time, ask them, "What does that look like for you," so you can tailor your answer to address their concern.

Use the "feel, felt, found" language to connect with your prospect. "I understand how you feel . . . I felt that way too . . . but I have found . . ."

Lastly, **don't attempt to convince people to join this business**. We are here to help people and put this in their laps, not convince them to join us. We are looking for people who want to do this, we shouldn't have to convince anyone to use the products nor join us in business. If you have to do that, you'll have a real tough time building this.

Time Isn't Right—

"I'm looking for busy people because I've learned that busy people get things done. I understand how you feel, I wasn't sure how I was going to fit this in, but most of us work this business in very part-time hours around everything else on our plates. It requires consistent efforts and doing a little bit each day and working it into your everyday life and conversations. And let's be honest, we can find time for the things that are a priority; the things that we really want."

Dig in further to what your prospect would like to do with this. "So, you're telling me you'd want to build an exit strategy from your job/be able to afford vacations/etc. In five to fifteen hours a week—ten minutes here, twenty minutes here, a half hour there, you can invest your time in achieving those goals. Are you willing to invest that time toward (their why)? This business can end up rewarding you with much more time and flexibility than you currently have. But you've got to want it."

If they keep pushing the "no-time" issue: "I'd love to present the information to you because even if this is not for you at this time, you may know of someone that this may be right for. The interest in my business is building big in your area, right now!" (Referrals are a powerful way to build your business. Also, ask your prospect if you may contact them at a later date . . . and if they say yes, mark it in your calendar).

Money—

"What if I can teach you a simple way to make the money back with our fast start bonuses? Or get a complete refund of your business kit?" This is a business, and we want people who recognize the opportunity/potential and use the investment as a motivation to pay it back quickly vs. a hesitation for people to get started.

Don't Want to Bother Friends—

"That is not what I do. I share products that change skin and businesses that enhance and change lives. I have a professional business, based on clinical products. I can teach you how to talk to people casually and conversationally you know and people you're referred to. And look, not everyone will want your products or want to join your business, but they might know someone who does!"

Point out: "Do you feel like Vanessa (the consultant who brought the conf call) has bothered you?" 100% of the time the answer is "no." "That is how this business is different, we grow and build based on relationships and we are actually coached and trained on how to do that authentically."

Mention that you are so thankful "so-and-so" "bothered you." We are not in the business of bothering people but helping them.

I'm Too Busy. I Don't Have Enough Time—

"Busy and successful people already have a track record of success, good work ethic, surround themselves with the same type of people, and know what hard work looks like."

"The majority of people who start their own business with Rejuvinat mold it around a full-time career . . . we are here to teach people how to work smarter, not harder."

"Most people work this business on very part time hours. Just consistent bits of effort, doing a little bit each day and working it into your everyday life and conversation, on your own time are what this is all about."

Further qualify as to what your prospect is looking for. Sometimes, your prospect is not right for your opportunity. Remind them that this business requires five to fifteen hours/week in the nooks and crannies. Do they have that much time to invest in a better future? A business that rewards them with much more free time than they invested. In short, it's a small investment that will reap huge rewards.

"Also important to note – unlike most jobs, your paycheck can increase without your hours increasing! That is the beauty of residual income."

Don't Know Anyone—

"I know it may seem that way, but here's what I've found. We all know several hundred people, and we'll help you jog your memory. And it's not necessarily who you know, but who THEY know. Plus, this business is a great way to get to know people as well. We will teach you tools to help you reach out. And remember, your target market is everyone with skin. Word of mouth is a powerful business! You never know who doesn't love what they see in the mirror or on their bank statement."

Pyramid—

"What do you mean by Pyramid?" (Pause) If they say "pyramid scheme," say, "Pyramids are illegal. With pyramids there is no selling of products. We have an amazing product and a very loyal customer base! Also, We are members of the DSA (Direct Selling Association) where we were awarded with their highest award called the RISING STAR AWARD, which is the highest award given in the industry. Also, the doctors still have proactive, their clinical practices and professorships at Stanford. They would never jeopardize their reputations or fortunes. What other questions do you have?"

If they say, "One of those things where you build a team and you make money off of them," etc., then say, "If you're asking if this is a network marketing model, yes absolutely. I wouldn't be doing it if it weren't. We get to build an organization of team members and customers, and we teach others to do the same. And we earn commissions for our organization that grown exponentially every month. Instead of getting paid because of my efforts, I get to earn based on the success of my whole organization. And unlike most jobs, where we'd never expect to earn more than our boss, it is not uncommon for someone to earn more than the person who invited them into the business. What other questions do you have?"

I'm Not a Salesperson—

"Great . . . I'm not looking for salespeople. I'm looking for passionate people who love to share the things they love. We're also looking for people who enjoy helping others. In fact, most people who are successful in this business have no prior sales experience. We can teach you how to do what we do.

"This is a relationship-driven business, without relationships and some commonality the trust factor isn't there . . . This is also something that we are trained on quite a bit."

I Want to Try the Product First, As I Can't Sell Anything I Don't Like—

"Actually, using our products is a part of our training. We are all walking billboards for how effective our products are, and once you see the results and people start commenting on your skin, you are going to want to be able to hit the ground running."

Or: "I was leaning that way too. Let me explain what helped me make the decision to jump into the business before trying the product first. Yes, I wanted to try the products. However, once I realized the deep discount on the products for the business kits. I didn't want to spend more money in the long run becoming a customer and then spending more $ and investing in the business . . . especially since I knew either way, I had the sixty-day money back guarantee. I figured I might as well try them and start talking. Not to mention, you could get your kit fee refunded . . . not so with a customer account! I paid my investment back in my first (xxx days) and you can too. I also realized I needed to really look at who's behind this company. Dr. Rejuvinat is the best-known dermatologist in the world. These doctors have a proven track record. I also know Nordstrom wouldn't put anything on their shelves if the products didn't work. But, if you still want to start out trying product first, then I'd love to help you get enrolled in my preferred customer program. You've at least allowed me to give you the flip side of the coin in regard to trying product first. So which way are you leaning?"

I'd Really Like to Start on the Smallest/ Cheapest Business Kit—

(Unless they have been a long-time customer and have absolutely everything) "My job is to set my partners up for success and from what you told me your goals are with this business. Starting out on anything other than the larger two business building kits won't help you achieve those goals."

"We always want to lead by example, because in this business "duplication" is something that can take someone's business VERY far. Your prospects will ask you what kit you joined before they sign up, and we want to be able to model for them how and why you chose what you did. In addition, you are not receiving any product, so you won't even be able to tell people what regimen you recommend or like the best."

If They Ask "What About the Mid-Range Kit"—

"Sure, that might be the right option for people who want a couple of regimens and wholesale products but don't have a huge interest in earning income from the business. The larger of the two kits are your best business building options and here's why: We are the marketing/advertising and we need to be using the tools and the products so we can share our experiences with people. You'll want/need to have them for your business launch events. The buy in is the deepest discount you're going to get receive on the products and if I can explain how you can pay your investment back in thirty to sixty days would that give you a better understanding as to why it's so important to start off correctly? Let's go over the larger two kits so you can see exactly what you get and start working on your list so you can see how quickly you can earn your investment back!"

At the End of the Conversation with Your Prospect—
"Just so I know the next step for you, on a scale of 1-10, what is your interest level?" If they respond to an eight or higher, I say "I'm concerned that we didn't answer all of your questions . . . what questions/concerns do you still have so that number could be higher?"

If the prospect says that they are a seven or below . . . ask them "Why not lower?" Their response will be what interests them about the business and an opportunity for a future yes.

If they have no other questions, ask them if they are ready to pick out their business building kit!

Acknowledgments

I need to thank my husband, Kale, first and foremost. Thank you for always believing in me and, despite being a private person, still encouraging me to be as effing loud as I want. Thank you for giving me the space to spend my "downtime" (ha) for the last two years with my face in a laptop, writing, editing, and promoting.

To my amazing children: Keegan, Riley, Macy, Lainey, and Rowan. You and your dad are the best team I've ever been a part of. I'm so lucky to be your mom.

I want to thank Row House Publishing for existing and for being brave enough to publish a story that no other publisher had the proverbial balls to do. Rebekah Borucki, president of Row House, thank you for creating a publishing house that so desperately needed to be created. Kristen McGuiness, thank you for believing in me and for pushing me to find the deeper story within the story, even when I didn't want to, and even if it did create fifty thousand more words for the editors. Thank you to the copy editors, sensitivity readers, cover designers, and all the people behind the scenes for making this book exactly what it needed to be.

Thank you to all the members, coaches, and volunteers who call Sober Mom Squad home. I could not do it without you!

Last, a simultaneous thank-you and deep apology to everyone who I messaged, recruited, pestered, refused to take no as an answer from, or sold a product to while with "Rejuvinat." You were all part of my awakening.

Bibliography

Introduction

Investopedia. "Multi-level Marketing." Accessed August 10, 2022. https://www
.investopedia.com/terms/m/multi-level-marketing.asp.

Hassan, Steven. "Steven Hassan's BITE Model of Authoritarian Control." Freedom
of Mind Resource Center. Accessed July 13, 2022. https://freedomofmind.com
/cult-mind-control/bite-model.

Taylor, Jon M. *The Case (for and) against Multi-level Marketing.* Bountiful, UT:
Consumer Awareness Institute, 2011. https://www.ftc.gov/sites/default/files
/documents/public_comments/trade-regulation-rule-disclosure-requirements
-and-prohibitions-concerning-business-opportunities-ftc.r511993-00008%C2
%A0/00008-57281.pdf.

Furst, Jennifer, and Julia Willoughby Nason, dirs. *LuLaRich;* Culver City, CA:
Cinemart, Story Force Entertainment, and Amazon Studios, 2021. https://www
.amazon.com/dp/B09CFXPNSX.

Blevins, Roberta. "Roberta Blevins." Accessed July 13, 2022. http://www
.robertablevins.com.

The Best Fake Friends You'll Ever Have

McLaren, Leah. "The Excruciating Loneliness of Being a New Mother." Today's
Parent. March 22, 2018. https://www.todaysparent.com/baby/postpartum-care
/the-excruciating-loneliness-of-being-a-new-mother.

Allender, Rachel. "Beyond Burnout. How the Mental Load Affects Moms and What
You Can Do about It." Mom's Hierarchy of Needs. Accessed July 13, 2022.
https://momshierarchyofneeds.com/2017/08/24/beyond-burn-out-no-youre-not
-alone-how-to-relieve-the-mental-load.

Tarver, Helen. "Ironically, Becoming a Mom Can Be Incredibly Lonely and
Isolating." The Roots of Loneliness Project. Accessed July 13, 2022. https://www
.rootsofloneliness.com/motherhood-loneliness.

Bibliography

Dell'Antonia, KJ. "Sororities: Sisterhood with More Than One Price Tag." *New York Times*. October 30, 2014. https://parenting.blogs.nytimes.com/2014/10/30 /sororities-sisterhood-with-more-than-one-price-tag.

Montell, Amanda. *Cultish: The Language of Fanaticism*. New York: Harper Wave, 2021.

Hassan, Steven. "Steven Hassan's BITE Model of Authoritarian Control." Freedom of Mind Resource Center. January 2021. https://freedomofmind.com/cult-mind -control/bite-model.

Bushnell, Mona. "MLMs Are Preying on the Dream of Entrepreneurship." Business .com. Updated June 29, 2022. https://www.business.com/articles/mlms-target -women-and-immigrants.

Butterfield, Stephen. *Amway: The Cult of Free Enterprise*. Boston: South End Press, 1999.

Pyramid Scheme Alert. "Study of Ten Major MLMs and Amway/Quixtar Show Huge Consumer Losses and Pyramid Recruitment." June 2008. https://www .pyramidschemealert.org/PSAMain/news/MythofIncomeReport.html.

Mah, Alice, and Carpenter, Mick. "Community." *The Blackwell Encyclopedia of Sociology*. Malden, MA: Blackwell Publishing, 2016.

Andrew, Alison, Orazio Attanasio, Britta Augsburg, Jere Behrman, Monimalika Day, Pamela Jervis, Costas Meghir, and Angus Phimister. "Mothers' Social Networks and Socioeconomic Gradients of Isolation." Cowles Foundation for Research in Economics, Yale University. Accessed July 13, 2022. https://cowles.yale.edu/sites /default/files/2022-08/d2261_1.pdf.

Markovits, Daniel. *The Meritocracy Trap: How America's Foundational Myth Feeds Inequality, Dismantles the Middle Class, and Devours the Elite*. New York: Penguin Press, 2019.

Illing, Sean. "How Meritocracy Harms Everyone, Even the Winners." Vox. Accessed July 13, 2022. https://www.vox.com/identities/2019/10/21/20897021 /meritocracy-economic-mobility-daniel-markovits.

I'm Positive That You Suck

Taylor, Jon M. *The Case (for and) against Multi-level Marketing*. Bountiful, UT: Consumer Awareness Institute, 2011. https://www.ftc.gov/sites/default/files /documents/public_comments/trade-regulation-rule-disclosure-requirements -and-prohibitions-concerning-business-opportunities-ftc.r511993-00008 %C2%A0/00008-57281.pdf.

Laura. "Why Are Pyramid Schemes a Scam?" Relatively Interesting. Accessed July 13, 2022. https://www.relativelyinteresting.com/pyramid-schemes-explained -and-why-they-are-a-scam.

U.S. Securities and Exchange Commission. "Beware of Pyramid Schemes Posing as Multi-level Marketing Programs." October 1, 2013. https://www.sec.gov/oiea /investor-alerts-bulletins/investor-alerts-ia_pyramidhtm.html.

Brooks, Douglas M. "Coercive Techniques in Business Opportunity Cults." Anti-MLM Coalition. Accessed July 13, 2022. https://antimlmcoalition.files .wordpress.com/2018/02/coercive-techniques-brooks.pdf.

Bond, Casey. "How MLM's and Cults Use the Same Mind Control Techniques." Huffpost. August 13, 2019. https://www.huffpost.com/entry/multilevel -marketing-companies-mlms-cults-similarities_l_5d49f8c2e4b09e72973df3d3.

Hassan, Steven. "Steven Hassan's BITE Model of Authoritarian Control." Freedom of Mind Resource Center. January 2021. https://freedomofmind.com/cult-mind -control/bite-model.

Jason Jones. "Retention: Keep Trying and Buying" and "Why Are We Where We Are with MLM?" Multilevel Marketing: The Consumer Protection Challenge Virtual Conference, The College of New Jersey School of Business, June 2022. https://www.mlmconference.com.

Goodman, Whitney. *Toxic Positivity: Keeping It Real in a World Obsessed with Being Happy.* New York: TarcherPerigee, 2022.

Talented Ladies Club. "Why 80% of Participants in an MLM Will Earn Less Than 70 Cents an Hour (Before Expenses)." Accessed July 13, 2022. https://www .talentedladiesclub.com/articles/why-80-of-participants-in-an-mlm-will-earn -less-than-70-cents-an-hour-before-expenses.

Sung, Morgan. "Kim Kardashian Told Women to 'Get . . . Up and Work.'" NBC News. March 10, 2022. https://www.nbcnews.com/pop-culture/celebrity /kim-kardashian-told-women-get-work-people-are-saying-s-hypocritical -rcna19547.

DeAngelis, Tori. "Class Differences." *Monitor on Psychology* 46, no. 2 (February 2015): 62. https://www.apa.org/monitor/2015/02/class-differences.

Gerdeman, Dina. "Want to Be Happier? Make More Free Time." *Forbes.* February 25, 2021. https://www.forbes.com/sites/hbsworkingknowledge/2021/02/05/want -to-be-happier-make-more-free-time/?sh=7dac99fb5c0d.

The Ladybosses

Fleck, Alissa. "How Women Making Men Rich Has Been Misbranded as Feminism." HuffPost. August 23, 2017. https://www.huffpost.com/entry/this-is -how-women-making-men-rich-has-been-misbranded_b_599d163de4b0b87 d38cbe631.

Wood, Jessica. "The Lies of the Bossbabes—How MLMs Are Holding Back Feminism." Medium. January 10, 2019. https://medium.com/@woodthewriter

/the-lies-of-the-bossbabes-how-mlms-are-holding-back-feminism
-9cf5607c746e.

Rosenberg, Gabe. "91 Percent of Women Feel Misunderstood by Advertisers."
Contently. July 1, 2019. https://contently.com/2014/07/01/study-91-percent
-of-women-feel-misunderstood-by-advertisers.

Maheshwari, Sapna. "3% Conference Spotlights Hurdles for Women at Ad
Agencies." *New York Times*. November 5, 2017. https://www.nytimes
.com/2017/11/05/business/media/women-advertising-3-percent.html.

Freundlich, Tamar. "Marketing to Women: What We Can Learn from the Past
Century." Promo. March 2, 2020. https://promo.com/blog/marketing-to-women
-what-we-can-learn-from-the-past-century.

Burch, Jessica Kay. "'Soap and Hope': Direct Sales and the Culture of Work
and Capitalism in Postwar America." PhD diss., Vanderbilt University,
August 2015. https://ir.vanderbilt.edu/bitstream/handle/1803/15447/BURCH
.pdf?sequence=1.

Rogers, Rikki. "What to Make of 'Female Empowerment' Marketing." Women's
Media Center. August 14, 2014. https://womensmediacenter.com/news-features
/what-to-make-of-female-empowerment-marketing.

Iqbal, Nosheen. "Femvertising: How Brands Are Selling #Empowerment to
Women." *Guardian*. October 12, 2015. https://www.theguardian.com/lifeandstyle
/2015/oct/12/femvertising-branded-feminism.

Baker, Elizabeth. "MLM Culture: Feminism and the Myth of Having It All."
Houston Mom Collective. September 19, 2021. https://houston.momcollective
.com/mlm-culture-feminism-and-the-myth-of-having-it-all.

Berry, Beth. *Motherwhelmed: Challenging Norms, Untangling Truths, and Restoring
Our Worth to the World*. USA: Revolution from Home, 2020.

Berry, Beth. "Why Modern-Day Motherhood Feels So Frustrating." Revolution
from Home. January 16, 2018. https://revolutionfromhome.com/2018/01
/modern-day-motherhood-feels-frustrating.

Amway. "Leadership at Amway Global." Accessed July 13, 2022. https://www
.amwayglobal.com/newsroom/leadership-team.

Wikipedia. "Amway." Accessed July 13, 2022. https://en.wikipedia.org/wiki
/Amway.

Federal Trade Commission. "Amway v. FTC." Accessed July 13, 2022. https://www
.ftc.gov/sites/default/files/documents/commission_decision_volumes/volume-93
/ftc_volume_decision_93_january_-_june_1979pages_618-738.pdf.

Business for Home. "The Top Female Direct Selling CEO 202 Poll." October 6,
2020. https://www.businessforhome.org/2020/10/the-top-female-direct-selling
-ceo-2020-poll.

Castle, Eliza. "Why We Need to Talk about White Feminism." Bustle. August 11, 2015. https://www.bustle.com/articles/103459-4-reasons-white-feminism-has -to-be-addressed-because-womens-empowerment-includes-everyone-video.

Jankunaite, Raimonda. "What Does Women Empowerment Really Mean?" SWAAY. March 10, 2021. https://swaay.com/what-does-women-empowerment -really-mean.

Oluo, Ijeoma. *So You Want to Talk about Race*. New York: Seal Press, 2019.

Sugiuchi, Deirdre. "White Supremacy Is Americas Original Pyramid Scheme." Electric Lit. Accessed July 13, 2022. https://electricliterature.com/white -supremacy-is-americas-original-pyramid-scheme.

Chudleigh, Hannah. "The New Face of Business: Comparing Male and Female Gender Stereotypes in Multi-level Marketing Facebook Posts in India." MA diss. Brigham Young University, 2019. https://scholarsarchive.byu.edu/cgi /viewcontent.cgi?article=8513&context=etd.

Stein, Alexandra. *Terror, Love and Brainwashing: Attachment in Cults and Totalitarian Systems*. Oxfordshire: Routledge, 2016.

Resnick, Ariane. "What Is Trauma Bonding?" Verywell MIND. Accessed July 13, 2022. https://www.verywellmind.com/trauma-bonding-5207136.

Stein, Alexandra. "Cults Are Terrifying. But They're Even Worse for Women." NBC News Think. April 2, 2018. https://www.nbcnews.com/think/opinion/cults -are-terrifying-they-re-even-worse-women-ncna862051.

Margolies, Lynn. "Competition among Women: Myth and Reality." Psych Central. May 17, 2016. https://psychcentral.com/lib/competition-among-women-myth -and-reality#1.

Jgln, Katie. "Women Still Grow Up Seeing Each Other as Competition." Medium. July 22, 2021. https://medium.com/the-virago/women-still-grow-up-seeing-each -other-as-competition-a02696a4d825.

Barash, Susan. *Tripping the Prom Queen: The Truth about Women and Rivalry*. New York: St. Martin's Press, 2006.

North, Gary. "The Feminine Mistake: The Economics of Women's Liberation." Foundation for Economic Education. January 1, 1971. https://fee.org/articles /the-feminine-mistake-the-economics-of-womens-liberation.

Furst, Jennifer, and Julia Willoughby Nason, dirs. *LuLaRich*; Culver City, CA: Cinemart, Story Force Entertainment, and Amazon Studios, 2021. https://www .amazon.com/dp/B09CFXPNSX/?ref=DVM_US_DL_SL_GO_AST_21LULR _mkw_sr6dBADoU-dc&mrntrk=pcrid_545566619447_slid__pgrid_132794832 411_pgeo_9011457_x__ptid_kwd-1407150340482&gclid=Cj0KCQjw_7KXBh CoARIsAPdPTfi-h5Dh9lqAFESycJ7tJHFjVIZyKALb5C3JUZ88qWK3QJKsj E9-0RQaAiaFEALw_wcB.

Martin, Hannah. "Seven Lies an MLM Rep Will Tell You and the Truth You Need to Know." Talented Ladies Club. Accessed July 13, 2022. https://www

.talentedladiesclub.com/articles/seven-lies-an-mlm-rep-will-tell-you-and-the
-real-truth-you-need-to-know.

Beatty, Mike. "167 MLM Income Disclosure Statements Reveals 92.3% of Members
Lose Money." Make Time Online. April 21, 2021. https://maketimeonline.com
/mlm-income-disclosure-statements.

Federal Trade Commission Consumer Advice. "Multi-level Marketing Businesses
and Pyramid Schemes." Accessed July 13, 2022. https://consumer.ftc.gov/articles
/multi-level-marketing-businesses-pyramid-schemes.

Naikoi, Josie. "Not the Good Girl." YouTube Channel. Accessed July 13, 2022.
https://www.youtube.com/c/JosieNaikoi.

That Time of the Month

Crownless Princess. "Front Loading." July 23, 2017. https://crownless-princesses
.writeas.com/front-loading.

MLM Legal. "What Is 'Front Loading' or 'Inventory-Loading?'" July 30, 2013.
http://mlmlegal.com/MLMBlog/what-is-front-loading-or-inventory-loading
/#:~:text=The%20FTC%20includes%20front%20loading,to%20engage%20in
%20the%20opportunity.

A (MLM) Skeptic. "MLM Basics: Inventory Loading, and Front-Loading." October
24, 2012. http://amlmskeptic.blogspot.com/2012/10/mlm-basics-inventory
-loading-and-front.html.

Rawlins, Kenny. "Let's Talk Stacking! Part 1: What Is Stacking in an MLM?
[Definition + How It Works]." Infotrax. February 15, 2021. https://www
.infotraxsys.com/insights/direct-selling-mlm-network-marketing-or-party-plan.

Lots of Dollars and Absolutely No Sense

FitzPatrick, Robert. *Ponzinomics: The Untold Story of Multi-level Marketing.*
Charlotte, NC: FitzPatrick Management Inc, 2020.

Schochet, Leila. "The Child Care Crisis Is Keeping Women Out of the Workforce."
American Progress. March 28, 2019. https://www.americanprogress.org/article
/child-care-crisis-keeping-women-workforce.

Yvonne, Celeste. *It's Not about the Wine: The Loaded Truth behind Mommy Wine
Culture.* Minneapolis: Broadleaf Books, 2023.

Riess, Jana. "10 Reasons Mormons Dominate Multi-level Marketing Companies."
Religion News Service. June 20, 2017. https://religionnews.com/2017/06/20/10
-reasons-mormons-dominate-multi-level-marketing-companies.

Palmer, Erica. "LDS Mothers Balance Career Aspirations with Divine Calling of
Motherhood." The Daily Universe. April 38, 2016. https://universe.byu.edu/2016/04
/28/lds-mothers-balance-career-aspirations-with-divine-calling-of-motherhood1.

Thirty-One Gifts. Accessed July 13, 2022. https://www.mythirtyone.com.

McNeal, Stephanie. "These Women Say an Essential Oil MLM Has Been Taken Over by Satan. Yes, Really." BuzzFeed News. February 22, 2022. https://www.buzzfeednews.com/article/stephaniemcneal/young-living-essential-oils-satanic.

Montell, Amanda. *Cultish: The Language of Fanaticism*. New York: Harper Wave, 2021.

"Licking" Things to Claim Them as Your Own

Graham, Megan. "MLM Sellers Are Asking for Cash to Donate Products to Health Workers, but Experts Say It's a Marketing Ploy." CNBC. April 4, 2020. https://www.cnbc.com/2020/04/04/mlm-sellers-asking-for-donations-for-health-workers-marketing-ploy.html.

McLeod, Lisa Earle. "Is Your Sales Team Addicted to Dopamine?" *Forbes*. February 21, 2018. https://www.forbes.com/sites/lisaearlemcleod/2018/02/21/is-your-sales-team-addicted-to-dopamine/?sh=721fb8875107.

FitzPatrick, Robert. *The Myth of Income Opportunity in Multi-level Marketing*. Charlotte, NC: Pink Truth, 2005. https://pinktruth.com/wp-content/uploads/fitzpatrick-mlm-study.pdf.

Kavallaris, Nikos. "An Economic Model of Multi-level Marketing." *PLOS One*. July 21, 2021. https://www.ncbi.nlm.nih.gov/pmc/articles/PMC8291665.

Consumer Fraud Reporting. "The Market Saturation Problem of Multi-level Marketing—Why It IS a Scam." Accessed July 13, 2022. https://www.consumerfraudreporting.org/MLM_saturation.php.

Pyramid Scheme Alert. "Saturation Reality and the Myth of MLM Growth." July 20, 2015. https://www.pyramidschemealert.org/saturation-and-the-myth-of-mlm-growth.

Taylor, Jon M. *The Case (for and) against Multi-level Marketing*. Bountiful, UT: Consumer Awareness Institute, 2011. https://www.ftc.gov/sites/default/files/documents/public_comments/trade-regulation-rule-disclosure-requirements-and-prohibitions-concerning-business-opportunities-ftc.r511993-00009%C2%A0/00009-57282.pdf.

The Party Never Ends and Neither Does Your Anxiety

Stegall, Hailee. "Sorority Rush Bears Frightening Similarities to Cult Recruitment." *Rocky Mountain Collegian*. October 10, 2021. https://collegian.com/articles/opinion/2021/10/category-opinion-stegall-sorority-rush-bears-frightening-similarities-to-cult-recruitment.

Bella, Darrel. "The Benefits of Incentive Travel for Both Employees & Companies." *The Luxury Signature*. July 13, 2022. https://www.theluxurysignature.com/2014/11/01/benefits-incentive-travel-both-employees-companies.

Worley, Savannah. "Dear White Women: Here's Why It's Hard to Be Friends with You." *Medium*. April 19, 2021. https://aninjusticemag.com/dear-white-women-heres-why-it-s-hard-to-be-friends-with-you-61ba6e497f1a.

It's Lonely (and Ugly) at the Top

Martin, Hannah. "Why There's No Such Thing as a Free MLM Car." *Talented Ladies Club*. Accessed July 13, 2022. https://www.talentedladiesclub.com/articles/why-theres-no-such-thing-as-a-free-mlm-car.

Ferrant, Gaëlle, Luca Maria Pesando, and Keiko Nowacka. "Unpaid Care Work: The Missing Link in the Analysis of Gender Gaps in Labour Outcomes." *OECD Development Centre*. December 2014. https://www.oecd.org/dev/development-gender/Unpaid_care_work.pdf.

Bland, David. "The Troubling Rise of the Anti-influencer." *Social Selling News*. April 1, 2021. https://socialsellingnews.com/link/the-troubling-rise-of-the-anti-influencer-5978.

Direct Selling Association. "DSA Industry Fact Sheets." Accessed July 13, 2022. https://www.dsa.org/statistics-insights/factsheets.

Direct Selling Association. "Direct Selling in the United States: 2017 Facts and Data." Accessed July 13, 2022. https://www.dsa.org/docs/default-source/research/dsa_2017_factsanddata_2018.pdf.

US Census Bureau. "Quick Facts, United States." Accessed July 13, 2022. https://www.census.gov/quickfacts/fact/table/US/PST045219.

Elbow, Elbow, Wrist, Wrist

Prakash, Neha. "The Good, the Bad, and the Very Surprising of Mom Influencing." *Marie Claire*. April 8, 2021. https://www.marieclaire.com/culture/a35477522/jo-piazza-mom-influencers-podcast-interview.

Kimes, Mina. "Drew Brees Has a Dream He'd Like to Sell You." *ESPN Magazine*. March 15, 2016. https://www.espn.com/espn/feature/story/_/id/14972197/questions-surround-advocare-nutrition-empire-endorsed-saints-qb-drew-brees.

Gressin, Seena. "FTC: AdvoCare Business Model Was Pyramid Scheme." *Federal Trade Commission Consumer Advice*. October 2, 2019. https://consumer.ftc.gov/consumer-alerts/2019/10/ftc-advocare-business-model-was-pyramid-scheme.

Gibson, Kate. "AdvoCare Fined $150 Million as FTC Calls It a Pyramid Scheme." CBS News. October 2, 2019. https://www.cbsnews.com/news/advocare-fined-150-million-as-ftc-calls-it-a-pyramid-scheme.

Chapman, Gray. "MLMs Take the Worst Parts of the Gig Economy, Then Make You Pay." Racked. September 13, 2017. http://www.racked.com/2017/9/13/16255060/mlms-gig-economy-hustle.

Truth in Advertising. "FTC v. Vemma Pyramid Lawsuit Documents." Accessed July 13, 2022. https://truthinadvertising.org/evidence/ftc-vemma-pyramid-docs.

Federal Trade Commission. "Nu Skin to Pay 1.5 Million Penalty to Resolve FTC Charges over Fat-Loss Claims for Supplements." August 6, 1997. https://www.ftc.gov/news-events/news/press-releases/1997/08/nu-skin-pay-15-million-penalty-resolve-ftc-charges-over-fat-loss-claims-supplements.

Federal Trade Commission. "Herbalife Will Restructure Its Multi-level Marketing Operations and Pay $200 Million for Consumer Redress to Settle FTC Charges." July 15, 2016. https://www.ftc.gov/news-events/news/press-releases/2016/07/herbalife-will-restructure-its-multi-level-marketing-operations-pay-200-million-consumer-redress.

Gressin, Seena. "FTC Alleges Neoria, Formerly Known as Nerium, Operating Illegal Pyramid Scheme." Federal Trade Commission. November 4, 2019. https://www.ftc.gov/business-guidance/blog/2019/11/ftc-alleges-neora-formerly-known-nerium-operates-illegal-pyramid-scheme.

Federal Trade Commission. "Serious Problems with the FTC's Revised Business Opportunity Rule." Accessed July 13, 2022. https://www.ftc.gov/sites/default/files/documents/public_comments/business-opportunity-rule-535221-00006/535221-00006.pdf.

Hanks, Angela, Christian E. Weller, and Danyelle Solomon. "Systematic Inequality: How America's Structural Racism Helped Create the Black-White Wealth Gap." American Progress. February 21, 2018. https://www.americanprogress.org/article/systematic-inequality.

Brooks, Douglas. "Advisor to the Pyramid Scheme Alert Board of Directors." Pyramid Scheme Alert. Accessed July 13, 2022. https://www.pyramidschemealert.org/douglas-m-brooks-esq.

Stroud, Matt. "How Lobbying Dollars Prop Up Pyramid Schemes." The Verge. April 8, 2014. https://www.theverge.com/2014/4/8/5590550/alleged-pyramid-schemes-lobbying-ftc.

Goodenow, Gary Langan. "The SEC and Multilevel Marketing." MLM Watch. August 16, 2004. https://quackwatch.org/mlm/legal/sec.

Patten, Bonnie. "An In-Depth Examination of Self-Regulation in the MLM Industry." Truth in Advertising. May 24, 2022. https://truthinadvertising.org/blog/the-dssrc-would-benefit-from-an-ftc-earnings-claim-rule.

Federal Trade Commission. "FTC Proposes New Business Opportunity Rule."
April 5, 2006. https://www.ftc.gov/news-events/press-releases/2006/04/ftc
-proposes-new-business-opportunity-rule.

Stewart, Emily. " MLM's Might Not Be Able to Get Away with Their Shady
Promises Much Longer." Vox. October 22, 2021. https://www.vox.com/the-goods
/22732586/ftc-mlm-rohit-chopra-business-opportunity-rule.

Pray to the Gurus and Goddesses

Pyramid Scheme Alert. "Saturation Reality and the Myth of MLM 'Growth.'"
July 20, 2015. https://www.pyramidschemealert.org/saturation-and-the-myth
-of-mlm-growth.

FitzPatrick, Robert. *The Myth of Income Opportunity in Multi-level Marketing.*
Charlotte, NC: Pink Truth, 2005. https://pinktruth.com/wp-content/uploads
/fitzpatrick-mlm-study.pdf.

Taylor, Jon M. *The Case (for and) against Multi-level Marketing.* Bountiful, UT:
Consumer Awareness Institute, 2011. https://www.ftc.gov/sites/default/files
/documents/public_comments/trade-regulation-rule-disclosure-requirements
-and-prohibitions-concerning-business-opportunities-ftc.r511993-00009%C2
%A0/00009-57282.pdf.

Richardson, Emma. "The Age of the Influencer—How It All Began." Influencer
Matchmaker. Accessed July 13, 2022. https://influencermatchmaker.co.uk/blog
/age-influencer-how-it-all-began.

Grose, Jessica. "When Grown-Ups Have Imaginary Friends." *New York Times.*
May 5, 2021. https://www.nytimes.com/2021/05/05/parenting/influencers-social
-media-relationships.html.

Abers, Rachael K. "What Our Obsession with *Inventing Anna* Tells Us about the
Age of the Personal Brand." The Week. February 16, 2022. https://theweek.com
/culture/entertainment/1010238/what-our-fascination-with-anna-delvey-shows
-us-about-the-age-of-the.

Abad-Santos, Alex. "The Death of the Girlboss." Vox. June 7, 2021. https://www.vox
.com/22466574/gaslight-gatekeep-girlboss-meaning.

Snyder, Abby. "Gaslight, Gatekeep: How 'Girlboss' Went from Aspirational to
Insulting." *Michigan Daily.* November 16, 2021. https://www.michigandaily
.com/statement/gaslight-gatekeep-how-girlboss-went-from-aspirational-to
-insulting.

Abrams, Sameer. "Sheryl Sandberg's Legacy." *New York Times.* June 2, 2022. https://
www.nytimes.com/2022/06/02/technology/sheryl-sandberg-legacy.html.

Hajjaji, Danya. " Rachel Hollis Video Controversy Explained as Housekeeper
Remarks Spark Backlash," *Newsweek.* April 30, 2021. https://www.newsweek.com
/rachel-hollis-video-controversy-explained-1587879.

Bibliography

Anderson, Will. "Beware the 'Christian' Pitch to Join Multilevel Marketing." The Gospel Coalition. January 28, 2022. https://www.thegospelcoalition.org/article /multilevel-marketing-christians.

Cult Defectors Pay the Price

Williams, Megan. *Cutting Ties: Healing after MLM.* Self-published, Amazon Digital Services, 2021, Kindle.

Federal Trade Commission. "When a Business Offer or Coaching Program Is a Scam." Accessed July 13, 2022. https://consumer.ftc.gov/articles/when-business -offer-or-coaching-program-scam.

Fagan, Abigail. "How to Find a Legitimate Coach." *Psychology Today.* November 20, 2021. http://psychologytoday.com/us/blog/coaching-corner/202111/how-find -legitimate-coach.

Tagle, Schneider. "Diet Culture Is Everywhere. Here's How to Fight It." National Public Radio. January 4, 2022. https://www.npr.org/2021/12/23/1067210075 /what-if-the-best-diet-is-to-reject-diet-culture.

Dooner, Caroline. *The Fuck It Diet: Eating Should Be Easy.* New York: Harper Wave 2019.

Mull, Amanda. "I Gooped Myself." *Atlantic.* August 26, 2019. https://www .theatlantic.com/health/archive/2019/08/what-goop-really-sells-women/596773.

Stillwell, Chloe. "Attention Rich White Women: You're Cordially Invited to Sail with Goop." Mic. August 18, 2021. https://www.mic.com/p/attention-rich -white-women-youre-cordially-invited-to-sail-with-goop-84082814.

Fitch, Kate. "Multi-level Marketing in Recovery: A Special Report." Colorado Mental Wellness Network. Accessed July 13, 2022. https://cmwn.org /colorado-mental-wellness-network-blog/special-reports/mlm-recovery.

Wang, Wendy. "The 'Leisure Gap' between Mothers and Fathers." Pew Research Center. October 17, 2013. https://www.pewresearch.org/fact-tank/2013/10/17 /the-leisure-gap-between-mothers-and-fathers.

You Can Check Out, but You Can Never Leave

Federal Trade Commission. "FTC Sends Warning Letters to Multi-level Marketers Regarding Health and Earnings Claims They or Their Participants Are Making Related to Coronavirus." April 24, 2020. https://www.ftc.gov/news-events/news /press-releases/2020/04/ftc-sends-warning-letters-multi-level-marketers -regarding-health-earnings-claims-they-or-their.

Vesoulis, Abby, and Dockterman, Eliana. "Pandemic Schemes: How Multilevel Marketing Distributors Are Using the Internet—and Coronavirus—to Grow

Their Businesses." *Time.* July 9, 2020. https://time.com/5864712/multilevel
-marketing-schemes-coronavirus.

Voytko, Lisette. "FTC Warns 16 Multi-level Marketing Companies about
Coronavirus Fraud." *Forbes.* June 9, 2020. https://www.forbes.com/sites
/lisettevoytko/2020/06/09/ftc-warns-16-multi-level-marketing-companies
-about-coronavirus-fraud/?sh=1704edc87b9d.

Laura. "Why Are Pyramid Schemes a Scam?" Relatively Interesting. Accessed
July 13, 2022. https://www.relativelyinteresting.com/pyramid-schemes-explained
-and-why-they-are-a-scam.

Influence Watch. "Environmental Working Group (EWG)." Accessed July 13, 2022.
https://www.influencewatch.org/non-profit/environmental-working-group.

AG Daily. "Food Science Babe: The Dirty Deception of the 'Dirty Dozen.'" March 18,
2021. https://www.agdaily.com/insights/dirty-deception-ewg-dirty-dozen.

Patten, Bonnie. "TINA.org Pushes for New Enforcement Tactic against MLM
Industry." Truth in Advertising. June 30, 2021. https://www.truthinadvertising
.org/tina-pushes-new-enforcement-tactic-against-mlm-industry.

Truth in Advertising. "Direct Selling in the United States: An Industry in Decline
(2008–2018)." Accessed July 13, 2022. https://www.truthinadvertising.org/wp
-content/uploads/2019/10/DSA-Infographic.png.

Graham, Megan. "MLM Sellers Are Asking for Cash to Donate Products to Health
Workers, but Experts Say It's a Marketing Ploy." CNBC. Accessed July 13, 2022.
https://www.cnbc.com/2020/04/04/mlm-sellers-asking-for-donations-for-health
-workers-marketing-ploy.html.

Kochhar, Rakesh. "Fewer Mothers and Fathers in the U.S. Are Working Due to
Covid-19 Downturn; Those at Work Have Cut Hours." PEW Research Center.
October 22, 2020. https://www.pewresearch.org/fact-tank/2020/10/22/fewer
-mothers-and-fathers-in-u-s-are-working-due-to-covid-19-downturn-those
-at-work-have-cut-hours.

Pyramid Scheme Termination Cause. "Saturation Reality and the Myth of MLM
'Growth.'" July 20, 2015. https://www.pstermination.org/38-psa.

Escaping the Pyramid

Cima, Roseann. "The KKK Was Originally a Giant, Lucrative Pyramid Scheme."
Quartz. October 30, 2016. https://qz.com/806978/the-kkk-was-once-a-giant
-pyramid-scheme-exploiting-racism-for-tons-of-money.

Fryer, Roland, and Steven Levitt. "Hatred and Profits: Under the Hood of the Ku
Klux Klan." Harvard Scholar. February 2011. https://scholar.harvard.edu/files
/fryer/files/hatred_and_profits_under_the_hood_of_the_ku_klux_klan.pdf?m
=1360041666.

Frenkel, Sheera, Ben Decker, and Davey Alba. "How the 'Plandemic' Movie and Its Falsehoods Spread Widely Online." *New York Times.* Accessed July 13, 2022. https://www.nytimes.com/2020/05/20/technology/plandemic-movie-youtube -facebook-coronavirus.html.

Tiffany, Kaitlyn. "This Will Change Your Life: Why the Grandiose Promises of Multilevel Marketing and QAnon Conspiracy Theories Go Hand in Hand." *Atlantic.* October 28, 2020. https://www.theatlantic.com/technology/archive /2020/10/why-multilevel-marketing-and-qanon-go-hand-hand/616885.

Sommer, Will. "QAnon Leaders Push Followers into Multi-level Marketing." Daily Beast. April 15, 2022. https://www.thedailybeast.com/qanon-leaders-push -followers-into-multi-level-marketing.

Pink Truth. "Should I Put Mary Kay on My Resumé?" September 2, 2020. https:// www.pinktruth.com/2023/08/17/should-you-put-mary-kay-on-your-resume/.

Green, Alison. "Should People Who Sell MLM Products Put 'Business Owner' on Their Resumes?" Ask a Manager. April 22, 2020. https://www.askamanager.org /2020/04/should-people-who-sell-mlm-products-put-business-owner-on-their -resumes.html.

Vance, Brittany. "Why You Must Nix MLM Experience from Your Resume." The American Genius. June 23, 2021. https://theamericangenius.com/business -marketing/why-you-must-nix-mlm-experience-from-your-resume.

US Department of the Treasury. "Paycheck Protection Program." Accessed July 13, 2022. https://home.treasury.gov/policy-issues/coronavirus/assistance-for-small -businesses/paycheck-protection-program.

Life Takes on a New Shape (and It's Not a Pyramid)

Scheibeler, Eric. *Merchants of Deception.* Charleston, SC: BookSurge, 2009.

Resources

Please note: There are dozens of websites, Instagram accounts, YouTube channels, and other information on the topic. This is not a personal endorsement of these creators, or their politics, lives, affiliations, or otherwise. This is simply a list of the resources that I have used in my research, in my exit from my MLM, and those that use factual, evidence-based information in their content. Use personal agency.

Legal/Consumer-Protection Resources and How to Report

Competition and Consumer Protection Agencies Worldwide: https://www.ftc.gov /policy/international/competition-consumer-protection-authorities-worldwide

Consumer Fraud Reporting: A resource to protect yourself and report the latest frauds, scams, spams, fakes, identity theft hacks, and hoaxes. http://www .consumerfraudreporting.org/MLM.php

Federal Trade Commission—Consumer Advice: Money-Making Opportunities and Investments: Learn how to spot the signs of business coaching schemes, investment scams, and other scams that promise a big payoff. https://consumer .ftc.gov/jobs-and-making-money/money-making-opportunities-and-investments

Federal Trade Commission: Report false income and health claims. https:// reportfraud.ftc.gov

National Association of Attorneys General, Find my AG. Report scams and schemes to your state Attorney General's office. https://www.naag.org/find -my-ag

Open States Find Your Legislator. Look up your legislator so you can urge them to take action against scams. https://openstates.org/find_your_legislator

Small Business Administration Complaint Submission Form: Submit a complaint to the SBA about PPP loan fraud. https://sbax.sba.gov/oigcss

Books

200% of Nothing: An Eye-Opening Tour through the Twists and Turns of Math Abuse and Innumeracy by A. K. Dewdney

All That Glitters Is Not God: Breaking Free from the Sweet Deceit of Multi-level Marketing by Athena Dean

Amway Motivational Organizations: Behind the Smoke and Mirrors by Ruth Carter

Combating Mind Control by Steven Hassan

Consumed by Success: Reaching the Top and Finding That God Wasn't There by Athena Dean

Cultish: The Language of Fanaticism by Amanda Montell

Cutting Ties: Healing after MLM by Megan C. Williams

False Profits: Seeking Financial and Spiritual Deliverance in Multi-level Marketing and Pyramid Schemes by Robert L. FitzPatrick and Joyce K. Reynolds

Freedom of Mind: Helping Loved Ones Leave Controlling People, Cults, and Beliefs by Steven Hassan

Merchants of Deception: An Insider's Chilling Look at the Worldwide, Multi-billion Dollar Conspiracy of Lies That Is Amway and Its Motivational Organizations by Eric Scheibeler

Ponzinomics: The Untold Story of Multi-level Marketing by Robert L. FitzPatrick

Scarred: The True Story of How I Escaped NXIVM, the Cult That Bound My Life by Sarah Edmondson with Kristine Gasbarre

Websites

I Got Out: A consortium of cult survivors. http://Igotout.org

Freedom of Mind: Steven Hassan's BITE Model. https://freedomofmind.com /cult-mind-control/bite-model

MLM-TheTruth: Research and analysis of MLMs by Dr. Jon Taylor. https://www .ftc.gov/sites/default/files/documents/public_comments/trade-regulation-rule -disclosure-requirements-and-prohibitions-concerning-business-opportunities -ftc.r511993-00017%C2%A0/00017-57317.pdf

Resources

MLMChange.org: Promoting Meaningful, Incremental, and Systemic Change in an Inherently Predatory Business Structure. https://mlmchange.org

Quackwatch, the Skeptical Guide to Multilevel Marketing: A copious list of articles, victim reports, and government regulatory action, operated by Stephen Barrett, MD. https://quackwatch.org/mlm

Talented Ladies Club: Multiple articles about MLMs. https://www.talentedladiesclub.com/?s=mlm

The Anti-MLM Coalition: UK-based site sharing information about the MLM industry, with facts, research and testimonies. https://mlmtruth.org

Podcasts

A Little Bit Culty

Coffee and Cults

Cult Liter with Spencer Henry

Cult or Just Weird: Season 1, Episodes 9 and 10

Cult Podcast

The Cult Vault

The Downline

The Dream: Season 1

From Huns to Humans

Hey Hun, You Woke Up! Victim Voices

Illegal Tender: Season 4

iilluminaughtii

IndoctriNation: Season 2, Episode 4 ("Escape from NXIVM")

The Influence Continuum with Dr. Steven Hassan

Life after MLM

Maintenance Phase

The Persuasion Pitch

Ponzinomics 101

Scientology: Fair Game

Sounds Like a Cult

That's a Cult? Episode 2

Trust Me: Cults, Extreme Belief, and Manipulation

Was I In A Cult?

Movies/Documentaries

BBC Secrets of the Multi-level Millionaires

Betting on Zero

LuLaRich

The Vow

(Un)Well

YouTube Channels

Briannah Jewel

CC Suarez

Cruel World Happy Mind

Deanna Mims

Erin Bies

Hannah Alonzo: Anti-MLM &
Scam Commentary

Isabella Lanter: Scam
Commentary

Jessica Hickson: Retired Hunbot

Josie Naikoi: Not the Good Girl

Julie Anderson

JulieJo: Commentary, Reaction,
Anti-Scam

Keya's World

Kiki Chanel

Kyla James

Roberta Blevins

Savannah Marie: Anti-MLM
Commentary

Savy Writes Books

The Antibot

About the Author

EMILY LYNN PAULSON is the author of *Highlight Real*, a speaker, and the founder of Sober Mom Squad. Her powerful TEDx Talks challenge the status quo of parenting, alcohol use, and feminism as we know it. Paulson has also been featured by *Today*, the *New York Times*, the *Washington Post*, the *Seattle Times*, *Next Question with Katie Couric*, and the *Tamron Hall Show* as a leading voice in the recovery and sobriety community. She lives in Central Oregon with her husband and their five children.